TOYOTA UNDER FIRE

LESSONS FOR TURNING CRISIS INTO OPPORTUNITY

JEFFREY K. LIKER
TIMOTHY N. OGDEN

NEW YORK   CHICAGO   SAN FRANCISCO
LISBON   LONDON   MADRID   MEXICO CITY   MILAN
NEW DELHI   SAN JUAN   SEOUL   SINGAPORE
SYDNEY   TORONTO

1 2 3 4 5 6 7 8 9 0 DOC/DOC 1 6 5 4 3 2 1

ISBN: 978-0-07-176299-1 (print book)
MHID: 0-07-176299-X

ISBN: 978-0-07-176307-3 (e-book)
MHID: 0-07-176307-4

Interior design by Mauna Eichner and Lee Fukui

McGraw-Hill books are available at special quantity discounts to use as premiums and sales promotions, or for use in corporate training programs. To contact a representative, please e-mail us at bulksales@mcgraw-hill.com.

This book is printed on acid-free paper.

Contents

Foreword

Reports of Toyota's demise following the sudden acceleration crisis in 2009–2010 were greatly exaggerated. Initial accounts of Toyota's response to a mountain of public concern about Toyota's vehicle safety were quick to allege a number of severe flaws in Toyota's culture. The crisis, indeed, cost Toyota dearly in recall costs, and loss of sales and reputation. A brand that for so long had been synonymous with reliability, customer focus, environmental responsibility, and world-class quality was all of a sudden portrayed in the most negative way by analysts and the press. And yet, a year later, not only has Toyota turned the corner, but it has used the crisis as an opportunity to further strengthen key processes. As it turned out, it was the very culture that was all too quickly blamed for the poor management of the crisis that ended up saving the day.

Treatises on crisis management normally focus on immediate damage control, PR strategies, and clever contingency plans. At a time of crisis, leaders may be hailed as heroes for taking "bold action," or they may be hung in the court of public opinion—as was the case with BP's CEO Tony Hayward following the oil spill in the Gulf of Mexico.

Numerous analysts and experts accused Toyota's leaders of responding late and insufficiently to the crisis, of denying or even trying to hide the facts, of putting profits before safety. But the ultimate test lay not in what senior leaders said and did in the days and weeks following the incident but in how the culture responded in the weeks and months thereafter. The defining moment of Toyota's response was not a specific pronouncement by an executive in Japan or the United States but how Toyota's staff turned its energy to finding ways to improve, how Toyota's hundreds of customer service representatives responded to the tens of thousands of calls received daily from concerned customers, and how dealers worked relentlessly to rebuild trust with Toyota's customers.

The decision not to outsource customer service to a low-wage call center turned out to be instrumental in Toyota's capacity to deal with the crisis, because it allowed its most precious resource, its culture, to take charge when it was most needed. Toyota's *hansei* philosophy—the expectation that one ought to accept responsibility for mistakes, learn from them, and avoid placing blame elsewhere—and its engrained "customer-first" value proved to be more valuable than any communication strategy money could buy.

Liker and Ogden's thorough account of the recall crisis brings home a central message that is relevant across industries and around the world and that is captured in the closing chapter of the book: the idea that "turning crisis into opportunity is all about culture. It's not about PR strategies, or charismatic leadership, or vision, or any specific action by any individual. It's not about policies or procedures or risk mitigation processes. It's about the actions that have been programmed into the individuals and teams that make up a company before the crisis starts."

As a business leader, when all is said and done, all you've got, really, is your organizational culture. Your technology can be reverse engineered, if not directly bought in the open market.

Capital can be raised by others from the very same sources you raised yours. Factories can be built or bought by others. Distribution contracts can be signed or snatched from under your feet. But what no one can exactly replicate (perhaps not even yourself if you tried to do it again from scratch) is your culture: the complex system of shared beliefs, norms, and values; the patterns of interaction and expectations of conduct that are implicitly and automatically rewarded or punished; the words and shared meanings that shape narratives and conversations; the founding stories; the implicit mechanisms of coordination and collaboration that are so hard to pin down yet are the very essence of your organization.

Culture is, in the terminology of management scholars, an intangible asset, a key strategic resource, and a source of sustainable competitive advantage because it is path dependent and therefore unique to each organization; because it yields value in terms of productivity, customer service, or innovation; because it is nearly impossible to deconstruct and reproduce; and because it is not available for others to acquire. And yet, the very reasons that make culture so valuable make it also extraordinarily complex to manage. Culture cannot be created at will or mandated from above. A corporate culture emerges from a history of interactions inside and outside an organization, beginning with a set of values the founders projected into the organization they created, and shaped by the actions and choices of the leaders at all levels of the organization who followed. Culture is built over years, not over off-sites.

Culture is tested at times of crisis: when conflicting priorities arise, when unexpected events threaten the very survival of an organization, when multiple paths of action are presented and conflicting views of the world take hold. During those times, culture helps make sense of the new reality, frames decisions, and defines priorities. But a culture can also break down or be abandoned under stress unless leaders meaningfully reinforce it, even in the midst of a crisis. Strong cultures can, in fact, be built and sustained only by leaders with strong ethical backbones.

The last decade has witnessed a series of business failures—from Enron, to WorldCom, to AIG, Washington Mutual, or Lehman Brothers—that have cost employees, shareholders, and taxpayers trillions of dollars. Millions of jobs have been lost, national economies have shrunk, and public deficits have ballooned as a consequence. A myriad of explanations have been offered, but one consistent factor underlay each of those organizations: a culture shaped by leaders who put profit maximization above any other objective and who were willing to push their business to the edge of what was legally permissible or morally acceptable, under the pretense of creating shareholder value.

Those are some of the accusations that were leveled at Toyota at the height of the crisis. After reading this book, it will be abundantly clear that those accusations couldn't have been more off base. In the challenges of the recession and the recall crisis, Toyota leaders weren't passing the buck or looking for someone else to blame. They were guiding the organization to reinvest in a strong culture of continuous improvement and putting customers first. Toyota leaders were making sure that the company was investing in people and looking toward the long term, not just the next quarterly report.

In an effort to begin the long and painstaking process of creating a business management culture that prioritizes honesty, integrity, and creating real value, five years ago Thunderbird established a management version of the ancient Hippocratic Oath physicians have taken for 2,400 years. The Thunderbird Oath of

Honor is now an integral part of our academic culture, from the admissions process, to the curriculum, to, most notably, the graduation ceremonies.

The explicit, public commitment of taking the Oath has changed the culture of Thunderbird for good: it has shaped conversations inside and outside the classroom, and it has helped remind faculty, staff, students, and alumni of the tremendous responsibilities management has in society to create sustainable prosperity worldwide.

In the last few years, the movement has spread. A group of Harvard Business School students launched the MBA Oath in 2009, and student groups around the world have signed on. A group of Young Global Leaders at the World Economic Forum created a Global Business Oath to encourage CEOs to make a public commitment to professional ethics. And a coalition of faculty, business leaders, students, and international organizations has established the Oath Project Foundation to help catalyze a movement to shape the values of managers around the world. The history of the Oath is a great example of how difficult it is to change culture as well as an example of the tremendous impact a change of culture can have in shaping conduct. Toyota's reaction to the recall crisis, the company's ability to turn crisis into opportunity for improvement, is another.

Effective leadership is not defined by heroic acts at times of crisis, or by clever decisions along a complex contingency tree, but by consistent efforts to nurture and strengthen an effective, adaptable, principled culture. And those efforts can be made only by leaders who have strong principles themselves. These efforts, as Liker and Ogden point out, start long before any crisis. The critical role of leaders at a time of crisis is not to personally resolve it, but to serve as role models of the values and culture of the company, to send a message that those values are even more important when facing challenges.

I encourage you to take inspiration from Toyota and to take a long, hard look at your values and the culture of your organization. If you aren't convinced that you and your company can turn crisis into opportunity, that you would be able to face problems honestly, take responsibility, and work toward improvement no matter what the circumstances, then make it your goal to start changing your culture. Whether that's via a public commitment similar to the Global Business Oath or by taking on entrenched policies that reward the wrong behaviors or some other step, I encourage you to get started today. You never know when a crisis will strike, and when it does it will be too late to begin the process of change.

ÁNGEL CABRERA
President, Thunderbird School
of Global Management

Preface

Everyone who has ever driven a car has experienced those moments when the car seems to take on a life of its own, when it seems to be about to, or in fact does, escape from our control. That's why the harrowing recording of the Saylor family's desperate call for help to 911, while their loaner Lexus vehicle was roaring out of control on a San Diego freeway in August 2009, caught the national attention. All four passengers in the vehicle died when the car crashed before their plea for help could be answered.

The Saylors' tragic ride epitomizes our worst fears about our cars. Since we use them daily, it's easy to forget that we are directing thousands of pounds of steel at speeds twice as fast as a racehorse at full gallop, with only a small wheel and a couple of pedals to keep it all under control. What if those controls stopped obeying us? What if these magnificent feats of engineering took on a life of their own? A brief survey of hit movies over the last two decades shows that this fear is quite prevalent in our subconscious.

The fact that Mark Saylor was a veteran California Highway Patrol officer added to the fear and confusion. If a police officer couldn't bring the car under control, who could? Understandably, the public wanted answers. Could this happen to them?

Thus the Saylors' tragic and unnecessary deaths, four lives among the more than 30,000 that are lost on American highways each year, began one of the most prolonged and intense periods of scrutiny of an automobile manufacturer in 20 years. That scrutiny was focused on Toyota, which up until that point had been widely regarded, and rightly so, as the manufacturer of the safest and most reliable cars on the road. Over the course of the next six months, Toyota would recall more than 10 million vehicles. It would be accused in the national media of turning a blind eye to customer safety, of losing its way and putting profits before quality, and of deliberately hiding electronic defects that could make vehicles unstoppable.

In the media frenzy of reporting on the troubles of this iconic company, details would be lost, such as the fact that what happened to the Saylors was the result of a dealership's not following Toyota procedures and putting the wrong, outsized floor mat into the Saylors' loaner vehicle without securing it; the mat then jammed the accelerator pedal, causing the accident. Nor would it be noticed that there was no forensic evidence of electronics issues in any of the many accidents investigated. Nonetheless, Toyota's public image, so carefully cultivated over 50 years by focusing relentlessly on continuous improvement and serving customers, was severely damaged. From being a paragon of corporate citizenship, it became the butt of late-night jokes. This started in the United States, and at first Toyota viewed it as a regional perception problem that could be handled by management in the United States, but in the Internet age, nothing stays local for very long, and it soon became a global crisis.

If the start of the crisis was the Saylor accident, you can view February 8, 2011 as a major milestone—that's when the National Highway Transportation Safety Administration released the details of a 10-month, $1.5 million intensive study of Toyota electronics led by NASA. Summarizing the results, Secretary of Transportation Ray LaHood, who had fiercely criticized Toyota during the crisis, said, "The verdict is in. There is no electronic-based cause for un-intended high-speed acceleration in Toyotas. Period."

But a year earlier, when the crisis was blazing out of control, the allegations against Toyota came as quite a shock to my system. When the Saylors' accident happened, Tim and I were putting the finishing touches on some research into how Toyota builds leaders. I had visited Toyota plants and offices throughout the United States and marveled at how Toyota did not lay associates off, but rather kept them fully engaged in training and *kaizen* (continuous improvement), so that the company would emerge stronger when the recession let up. The recession, though, was beginning to look like small fry compared to the firestorm of criticism that the company was now facing.

The allegations about Toyota made no sense to me. When I started my academic career in 1982, I was a bona fide cynic. Like most people, I believed that executives of large corporations were concerned with only three things—profits, profits, and profits. I had studied many highly praised management programs to "empower" the workforce that, on close examination, had yielded only temporary gains and minor cosmetic improvements in the look of the workplace as employees subverted attempts to be manipulated by uncommitted managers. Then I came upon Toyota in 1983, and my career would never be the same. For the first time in my research, I saw a company in which managers really did invest in developing their employees; in which teamwork was rewarded over individual grandstanding; in which the workers exerted just as much effort when the boss was away as when he was looking over their shoulders. What Toyota managers and team members told me in interviews was borne out by what I saw in the manufacturing plants and learned from former Toyota employees who became my colleagues. Of course, the quality and productivity data spoke for themselves. When I first told American manufacturing executives about Toyota's benchmarks, they told me that those numbers were impossible.

Most important, what I saw when I visited Toyota wasn't some new management initiative or a one-month quality and teamwork campaign. Toyota's approach to leadership and operational excellence was based on a philosophy and culture, now known as the Toyota Way, that extended back to the company's founding as a maker of automatic looms before the turn of the twentieth century. While almost everything about the company had changed at the surface level during that time, the commitment to the culture and philosophy of continuous improvement, respect for people, contributing to society, and putting customers first hadn't changed at all. My cold-hearted skepticism slowly turned to warm-hearted enthusiasm.

Since then, I've dedicated my career to understanding the Toyota Way as best I can and helping other companies and their leaders to learn what they can from Toyota's management system and philosophy. I've spent tens of thousands of hours watching and learning at Toyota and helping other companies apply Toyota principles—and I have witnessed dramatic improvement in those other companies when they did so.

In all that time, I had never had reason to doubt the sincerity of Toyota's commitment to quality, safety, and putting customers first. But suddenly the press reports were painting a picture of a company that looked nothing like the one I knew.

My first instinct was to write a storm of letters to the editor and opinion columns defending Toyota. I was stunned to see colleagues who made a living teaching Toyota principles quoted in the press as saying that Toyota had lost its way and had put growth and profitability ahead of people and safety. I wanted to jump into the fray and fight for Toyota's reputation. But then a longtime friend, John Shook, who had spent years as a Toyota manager, pointed out to me that if I leaped to Toyota's defense, I would not be following the Toyota Way.*

The Toyota Way demands that any problem be thoroughly investigated before any conclusions are reached. It demands that problem solvers "go and see" the problem firsthand and not rely on abstract, thirdhand reports. It demands thoughtful and critical reflection to find root causes and develop effective solutions. Most of all, it demands that every team member openly bring problems to the surface and work to continuously improve what is within their control. I wasn't doing any of those things. Whether Toyota was living up to its principles or not, I wasn't.

So Tim and I began a process of trying to live out the Toyota Way as we examined the allegations and tried to uncover the facts. We quickly found ourselves in a losing race, trying to investigate every allegation against Toyota. Tracking down every police report, every NHTSA filing, and every field report, we realized, would be a lifetime pursuit (if not more). We then stepped back and asked: What is our purpose in this investigation? Was it to document in detail every case of a sudden unintended acceleration complaint; become experts on electronic systems; document day by day what Toyota did, what the government did, and who said what to whom? We finally concluded that we were not investigative reporters, but that we had the opportunity to do something more meaningful and useful than an exhaustive forensic investigation. We had the opportunity to examine how Toyota had responded to a serious crisis and to relate the lessons to be learned for others.

---

*John Shook was the first American to become a Toyota manager in Japan and is currently CEO of the Lean Enterprise Institute.

Thus, we make no claims that this book is comprehensive or that we've uncovered every fact or detail related to Toyota's recall crisis. We've done our best to be thorough and complete while also being succinct. There is a great deal of detail from our investigations and interviews that doesn't appear in the book, because this book is not intended to be a defense of Toyota or investigative journalism. Instead, we've tried to provide the materials that are relevant to understanding the crisis and what others can learn from it. The hard times Toyota was living through allowed us to see Toyota in a different context than ever before.

Since I'd been studying Toyota, the company had had a nonstop record of success. The years from 2003 to 2008 were the most profitable five years in the company's history. In fact, Toyota Motor Corporation had been profitable for almost 50 years running, continually gaining market share. This was the first time I had seen Toyota operate during truly bad times, during a crisis. It's one thing to pledge a commitment to long-term thinking and putting people first when you're winning. Doing so when you're under fire is a whole different ball game. How would Toyota react? Could Toyota turn the dual crises of the Great Recession and the successive recalls, like other challenges it has faced, into an opportunity for improvement?

This was certainly not the first crisis that Toyota had faced. In fact, while this has been obscured by the record it has amassed, Toyota's entire history is one of facing severe challenges and responding successfully. The original company, Toyota Automated Loom Works, was founded in rural Japan in the 1890s as the country emerged from centuries of isolation to find that the world had left it behind. The automotive company as we know it today literally had to rebuild from the ashes of Japan after World War II, fighting through a period of near bankruptcy. It had proved remarkably resilient to any number of challenges and crises, from recessions to dramatic increases in the strength of the yen (which slashes profits) to the 1973 oil crisis to major spikes in the costs of raw materials such as steel. The company was a model of resilience, a company that could defy business cycles and maintain a steady path of growth and progress while other companies made knee-jerk decisions to retreat from investment, close plants, and lay off masses of employees. But the recession plus the recall crisis was a greater challenge by an order of magnitude than anything I had seen Toyota face.

At that point, Tim and I began talking about writing a book that ultimately became *Toyota under Fire*. We read everything we could find about what was happening and had happened at Toyota. It was certainly important to ground our analysis in the facts and to separate fact from fiction on the most fundamental issues, particularly for the recall crisis. I called friends and contacts inside and outside the company. Toyota itself granted us unique access to its executives, managers, and team members so that we could go and see and draw our own conclusions. We began doing our best to find out what lessons Toyota was learning and what lessons others could learn from Toyota's experience managing through these crises.

Our instincts that there were important lessons to be learned were borne out as Toyota began to recover from the negative firestorm. Market share, recognition for quality, and profitability began recovering quickly. More and more data came out suggesting that many of the accusations against Toyota had little basis in fact. Various media reports were shown to be inaccurate; supposedly independent experts who were criticizing Toyota were revealed to be on the payroll of trial attorneys who were suing Toyota. While the company had not fully recovered from either the Great Recession or the recall crisis, it had bounced back remarkably quickly. Even more noteworthy, it turned these crises into opportunities to further the company's long-term goals.

There's a widely held belief, often cited in business management circles, that the Chinese pictogram for the word *crisis* is made up of characters meaning "danger" and "opportunity." This is certainly a comforting thought for managers who are facing hard times—that the dark clouds have a silver lining. Unfortunately, both literally and figuratively, this belief is a myth. The meme about the Chinese character was started by a management consultant who had been studying Chinese for only a few months and as a result misinterpreted the characters. The idea that a crisis is an opportunity is belied by the many businesses that have only just scraped along during the recession, having slashed jobs and investment in their future.

In fact, as John Shook warned me, looking at Toyota through rose-colored glasses distorts the facts. The company did suffer from the recession in the form of financial losses and from the recall crisis both financially and in the form of loss of reputation. When Toyota executives looked hard in the mirror, they found some serious weaknesses in the company that had developed as the company grew rapidly. Most important, they found that they had lost the intense focus on understanding customer concerns that had defined the company for most of its history. When customer concerns were identified, it took too long to respond, as the company had grown into a large global company with too much bureaucracy. The bureaucracy and some decision making isolated in Japan had also fueled the recall crisis and slowed Toyota's responsiveness to legitimate complaints by customers and the U.S. government.

Our investigations, and increasingly the data, suggest that as a result of facing these problems with brutal honesty, Toyota has managed the feat of not just weathering a crisis, but using that crisis as an opportunity to push itself further toward its long-term goals. It didn't do so by beginning some radical new program or bringing in new executives with "fresh ideas." In fact, as one article that was intended as criticism of Toyota for not being more aggressive in its business response noted, not a single associate at Toyota has involuntarily lost his or her job as a result of the dual crises. It's probably most accurate to say that Toyota turned crisis into opportunity not by doing something different, but by doing even more of what it had been doing before the recession or the recall crisis started.

Considering the nonstop battering that Toyota took, first from the recession and then from the full force of the U.S. media and various congressional committees, I was quite impressed by the resilience of the brand and the business rebound in the United States. Toyota's U.S. sales dropped precipitously by 16 percent in January 2010 and 9 percent in February 2010, even though overall vehicle sales in the United States had increased. By March, with uncharacteristically high sales incentives (although still about 30 percent below the U.S. average), Toyota boosted sales by 35 percent over the prior year, and sales of cars that had been recalled were up by 48 percent. By May, according to a list compiled by Reuters, the Camry, Corolla, RAV4, and Prius were among the 20 top-selling vehicles in the United States and the Camry had regained the crown as the bestselling midsized car. Even in November of 2010, when it seemed that Toyota sales had seriously lost ground to competitors, a closer look only at retail sales (eliminating the low-profit fleet sales, for example, to rental car companies) showed that Toyota had 17 percent of the retail sales market, compared to an average of 18.3 percent in 2009. This did represent a 1.3-percentage-point loss of share, but it still made Toyota the number one automaker in retail sales in the United States.

I was also impressed, given the lost sales and the high cost of the recalls, that in the fiscal year ending March 30, 2010, Toyota reported a global profit of $2.2 billion and has been profitable for each quarter since. An indicator of the strength of the Toyota brand was demonstrated in a Rice University automotive consumer survey in February 2010, at the worst of the recall crisis, that found that Toyota owners in the United States overwhelmingly supported the company, thought that it was handling the recalls properly, and would buy another Toyota. And by November 2010, *Consumer Reports* ranked 17 Toyota vehicles among "the most reliable" on the road, the most of any automaker. Perhaps more important, *CR* stated: "We believe that Toyota has adequately addressed the problem of unintended acceleration and that its new vehicles on sale now are fundamentally safe."

Yet, as we will see later in the book, some long-term damage was done, and Toyota realized that it still had a great deal of work to do if it was to regain its pristine image for quality and wanted to get even better than it had been before these crises. While Toyota was struggling to get through the crisis, it was becoming increasingly evident that its chief competitors in the United States, notably Ford and Hyundai, had been getting much stronger. Simply recovering is never enough in the Toyota Way. The goal is always to come out stronger and more competitive.

The reader will, of course, notice that while this book is about a global company, it has a predominantly U.S. bias. While the bad news spread throughout the world, the United States was the epicenter, particularly of the recall crisis. In fact, most of the U.S. media wrote articles about Toyota as if it were only a U.S. company and only the U.S. market for automobiles existed. Sales figures and quality data were published without even mentioning that they were from the United States only. The wake-up call for Toyota was that each region, and even each country, is different, and that the local social and political context has to be considered in every decision. Having all the most important decisions made in Japan by Japanese engineers and executives who were isolated from the *gemba* (where the issues were really happening) was discovered to be a critical weakness for this global company, and there was a great deal to be done to listen to customers in every country and to give team members who were locally at the *gemba* more authority.

That's the story we've set out to tell here: how Toyota responded to being under fire, with a primary focus on the epicenter—the United States. This book is the culmination of more than two years of investigation starting in the midst of the global recession, including visits to Toyota plants and offices across the United States and Japan and interviews with President Akio Toyoda, board members, and senior executives in both locales, as well as Toyota team members, dealers, and independent experts on the automotive industry. I spent several days in each of the plants that were hit hardest during the depth of the recession, interviewing team members and getting a tour through their *kaizen* (improvement) activities. I observed a Camry being tested for sensitivity to electromagnetic interference in Japan. I watched as team members fielded customer questions in Toyota's call center in Torrance, California. I previewed training materials for a new quality professional training program.

We do not claim to be technical experts on sudden unintended acceleration or to know the details of all the discussions between Toyota and the government over recalls, but we are confident in our understanding at a big picture level and have done our best to provide a fair and accurate assessment of the most important events in this period. Tim and I spent hundreds of hours in interviews. We learned of heroic moments at Toyota, and executives did not hesitate to reflect harshly on serious gaps between current practices and the ideals of the Toyota Way. Throughout the book, we quote Toyota sources based on these interviews, except in cases where we explicitly cite a news report that quoted someone at Toyota. We also talked to independent automotive experts from *Consumer Reports*, Edmunds.com, thetruthaboutcars .com, and universities, as well as journalists, who shared detailed information and data that they had collected.

The worst thing to do in hard times is regress, which unfortunately is what too many companies seem to do. Toyota's greatest contribution to the world is as a model of real continuous improvement. Continuous improvement does not stop when there are setbacks. Setbacks are opportunities to look in the mirror, identify your weaknesses, and move to a new level of performance. The dual crises were yet another opportunity to galvanize all Toyota team members and partners toward a vision of improving quality and safety to a level never seen before in the auto industry. As always, there was no shortage of problems to work on.

The path through the crises to improvement was guided by the Toyota Way. The Toyota Way is a very deep philosophy, and there are many specific methods to be studied and mastered. But in another sense, the basic concepts are very straightforward. Face challenges with a clear head and positive energy. Hold fast to your core values and your vision for the company. Always start with the customer. Understand the problems that you face by analyzing the facts, including your own failings, and understanding the root causes. Thoroughly consider alternative solutions, then pick a path, develop a detailed plan, and execute with discipline and energy.

Perhaps most unusual is who is doing all these things. It is not the senior executives who at periodic crisis points turn the company around. It is not the staff quality experts and engineers who are figuring out how to solve the technical problems causing defects. Too often, we think you can take a company that is in crisis and turn it around simply by clearing out the old executives, bringing in the new, and, perhaps, adding a new department of experts on whatever caused the crisis. Top executives and staff departments certainly play important roles, but to get to continuous improvement, you need everyone to be both doing and thinking. In fact, the people doing the value-added work are in the best position to see and understand in detail the weaknesses and to find innovative ways to improve the product and processes. We are talking about the people who engineer and test the cars, those who build the cars, those who sell the cars, the maintenance people who are seeing problems every day, the people in contact with government agencies discussing whether to conduct a recall, and even the people who are at the phones talking to customers with concerns. It is the combined effort of hundreds of thousands of people globally who are highly motivated and developed to check, question, challenge, and improve that has made Toyota such a strong competitor. This is what we mean by culture—the collective values in action on a daily basis throughout the company.

The motivation and skills to continuously improve are not genetically inherited, but learned. All managers in Toyota are expected to be teachers and to develop in their students the art of continuous improvement. It is that culture of deeply training and developing people that Akio Toyoda concluded had weakened as Toyota grew so fast that there were not enough managers/teachers to go around and too many new hires who had not gone through the long, arduous process of becoming indoctrinated into the Toyota Way.

This is not to say that the Toyota Way evaporated from the company. The culture was always alive and strong in most parts of the company, but it needed to be awakened and raised to a higher level, particularly in technical and administrative areas dealing with translating customer complaints into improvements, responding to government concerns, and making recall decisions. The Toyota Way is far more than a set of truisms at Toyota.

These improvements are exactly what we witnessed at Toyota through these crises. You do not turn a culture off and on again like a light switch. Toyota's experience shows that with a strong culture built over decades of living the values, these actions are possible in the real world, even in a crisis, even while operating at a $4 billion loss, and even while being falsely accused by the media and politicians of reckless disregard for customers.

We are grateful to Toyota for opening its doors and sharing in great detail what it was doing to respond to the crisis. We were consistently encouraged by Toyota to provide our own unbiased interpretations about what we learned in a way that might benefit other companies going through a crisis. We think there are lessons for every company and every manager in Toyota's missteps and successes. We've worked hard to tell the Toyota story with candor, based on the facts, and with an eye toward what others can learn about navigating through very rocky waters.

One quick note: we interviewed a wide variety of people inside and outside Toyota during our research. Any direct quotes in the text, unless otherwise noted, are taken from those interviews. In quotes translated from Japanese, we have taken the liberty of lightly editing for grammar and clarity.

JEFFREY K. LIKER, PH.D.
Professor, Industrial and Operations Engineering,
University of Michigan; author, *The Toyota Way*

Acknowledgments

There are far more people that we would like to acknowledge for their help than we could possibly include without filling much of this book. We do want to start by acknowledging all those who gave generously of their time to share with us their perspective on what had happened to Toyota and often provide critical data. Toyota as a whole was gracious in opening its doors to us, making some of its busiest people available to us for interviews, efficiently organizing visits and tours, and taking the attitude that it would share what it knew, and it would be up to us to write what we believed to be true.

Here is a list of some of the people we interviewed within Toyota, but there were many managers and team members whom we talked to on various tours of the company's facilities. We are grateful to them all.

Toyota Motor Corporation (TMC), Japan

Akio Toyoda, President and Representative Director

Atsushi Niimi, Executive Vice President, Global Manufacturing and Production Engineering; and Representative Director

Yukitoshi Funo, Executive Vice President, Global Government and Public Affairs; and Representative Director

Shinichi Sasaki, Executive Vice President, Global Quality and Support Services; and Representative Director

Takeshi Uchiyamada, Executive Vice President, Global R&D; and Representative Director

Shigeru Hayakawa, Vice President, Corporate Citizenship and Public Affairs; and Managing Officer

Takahiro Fujioka, Vice President, TQM Promotion Office and Manufacturing Plants; and Managing Officer

Katsutada Masumoto, Vice President, Sales Parts and Logistics and Customer Service Planning; and Managing Officer

Shinji Miyamoto, General Manager, Quality Division

Katsutoshi Sagata, General Manager, Design Quality Innovation Division

Hirohisa Kishi, General Manager, Engine Management System Development

Masayuki Noda, General Manager, Electronics Laboratory Planning Department

Toyota Engineering and Manufacturing, North America (TEMA)

Tetsuo Agata, President and Chief Operating Officer, TEMA; and Senior Managing Director, Toyota Motor Corporation

Steve St. Angelo, Chief Quality Officer, North America; Chairman, Toyota Motor Manufacturing Kentucky and Toyota Motor Manufacturing Mississippi; Executive Vice President, TEMA; and Managing Officer, Toyota Motor Corporation

Dino Triantafyllos, Vice President, Quality Division, and Regional Product Safety Executive, TEMA

Bob Young, General Manager, Purchasing

Jason Reid, Assistant General Manager, Purchasing

Tim Turner, Team Leader, Toyota Motor Manufacturing Kentucky

Renee McIntosh, Team Member, Toyota Motor Manufacturing Kentucky

Steve Turley, Team Member, Toyota Motor Manufacturing Kentucky

Vinodh Venugopal, General Manager, Quality Engineering & Quality Control, Toyota Motor Manufacturing Kentucky

Wil James, President, Toyota Motor Manufacturing Kentucky

Norm Bafunno, President, Toyota Motor Manufacturing Indiana

Dan Antis, Plant Manager, Toyota Motor Manufacturing Texas

Toyota Motor Sales, USA (TMS)

James E. Lentz, President and Chief Operating Officer; and Managing Officer, TMC

Robert Carter, Group Vice President and General Manager, Toyota Division

Robert M. Waltz, Vice President, Product Quality and Service Support

Mike Michels, Vice President, External Communications

Irving A. Miller, former Group Vice President, Corporate Communications

Brian Lyons, Safety & Quality Communications Manager

Nancy Fein, Vice President, Customer Relations

Paul Williamsen, National Manager, Lexus College

Toyota Motor North America, Inc. (TMA)

Dian Ogilvie, Senior Vice President and Secretary, Toyota Motor North America, Inc.

James M. Wiseman, Chief Communications Officer and Group Vice President, Corporate Communications, Toyota Motor North America, Inc.

Toyota Technical Center, Inc. (U.S.A.)

Greg Bernas, Chief Engineer, Toyota Technical Center

Bruce Brownlee, Senior Executive Administrator for External Affairs, Toyota Technical Center

Kristen Tabar, General Manager—Electronics Systems 2, Toyota Technical Center

Among all of these people, we'd especially like to thank Jim Wiseman, Steve St. Angelo, and Brian Lyons, who constantly went above and beyond the call of duty to help us get questions answered and track down technical details and documents.

We'd also like to thank the numerous individuals at independently owned Toyota dealerships around the country who took the time to speak with us and share their experiences.

Colleagues, Experts, Journalists, Analysts, and Friends

There were many other people who took time to share their insights and expertise with us whom we'd like to acknowledge:

Jeremy Anwyl, CEO, and Jeannine Fallon, Executive Director, Corporate Communications, Edmunds.com

David Champion, Senior Analyst, *Consumer Reports*

Edward Niedermayer, Editor-in-Chief, thetruthaboutcars.com

Bertel Schmitt, Editor, thetruthaboutcars.com

John Cook, Gawker Media

Micheline Maynard, former Detroit bureau chief,
New York Times

Richard Schmidt, Professor Emeritus of Psychology, UCLA

We also must acknowledge the yeoman work of James Franz, a lean advisor colleague of Jeff's who did the dirty work of searching many archives for detailed data on articles published, sales, income, and other such information.

John Shook was a major influence on the tone and approach to the book through a series of conversations with Jeff. John was the first American to become a Toyota manager in Japan and is now the CEO of the Lean Enterprise Institute. John shared his deep insights based on past experience and current contact with Toyota and challenged Jeff to keep a critical eye and always engage in *hansei*.

Tim would like to especially acknowledge his business partner, Laura Starita, who kept the business fires burning, and his wife, Catherine Ogden, who kept the home fires burning so that he could spend the many hours necessary to get the book done so quickly. And Jeff would like to thank his wife, Deborah Liker, for her support through the Toyota crisis and for her patience while he wrote his ninth book about Toyota, his son, Jesse, for his usual sage advice, and his daughter, Emma, for her warmth and caring.

Other people who helped out by doing background research, reading drafts, and providing advice include Anders Gustafson, Stephanie Falktoft, and Kelsey Lafferty. We appreciate all their efforts.

ONE

The Most Admired Company in the World

> *It is essential that our global leadership team embrace the concepts of the Toyota Way as we achieve our business goals in host countries which have a wide variety of customs, traditions, and business practices.*
>
> —THEN PRESIDENT FUJIO CHO IN THE
> PREAMBLE TO *THE TOYOTA WAY 2001*

As 2007 ended, it would be no exaggeration to say that Toyota was on top of the world. While you could argue whether it was the largest car company in the world, depending on what measurements you used, there was no question that it was the dominant car company globally. Toyota was the firm that all others benchmarked themselves against. It was far more profitable than its major American competitors. In fact, it had been continuously profitable for almost 50 years, a record that rivaled that of any global 1000 firm and was unheard of in manufacturing industries.

Its growth and profitability were driven by its extraordinary record of quality and customer satisfaction. It dominated annual quality awards and value-for-money rankings. Toyota's vehicles held their value much better than its competitors' products. Customer loyalty was tops in the industry. The company was profitable in every vehicle segment, from small cars to massive SUVs. It had even made the Prius—the world's first mass-production hybrid—profitable, a feat that, when the vehicle was launched, industry observers had claimed could never happen.

But Toyota's position was more dominant than even these impressive figures might suggest. Toyota had literally revolutionized manufacturing, process engineering, and quality, setting new standards for operational excellence that had become goals for companies in many industries. Toyota changed the way a large portion of the world thinks about quality and how to continuously improve any process. Today, almost every large organization, regardless of its sector or country, at least speaks the jargon of built-in quality, lean, and just-in-time operation, although only a select few have carried the concepts to anything approaching the level that Toyota has.

At the end of 2007, it seemed that everyone loved Toyota, even such diverse constituencies as Wall Street investors and hard-core environmentalists. Millions of books explaining Toyota's approach were sold, not least *The Toyota Way*, and companies were spending billions of dollars trying to understand, learn from, and replicate the Toyota model.*

It's Toyota's overwhelming success that makes it hard to believe today that there was a time when "Made in Japan" was a synonym for junk rather than high quality, or when American car companies had a stranglehold on the global car business. Or that Toyota Motor Corporation began with a single self-taught

---

* Jeffrey K. Liker, *The Toyota Way* (New York: McGraw-Hill, 2004).

inventor tinkering with looms in an obscure rural village outside Nagoya, Japan, in the late 1800s.

So how did Toyota rise from the rural rice fields of a backward, unindustrialized country to the top of the world, the vantage point that made its fall from grace so shocking? That history is not just a curiosity. Indeed, understanding the underpinnings of Toyota's success is critical to understanding what happened at Toyota from 2008 to 2010 and how it acted and reacted under fire.

From Humble Beginnings

Toyota was born out of the tinkering of Sakichi Toyoda, who grew up the son of a poor carpenter in a region of rice farmers. In the late 1800s, as Japan was trying to catch up to the industrialized nations after over 200 years of being closed to the outside world, the Japanese government encouraged the growth of small-scale manufacturing across the country. This included village and even home-based mills. The women of Toyoda's family were involved with weaving—at the time a difficult, labor-intensive process undertaken with manual looms, using technology that had not changed much in a century.

Just like the inventor-heroes of Western lore, such as Alexander Graham Bell, Charles Babbage, James Watt, Guglielmo Marconi, Louis Pasteur, and Thomas Edison, Sakichi Toyoda tinkered in his workshop for decades, refining his loom designs by trial and error, hoping to ease the manual labor of his female relatives. His first manual wooden loom in 1891 immediately reduced that burden by using gravity and a foot pedal to move the loom's shuttle back and forth, doubling productivity. Over the next few years, he made a number of other improvements to his looms, and by 1896 he had produced a steam-driven power loom that quadrupled productivity. Toyoda's tinkering not only led him to automatic loom design, but necessarily also took him into engine design—after all, the automatic looms needed a power source. But his best-known innovation, an innovation that set the pattern for all of Toyota's future history, was a way of eliminating common mistakes in the weaving process.

Using a manual loom, it was easy to spot mistakes and quality problems—the process was quite slow, allowing the weaver to closely inspect the cloth continuously. But the faster rate of automatic looms meant that defects or problems were harder to spot. And when an error occurred—the most common problem was a thread breaking—the loom could keep running long after the product was ruined. For a cottage weaving shop, this was potentially disastrous. Such a shop couldn't afford to waste materials, so people were stationed at the "automatic" looms to shut them down in case there were problems.

Of course, that defeated a lot of the benefit of automation. In response, Sakichi Toyoda invented a mechanism that would stop the loom automatically as soon as a thread broke. As he put it, he "freed the person from the machine" so that people could spend their time doing value-added work instead of simply monitoring the machine. This and other innovations were so groundbreaking that Platt Brothers of England, the world's dominant loom maker, eventually bought the rights to one of Toyoda's most popular looms. The proceeds from the sale funded the start-up of Toyota Motor Corporation. Now referred to in Japan as the "king of inventors," Sakichi Toyoda also is credited as being a leader in fueling Japan's industrial revolution.

The Toyota Production System and Toyota Business Practices

Those with at least a passing knowledge of Toyota's approach to manufacturing will recognize the origin of the now famous *andon* cord in Sakichi Toyoda's "mistake-proof" loom. The *andon* cord is pulled by a worker in a production plant to stop the assembly line as soon as an error is detected (all of Toyota's automated equipment also has built-in error detection that will shut down the machine automatically). The basic philosophy of immediately identifying and eliminating mistakes and waste has been a core pillar of the company from the very beginning.

The shift from looms to motor vehicles was driven by Sakichi Toyoda's son Kiichiro, on the advice of his father. Sakichi believed that the firm needed to expand into other areas of manufacturing. In 1929, Kiichiro began traveling to the United States and Britain regularly, ostensibly to negotiate licensing terms for the company's loom technology. In reality, he was also learning all he could about automobile and machine tool factories to help guide him in setting up the automobile division at Toyoda Loom Works, which he did in 1933. By 1937, Toyota Motor Company (today known as Toyota Motor Corporation or TMC), was the center of the business.

It was Kiichiro Toyoda who, in a key document in the late 1930s laying out Toyota's operating philosophy, first penned the words "just-in-time," describing a continuous flow of materials from raw materials to the customer. The theory was put into practice under the leadership of another iconic figure in Toyota's history, Taiichi Ohno, who tried his first "pull system," building in response to customer pull, in 1948 and who first put into a plant, by 1953, what some now call a "supermarket."

Ohno's supermarket idea was inspired by a conversation with a friend who had recently visited the United States and described the American self-service supermarket. Before the widespread availability of refrigeration, inventory control in the grocery business was critical. Food spoiled quickly, and so grocers needed to keep a close eye on their inventory, keeping only enough on hand to meet a few days' demand. In modern terminology, supermarkets needed just-in-time inventory management, and that's exactly what they had.

The nascent Toyota Motor Company had a problem similar to that of supermarkets. While there was no danger of Toyota's inventory spoiling, the company simply didn't have the funds to keep inventory on hand. As a small outfit, it needed to conserve its very limited working capital as much as possible. Like American supermarkets, where goods like milk are put up on the shelf only in the quantity needed to replace what the customers take away, Toyota factories would eventually have internal "supermarkets" that replenished parts on the assembly line as they were needed.

The combination of Sakichi Toyoda's emphasis on eliminating mistakes and Kiichiro Toyoda's emphasis on and Taiichi Ohno's innovations in just-in-time inventory formed the basis of what has become known as the Toyota Production System (TPS). TPS, as it evolved and was refined over the course of the next 80 years, is the blueprint that guides Toyota's operations from suppliers to manufacturing to delivery of automobiles and service parts to dealerships. Above all, it focuses on the relentless pursuit of quality and the elimination of waste through continuous improvement by all workers and managers. That sounds like common sense today, but it was and is revolutionary. The dominant model of manufacturing systems before Toyota's rise as a global leader was the pursuit of economies of scale. This approach focused on driving down the cost of production by increasing the amount that was produced at every step of the process. Inevitably this caused a buildup of inventory, but that was perceived as a good thing. Quality problems could be tolerated because there were always more parts to pull from inventory. The belief was that reducing defects was far more expensive than maximizing efficiency and throwing away the flawed parts.

Toyota proved that the opposite was true. If you eliminated waste and quality problems, you could operate far more cheaply—and keep customers much happier. The process for eliminating waste and errors that Toyota has developed is founded on the insights of Taiichi Ohno. Ohno saw that if the company was to maintain Sakichi's commitment to catching and fixing problems and Kiichiro's commitment to just-in-time operation, it had to have a systematic way of solving problems throughout the company. His focus was on drilling down to the root cause of the problem by asking why five times.

The problem-solving process that Ohno started was later enhanced by ideas from an American who was dispatched to Japan by the U.S. government to assist in the rebuilding of Japan after World War II, Dr. W. Edwards Deming. Deming's ideas are the foundation of the modern quality movement. He taught Japanese managers about the importance of quality and a way of thinking about how to achieve it. Central to Deming's approach was a radical expansion of the definition of the word *customer*. Historically, customers were considered to be the end users of a product. Deming taught that "the customer" is also the next stage of a process. Thus, serving the customer in a manufacturing environment meant providing the next step in the assembly line with exactly what it needed, in terms of both quality and volume, at the exact time it was needed. When problems with serving customers were encountered, Deming advocated a highly systematic approach to solving them, known as the Plan-Do-Check-Act (PDCA) cycle.*

The PDCA cycle is fairly intuitive. Before you attempt to fix a problem, you need to make sure that you have a *plan* that is likely to succeed based on thorough study of the root cause of the problem, not just its symptoms. Once you have a plan for fixing the root cause, you *do* the solution in a test environment, *check* that the solution works, then *act* based on what you learn from the test environment, either improving the plan or moving on to another area that is in need of improvement. Thus, the PDCA cycle never ends—the final step always points to opportunities for further improvement.

The Toyota problem-solving process, known first as "practical problem solving," has evolved to today's version, called Toyota Business Practices (TBP). It is Toyota's approach to solving problems, from eliminating errors in individual jobs to setting the global strategy of the company

In summary, the TBP process begins with a statement of the problem, including the gap between the actual and the ideal conditions. This gap is then broken down into the most important problems that can be acted upon. These specific subproblems are then analyzed by asking "why?" until the root cause, not a surface cause, is found. Within Toyota, this is known as the Five Whys— the belief that to find the root cause of a problem, you have to ask "why" at least five times. Countermeasures are then identified, tried, and monitored, with further adjustments being made until the gap is eliminated and the next challenge identified.

---

* Deming adapted the PDCA cycle from William Shewhart.

The eight steps of TBP are

PLAN

1. Define the problem relative to the ideal.

2. Break down the problem into manageable pieces.

3. Identify the root cause.

4. Develop alternative solutions.

5. Evaluate and select the best solution based on what is known.

DO

6. Implement the solution (on a trial basis if possible).

CHECK

7. Check the impact of the solution.

ACT

8. Adjust, standardize, and spread based on what has been learned.

While TPS is mostly a system for manufacturing and repetitive processes, TBP takes the philosophy of TPS and applies it broadly to the entire enterprise, from manufacturing to engineering to sales, and even to strategic decision making. Toyota believes that this problem-solving process is essential to leadership—every leader, no matter what his role or department, is expected to be a master of TBP. Mastering this process allows even a leader with a background in finance or human resources, for instance, to contribute meaningfully on the shop floor, and also to view his own department's work as a set of processes that can be improved.

Another major contribution from Ohno was the development of standardized work. This is the concept that every job on the production line needs to be tightly defined and performed in the exact same way by every worker who is doing that job. Solving problems on the production line and continually improving performance simply couldn't be done without standardized work—it would be virtually impossible to isolate and correct any factors that were contributing to a defect or underperformance with the added variation of the same job being done in different ways. Many Westerners initially find the concept of standardized work distasteful, imagining a system that treats people like cogs or robots. On the contrary, standardized work allows line workers to think about what they are doing, why they are doing it, and how to improve it. Think of it this way: no one thinks of great actors like Sean Penn or Meryl Streep as drones or cogs. But they can't bring their creativity and insight to a role until they've memorized the script. Standardized work is like an actor's script. It's the basis on which a production worker can apply her skills to continuously improve a process. Without standardized work, TPS and TBP would be impossible.

Building on a Firm Cultural Foundation

The Toyota Production System is the foundation that is often credited with allowing Toyota to emerge from the small, devastated market of Japan in the 1950s and become the world's largest carmaker. Along the way, Toyota dramatically changed perspectives of what was possible in terms of the quality and productivity of design and manufacturing operations. But as any student of industrial organization or psychology, or even anyone familiar with the history of any large company, will tell you, processes and procedures are never enough to ensure excellence.

As management thinkers like Peter Drucker, Tom Peters, Jim Collins, and Peter Senge have demonstrated in their research and writing over the years, achieving consistent excellence is extraordinarily difficult and rare. Excellence, where it does occur, is a result of culture rather than just processes. Every company and every process is subject to the laws of entropy—things simply degrade over time. That can happen because people grow complacent or because circumstances change and yesterday's solutions no longer apply in today's context. For many companies, performance declines as a company grows beyond its founders and their passion.

The only way to combat the pervasive disease of entropy is culture—building an organization that constantly renews its commitment to excellence and to its core principles, an organization that can instill those principles and the founders' passion in each new generation of employees and leaders.

As demonstrated by its remarkably consistent growth and profitability, Toyota has built a culture that does exactly that. For most of Toyota's history, that culture was not formally codified or given an official name. It was simply handed down from employee to employee—a process that was possible because all of Toyota's leaders had spent their entire careers at the company. The model for training was the master-apprentice relationship. As Toyota grew globally, though, spreading the culture one-on-one with daily mentoring was not enough. There simply were not enough master trainers who had grown up in the culture available for all the new hires. In 2001, then president Fujio Cho, a student of Ohno and the first president of Toyota's Georgetown, Kentucky, plant, introduced the document formally defining the Toyota Way. This wasn't a new direction for Toyota; it was a codification of the culture that had been created by Sakichi and Kiichiro Toyoda and extended by leaders like Taiichi Ohno.

The Toyota Way 2001, as it is still called, is defined as a house with two pillars—respect for people and continuous improvement. Respect for people extends from the team members on the shop floor to every one of Toyota's vast network of partners and out to its customers and to the communities in which Toyota does business. Continuous improvement literally means continually improving products, processes, and even people at all levels of the organization. Some versions of the model show respect for people as the foundation of continuous improvement, since only highly developed people who care passionately about their work and about the company will put in the effort needed for continuous improvement. The twin pillars of respect for people and continuous improvement rest on a foundation of five core values that we summarize here.*

Spirit of Challenge

Toyota was founded on the willingness to tackle tough problems and work at them until they were solved. That was Sakichi Toyoda's approach to looms and Kiichiro Toyoda's approach to building a car company from scratch. Like the two founding Toyodas, every Toyota employee is expected not just to excel in his current role, but to take on the challenges of making needed improvements with enthusiasm. As *The Toyota Way 2001* puts it, "We accept challenges with a creative spirit and the courage to realize our own dreams without losing drive or energy."

Kaizen Mind

Kaizen is a mandate to constantly improve performance. *Kaizen* is now a fairly famous concept, and the term will be familiar to many readers. But the vast majority of people, we've found,

---

* The quotes in this section come from *The Toyota Way 2001*.

misunderstand *kaizen*. Too often it has come to mean assembling a special team to tackle a discrete improvement project, or perhaps organizing a *kaizen* "event" for a week to make a burst of changes. At Toyota, *kaizen* isn't a set of projects or special events. It's the way people in the company think at the most fundamental level, harking back to Deming's never-ending PDCA cycle.

There are two types of *kaizen*. The first is maintenance *kaizen*, the daily work of dealing with an unpredictable world. Maintenance *kaizen* is the process of reacting to the inevitable (some might call it Murphy's Law) mistakes, breakdowns, changes, and variations of everyday life in order to meet today's expected standard (for productivity, quality, cost, and safety).

Visitors to Toyota plants are often surprised by the high level of activity—including the responses to the frequent pull of an *andon* cord by team members on the production line throughout the plant at the first sign of any out-of-standard conditions. This intense activity and the problem solving that results is largely maintenance *kaizen*. Since these problems have the potential to shut down the line, maintenance *kaizen* is urgent and immediate, with the goal of bringing conditions back to the standard.

The second type of kaizen is improvement *kaizen*. This is the work of not just maintaining standards but raising the bar. Toyota inculcates in all employees the idea that the goal is perfection, and therefore that every process can be improved.

One of the core misunderstandings is how much effort Toyota puts into improvement *kaizen* on a daily basis. Many outsiders expect Toyota to have perfected most of its processes—after decades of *kaizen*, there can't be much room left for improvement, they reason. Fighting this perception, even among Toyota employees, is perhaps one of the reasons that "*kaizen* mind" is a core value of Toyota. You can't maintain the gains from a lean approach unless you focus relentlessly on continually improving all processes. As Taiichi Ohno would preach, no matter how many times it has been improved, every step in the production line is full of waste, and even if it is perfect today, conditions will change tomorrow, and waste will creep in. At the root of *kaizen* is the truth that nothing is perfect and everything can be improved.

This value and way of thinking often lead to misunderstanding of Toyota in the popular media. Throughout Toyota's history, you'll see statements from executives that the firm needs to "get back to basics." Fujio Cho would even say in speeches that the company has to "reinvent itself." These statements are usually interpreted as admissions of major corporate decline. Having a *kaizen* mind, though, means that it is always appropriate to go back to basics, to renew the focus on quality, and to critically evaluate today's condition, no matter how good you are compared to the past.

Genchi Genbutsu, *or Go and See to Deeply Understand*

It would seem that going to see something firsthand is simply a practical matter—although one that is infrequently practiced in most firms—rather than a value. The value of *genchi genbutsu* isn't just the specific act of going and seeing, but the philosophy of how leaders make decisions. In this sense, there are two main aspects of *genchi genbutsu*. First, decisions are made based on observed facts about the issue rather than on hunches, assumptions, or perceptions. The expectation is that no problem or issue will be addressed without the firm grasp of facts that comes from seeing and living with that issue firsthand. Second, decisions should be put into the hands of those who are closest to the problem, those who have gone to see it and who have a deep understanding of its causes and the impact of proposed solutions. The role of more senior leaders is not to judge the solution of those close to the problem as much as it is to judge the problem-solving process used to arrive at the proposed solution.

Teamwork

Most companies say that teamwork is critical to success, but saying this is much easier than living it. Dig a bit below the surface in most areas of human endeavor, whether it's a company or a sports team, and you'll find that people talk about teamwork, but are interested first in their individual accomplishments. At Toyota, the view that individual success can happen only within the team and that teams benefit from the personal growth of individuals is built into the promotion process (which focuses heavily on team behavior) and incentives for performance (where individual incentives are only a small component, while team-based incentives predominate). Teamwork does not mean that individuals are not responsible. Critical to Toyota's success is single-point accountability—one person's name goes up next to each item in an action plan. But in order to succeed, the individual responsible must work with the team, drawing on its collective talents, listening closely to all team members' opinions, working to build consensus, and ultimately giving any credit for success to the team.

Respect

In many ways, this is the most fundamental of the core values. Respect is a broader concept than the pillar of Respect for People, starting with the desire to contribute to society through producing the best possible products and services. This extends to respect for the community, customers, employees, and all business partners. It means that every Toyota team member must take responsibility for his actions and their effects on others.

One of the underappreciated facets of TPS is how it feeds into the Toyota Way and vice versa. It's one thing to say that the Toyota culture embraces the spirit of challenge. It's quite another to make sure that challenges are perpetually in front of everyone in the company. TPS deliberately creates a steady flow of challenges. This might seem odd—most companies have a hard enough time dealing with the challenges presented to them by demanding customers, evolving markets, and aggressive competitors. But one of the things that Taiichi Ohno understood about just-in-time production was that with so little inventory, there was no room for error. That's why standardized work and a systematic problem-solving process were imperative for the company. When you have inventory on hand, if a machine goes down or a process is operating at less than full efficiency, you have a buffer. But when you're operating in a just-in-time environment throughout the company, any hiccup rapidly reverberates up and down the production line. That means that you can't get by just slapping Band-Aids on problems or even with "good enough" solutions to a problem. The rest of the production line depends on problems being solved at the root cause so that they do not return.

That, in turn, is a driver for *kaizen* mind. Toyota needs every employee to always be thinking about how to improve processes—continuous improvement—just to keep up with the demands of TPS on a daily basis. Of course, it also requires willingness to "go and see" problems to make continuous improvement a living reality, teamwork so that solutions to problems work together to create a better whole. All of this, though, ultimately requires a culture of respect for employees, no matter what their level within the company. Executives and "lean experts" can never provide the amount and level of problem solving that is required if TPS is to function smoothly. Every team on the production line has to be doing effective problem solving every day.

That means that Toyota has to invest in team members so that they can *be* problem solvers and respect the solutions that the team members find. The expertise in using TPS and TBP for solving problems that even average team members have makes them the company's most valuable asset. Losing employees, for whatever reason, literally undermines the business model. It is no different from capital assets walking out the door. In general, the phrase *human capital* seems to demean human beings, lumping them in with machines and money in an undifferentiated mass. But at Toyota, the capital really is human. Machines can be replaced quickly. A team member with 10 years of experience in TPS and TBP can be replaced only by spending 10 years investing in the training of another employee. People are not the biggest bucket of variable cost at the company, they are the largest bucket of appreciating assets.

Growing to Lead in the United States and the World

The combination of TPS, TBP, and the culture of the Toyota Way is the competitive advantage that allowed Toyota to become the largest carmaker in Japan and expand into other markets in Asia. But in the 1960s, the combined Asian markets were easily dwarfed by the U.S. market.

When Toyota began planning to enter the U.S. market in the late 1950s, its strategy would have seemed laughable to anyone outside the company. Confront the biggest, most experienced car-makers in the world on their home turf? That perception was given even more credibility when Toyota's first attempt at selling a car in the United States was the disastrous Toyopet Crown, which was first imported to California. The car seemed to work fine by Japanese standards of the time, but it barely had the power to get up California hills. It was hastily recalled, and the few hundred that had been sold were shipped back to Japan until they could be upgraded. But Toyota returned to the U.S. market with better vehicles, ones more suited to American roads. By 1970, Toyota was the number two import plate in the United States, behind VW. Toyota got a further boost when the 1973 oil embargo created gas shortages and Americans began scrambling to buy small, fuel-efficient cars.

A small position in the U.S. market was never going to be enough, however. Senior executives at Toyota realized that if the company did not become a significant player in the United States, it would never have the size and scale necessary to permanently fend off the big American companies in any other market. But scaling in the United States would require producing cars in the United States—the company couldn't achieve its goal of being a top contender in the American market if it had to ship all the ve-hicles it sold across the Pacific. Producing cars outside of Japan was an uncertain prospect. Toyota's success was built on its unique cul-ture and approach. No one knew if the Toyota Way and TPS could work outside Japan with workers from other countries who had not spent their whole careers immersed in the culture.

Toyota decided that the least risky path for testing TPS with American workers was a joint venture with an American manu-facturer. Toyota knew that it had to lead the way in introducing TPS, but a joint venture partner could provide needed exper-tise in working with American suppliers and with the general

American financial and regulatory system. A joint venture was formed with GM in 1983, and a shuttered GM plant in California was reopened and named New United Motor Manufacturing, Inc. (NUMMI). The agreement with GM specified that the plant would build Chevy Novas; Toyota would be responsible for engineering and production, while GM provided the facility, supplier relationships, and capital. GM would get small, high-quality cars in its lineup, and Toyota would have a low-risk way to learn how to build its culture in the United States.

Given all the uncertainties—the first time TPS had been tried with a unionized American workforce,* the first joint venture between Toyota and GM—NUMMI was a huge risk, and success was by no means assured. The project was supervised by Tatsuro Toyoda, one of Kiichiro's sons and later president and then chairman of Toyota.

As it turned out, NUMMI was a huge success. Comparisons to an established GM small car plant in Framingham, Massachusetts, found that it took 19 hours to assemble a car at NUMMI compared to 31 hours at the GM plant, and with one-third the defects along the way. NUMMI had 80 percent less inventory, and its performance in its first year of production was comparable to that of its parent plant in Japan.† Toyota's ability to generate such high levels of quality and productivity in an American plant with American workers was what truly brought its revolutionary approach to manufacturing to the world's attention.

---

* Indeed, one of the reasons that the plant had been closed when it was GM-owned was that the local workforce was the worst in the United States in quality and basic discipline. Yet, as a condition of reopening the plant, the collective bargaining agreement required that 80 percent of these workers be rehired.

† Statistics are taken from James P. Womack, Daniel T. Jones, and Daniel Roos, *The Machine That Changed the World* (New York: Rawsons Associates, 1990).

NUMMI was a large part of the basis for the bestselling book *The Machine That Changed the World*, which introduced the term *lean manufacturing* to describe Toyota's approach as a new paradigm, as important as the shift from craft to mass production.

NUMMI was also successful enough to convince Toyota that it could expand production in North America. Just a few years later, Toyota announced its first wholly owned North American production facility, to be built in Georgetown, Kentucky. From there, Toyota went from success to success. The new facility, known as Toyota Motor Manufacturing Kentucky, racked up quality award after quality award. Meanwhile, Toyota's market share steadily grew. Each new product that the company introduced quickly became a leader in its category in terms of both quality and sales.

During the 1990s, Toyota was steadily gaining market share on GM. By the turn of the century, everyone saw the handwriting on the wall. Before long, Toyota would overcome GM as the world's leading car company. The only question was when. That was the context for Global Vision 2010, Toyota's vision for the decade, publicly announced in 2002.

At Toyota, setting companywide goals and 10-year strategies is the task of the most senior executives and the board of directors, as it is at any company. But that group at Toyota is unique— the board of directors is nearly 30 strong and is made up almost entirely of current and former executives. Every executive vice president of TMC is a member of the board, and former presidents remain on the board after they step down. So the companywide goals are not set by the current president and a small circle of advisors. Setting these goals is a consensus process that includes current, former, and future chief executives (who are always lifetime employees of Toyota), along with the senior leaders who are running the business daily around the world.

The high-level goals for 2010 included becoming more environmentally friendly in both vehicles and operations, creating innovative and exciting new vehicles, and becoming "the most admired automotive company in the world." These goals are fairly vague, of course, and they were broken down into targets related to profitability, quality, average fuel economy, and market share—specifically, in this case, 15 percent global market share, a figure that would push Toyota past GM as the world's largest automobile manufacturer. It was an audacious target that required almost doubling the size of the company, although in 2002, few doubted Toyota's ability to achieve it.

From 2002 to 2007, everything seemed very much on course. In fact, 2003 to 2007 was the most profitable five years in the company's history. At the beginning of 2008, Toyota was sprinting toward achieving its Global Vision 2010 goals. In North America, for instance, Toyota's aggressive push into the stronghold of American carmakers with vehicles like the Tundra full-size truck and the Sequoia, Highlander, and RAV4 SUVs was met with great success, success that was exceeded only by the wild popularity of the Prius hybrid. Shortly after bringing out the Tundra, Toyota announced that it would build a factory complex in San Antonio, Texas, to build Tundras in tandem with the original plant in Indiana (known as TMMI) where it was launched. In addition, new plants had opened or were planned in Ontario, Canada; Blue Springs, Mississippi; and Baja, Mexico. Certainly, investing in new plants in the United States and Canada while most of manufacturing was fleeing the country to low-wage developing economies set Toyota apart.

In 2008, the Camry was the best-selling vehicle in the United States, the eleventh time in 12 years that the car had won the sales crown. Lexus has also been the best-selling luxury brand more years than not since the turn of the millennium.

In the wake of crises to come, many pundits suggest that Toyota was growing too fast during this period, introducing quality problems and weakening the culture. But just before the recall crisis, in 2009, there was no sign of a slippage in quality: Toyota brands won 10 of the coveted J.D. Power initial quality awards for the best vehicles in a segment—more than any other automaker. The Toyota assembly plant in Higashi-Fuji, Japan, received the Platinum Plant Quality Award for producing vehicles yielding the fewest defects and malfunctions, averaging just 29 problems per 100 vehicles, while the industry average in 2009 was 108 problems per 100. *Consumer Reports* 2009 reliability rankings (which necessarily are looking at the prior year's vehicles) found that three of the five most reliable brands were Toyota makes (Toyota, Scion, and Lexus). The Prius was the most satisfying overall car. Lexus was the overall best in reliability (for the eighth time in 20 years), and the Sienna minivan was the top-rated nonluxury car.

Then, with the summit within reach and every part of the company seemingly stronger than it had ever been before, Toyota suddenly confronted one of the most difficult periods in its history. From the oil price spike in the spring and summer of 2008, to the Great Recession, to serious allegations of major safety and quality problems in the United States leading to the recall of millions of vehicles, the challenges, both external and self-inflicted, just kept coming.

How Toyota rose to those challenges and turned them into opportunities for continuous improvement is the story that we'll tell in the next three chapters. It's an important story for anyone who wants to be prepared when a crisis strikes, whatever its source. It sheds new light on how even the best will stumble—and what the best need to do to recover when they do.

TWO

The Oil Crisis and the Great Recession

It's up to us, in management, to create an environment in which every team member on the line takes control of quality, and works to streamline production without ever worrying about his own job security.

— THE TOYOTA WAY 2001

As 2008 began, it truly looked as if it was going to be Toyota's year. Toyota's passenger cars, large SUVs, and trucks were selling in record numbers. In America, Toyota's most profitable market, new plants were about to come on line, increasing capacity (and improving Toyota's margins and reducing currency valuation risk, since fewer vehicles would need to be shipped from Japan to meet demand).

But by the spring, oil prices began rising dramatically. And they didn't stop. The United States, with its love of large vehicles and its low gas prices from a global perspective, was particularly hard hit. By the summer of 2008, gasoline prices in the United States had almost doubled, topping the prices during the worst of the 1970s oil crises on an inflation-adjusted basis. In most of the country, regular gasoline was going for more than $4 a gallon; in states like California and New York, it was over $5. That meant that filling up the 20-gallon or larger tanks of large vehicles cost many people more than $100, a high enough threshold to make Americans question whether big was really better. Understandably, the sales of those large vehicles all but came to a halt. It was a shock to the American automobile industry similar to the 1973 oil embargo that opened the U.S. market significantly to small cars from Toyota and other Japanese manufacturers.

But now Toyota wasn't a small and scrappy challenger looking for a foothold in the U.S. market. It was the leading maker of automobiles in the world, and it had gained significant market share in the United States selling the large minivans, SUVs, and trucks that many Americans craved. So when sales of large, highly profitable vehicles like Tundra trucks and Sequoia SUVs inevitably plummeted, it hurt Toyota.

But unlike the "Detroit Three" (GM, Ford, and Chrysler), who relied almost entirely on their large vehicles for their profits, Toyota had significant buffers: its small, fuel-efficient vehicles, like the Corolla, Prius, Yaris, and RAV4, were profitable and would benefit from a shift in demand. So while its margins decreased, Toyota could operate at a global profit even with minimal sales of trucks and SUVs in the United States. That's one of the reasons why the company ensured not only that it could make small cars at a profit, but that via continuous improvement, profitability was stable or increasing over time. So while Detroit went into full panic mode during the summer of 2008, Toyota simply looked to adjust the mix of vehicles being produced, balancing supply and demand, and pressed on.

But then the bottom really fell out of the market in a way that Toyota did not anticipate. By the fall of 2008, there was no doubt that a major global recession was under way. Credit markets seized up—suddenly no loans were available. That's truly a crisis for the automotive industry, since most vehicles are financed. If consumers couldn't get auto loans, they couldn't buy cars. But of course it wasn't just a question of a lack of credit. Even consumers who still had access to credit or who could finance a car through other means stopped buying, afraid of what the future held. Pocketbooks everywhere were closed and locked.

There was an unprecedented collapse of automobile sales, not only in the United States, but around the world, and not just of large vehicles, but of all vehicles. The variety of countries in which Toyota operates and the variety of vehicles it makes profitably give it theoretical protection against economic instability: downturns in some parts of the world or some parts of the market will normally be offset by upswings in others. But in this case, all of the Group of Seven industrialized economies turned downward, and many others besides. There was no place to hide.

As each month passed, Toyota's North American year-over-year sales numbers plummeted further. By May 2009, sales were 40 percent below what they'd been the previous year. To add insult to injury, the U.S. dollar weakened by 15 percent in relation to the Japanese yen between July and December of 2008. Every 1 percent reduction in the strength of the dollar translated to roughly a $36 million decline in operating income for Toyota in yen terms. The combined impact of plummeting sales and the currency adjustment led to Toyota's first loss as a company since 1950—a loss of more than $4 billion for fiscal year 2009 on global sales of 7.6 million units, a drop of 1.3 million units from 2008.*

---

* We should note that in 2008, General Motors lost $30.9 billion, $9.6 billion in the fourth quarter alone. The firm's survival required that it be taken over by the U.S. government and that it cut tens of thousands of jobs. Ford, meanwhile, lost almost $15 billion in 2008 and had already lost $30 billion in the three years since 2006.

When the loss was announced, reporters began calling daily to ask for comment. "What will Toyota do now that it is in crisis? Whose decision was it to introduce the Tundra and build a new plant dedicated only to these large fuel guzzlers? Who is getting fired over the decision to build the new plants? Will the president be fired?" they asked.

Those are natural questions from the press when a company announces a $4 billion loss. We've become conditioned to the ways in which businesses react to losing money: executives lose their jobs; plants are closed down; people are laid off; projects are canceled; assets are sold. It's a fairly predictable recipe. In fact, it is the recipe that most of the automotive industry followed—and not just the American companies that were operating at marginal profitability or even at a loss before the recession. Nissan, for instance, dumped 12 new models and laid off more than 20,000 people. A CNN article in July of 2010 reported that the automobile industry in the United States alone laid off 300,000 workers because of plant closings;* the CEOs of Chrysler, GM, and Kia lost their jobs. The CEOs who kept their jobs generally wielded a sharp axe. Ford's CEO, Alan Mulally, was named to a think tank's list of CEOs with the highest pay who laid off the most workers—in his case, nearly 5,000 workers in 2009 on top of earlier cutbacks in 2008.†

At Toyota, a management transition had already been planned for 2009 before the recession hit: Akio Toyoda was to

---

* Chris Isidore, "7.9 Million Jobs Lost—Many Forever," CNNMoney.com, July 2, 2010; http://money.cnn.com/2010/07/02/news/economy/jobs_gone_forever/index.htm.

† *Huffington Post*, "The 10 Highest-Paid CEOs Who Laid Off the Most Workers: Institute for Policy Studies," September 1, 2010; http://www.huffington post.com/2010/09/01/ceo-pay-layoffs_n_701908.html#s133350.

succeed Katsuake Watanabe as president and CEO; Watanabe would become vice chairman of the board. Since this came in the midst of the collapse of sales and profitability as the recession hit full force, it was easy to infer that Watanabe was being "fired," and that Akio Toyoda was being brought in to "fix" the company. For example, consider this headline from CNN on January 20, 2009: "Japanese Automaker Reshuffles Ranks after Posting Drop in 2008 Sales."

That interpretation, which was not uncommon in the press, rests on a misunderstanding of Toyota's governance structure. Toyota is one of a small number of major Japanese companies that maintain the tradition of having an internal board of directors. Whereas the gold standard of corporate governance in American and European companies is a board made up primarily of independent outsiders, Toyota's board is almost entirely composed of lifetime Toyota executives. So, for instance, as the recession hit, Shoichiro Toyoda, Hiroshi Okuda, and Fujio Cho, the three presidents who preceded Katsuake Watanabe, were on the board. Other board members are primarily executive vice presidents who currently run or recently ran large portions of the company's operations.

If it weren't for Toyota's remarkable history of success, its governance structure would be highly suspect—it violates many of the taken-for-granted principles of good corporate governance today, which assumes that impartial outside eyes are essential to help companies make tough business decisions and remain innovative and competitive. Why does Toyota cling to this model? It's tied to the primacy of the Toyota Way and TPS at Toyota. The company, with good reason after more than 50 years, feels that outsiders who do not know TPS, have not lived the Toyota Way, and have not spent years refining their problem-solving capabilities in the Toyota Business Practices template simply cannot provide the kind of oversight and insight necessary for the company to maintain those central advantages. Outsiders would not understand management's decisions and how they were arrived at well enough to play the needed role on the board.

That being said, Toyota's board plays a very different role from that typically played by the boards of American companies. In American companies, where directors are primarily outsiders, many with full-time jobs of their own, the board meets somewhere between four and eight times a year to review a set of plans made by management. In contrast, a Toyota board member's full-time job is either being an executive of the company or just being a board member. Therefore, the board has the time to be intimately involved in exhaustive monitoring of both internal performance and external forces, which Toyota considers essential for sound strategy and planning. Board members spend a significant amount of their time at Toyota factories, literally walking the shop floor, and visiting offices and dealerships around the world. Toyota's value of *genchi genbutsu* demands their presence at the work site to check processes firsthand.* As a result, when the board sets operational goals and strategies, they are not the plans of a small group of current executives that have been signed off on by a board of outsiders after a high-level overview.

---

* There is also a separate global "board" of managing officers who are one level below the senior executives who serve on the board of directors. These managing officers run specific operations in a region, such as manufacturing or sales. For instance, Jim Lentz, CEO of Toyota Motor Sales, USA, and Tetsuo Agata, president of Toyota Engineering and Manufacturing North America, are managing officers. The managing officers regularly report to the board to give an even more detailed picture of daily operations.

Every board member is intimately and deeply involved in setting the plans in the first place, and most will lead the implementation of some part of the agreed-upon plans.

When the bottom fell out of the car market in late 2008, the board could not blame Katsuake Watanabe alone for the investments in expansion like new vehicles and new plants. Those investments were part of pursuing Global Vision 2010, and that wasn't Watanabe's plan alone; it was the board's plan. As president, Watanabe had some additional responsibility for daily operations, but others, like Fujio Cho, who had preceded him, and Akio Toyoda, who would succeed him, also were responsible for the company's strategic direction. While Watanabe publicly took responsibility for Toyota's losses, it was as the voice of the company, not as a lone ranger CEO who had pushed through an audacious plan and fallen short. So the transition from Katsuake Watanabe to Akio Toyoda was not the board reacting to the recession. Toyota Business Practices dictates using the "Five Whys" to get to the root cause of a problem, not the "Five Whos" to find and fire the guilty party.

But the board equally wasn't ignoring a $4 billion loss and a 40 percent drop in North American sales. And the Toyota Way does not allow the company to blame others or even conditions that are seemingly beyond the company's control for problems. The focus is always on finding ways to improve the company so that even external events can be appropriately handled without major damage to the company. In this case, the board concluded that there had been signs before the summer of 2008 that there was a bubble of high demand and that it would collapse at some point. For example, Atsushi Niimi, as the executive vice president responsible for global manufacturing, would not accept the argument that this was a crisis that was out of Toyota's control:

One reflection in hindsight is that, in the United States, at some point of time, we realized that the trucks were increasing in inventory. Our truck inventory was building up from the end of May through the beginning of June [2008]. Toyota's culture is to build only what is sold, only what is demanded from the market. But we did not keep true to this philosophy; we were not swift enough or quick enough.

Toyota's response to the Great Recession was radical—radical in that it didn't involve the expected steps: there were no fired executives, no massive layoffs, and no plant closings. Instead, it followed TBP and the Toyota Way to find ways to put the company on a solid footing during the worst of the downturn while continuing to invest in the future. That involved revisiting the company's 10-year plan, Global Vision 2010, and replacing it with Global Vision 2020. The long-term vision provided the guardrails and direction that would inform the short-term plan, created by the board's Emergency Profit Improvement Committee (EPIC), for returning the company to profitability. The work of the board on Global Vision 2020 and of EPIC were concurrent; for clarity's sake, we discuss them sequentially.

Global Vision 2020 and Responding to the Recession

The Toyota board of directors began to define its approach to the crisis with its usual intensive analysis. It listened to outside experts on short- and long-term economic trends. Managing officers made detailed reports about their regions. Directors and officers made personal visits to operations throughout the world.

The key long-term economic trends identified by Toyota's analysis in the spring of 2009 (paraphrased from Toyota sources) were

Rising Fuel Prices. Fossil fuel shortages will get more severe over time, driving up the prices of oil and gas. In the United States, the huge federal budget deficit will create pressure to increase taxes on gas, bringing U.S. prices more in line with those in the rest of the world. Prices will reapproach their 2008 peak and surpass it.

Environmental Consciousness. Not only has global warming shifted from a scientific curiosity to an accepted fact, but general environmental consciousness about air quality, recycling, and reuse is becoming a mainstream concern. It is not clear whether individual purchasers will pay extra for an environmentally conscious car, but legislation requiring low emissions will become increasingly strident.

The short-term trends that were identified were

Weakened Competition. Most competitors would fare worse than Toyota during the recession, downsizing and cutting R&D spending, which would further reduce their capability to design and build competitive products. In the United States, the Detroit Three were in a weakened state. This presented an opportunity to gain market share.

Pent-up Demand. North American vehicles in recent years have been scrapped at a rate of 13.5 million units per year, yet production in 2009 was operating at the annualized rate of 9 to 10 million units. Coming out of the recession, there would likely be a surge in demand.

Instilled Sense of Urgency. Toyota employees didn't need to be prodded into acquiring a mentality of crisis and scarcity—

they could see it in their own neighborhoods. As a result, they were ready and open to taking on the challenge of rapid change.

This analysis guided the formation of Global Vision 2020. That vision is of Toyota as a firm that integrates the cycles of nature and the cycles of industry. Toyota's aim over the decade was to "undertake *monozukuri* [a Japanese term that means 'the art of making things'] that strikes a harmonious balance with nature in order to carefully sustain the global environment." The slogan was to "open the frontiers of tomorrow through the energy of people and technology."

The long-term goals of Global Vision 2020 provided direction on responding to the recession—which investments were appropriate and in line with the company's long-term vision, and which were not. Global Vision 2020 set the agenda for R&D as a focus on fuel-efficient, environmentally friendly vehicles. Toyota's existing investments in hybrid technologies, including battery systems, electric motors, and other technology, as well as in alternative fuels like hydrogen, would be ramped up. The company would also seek partnerships with other leaders in the space—eventually leading to an investment in and partnership with Tesla Motors, a niche but fast-rising manufacturer of all-electric vehicles.

Concurrently with the work to develop Global Vision 2020, the board's Emergency Profit Improvement Committee initiated efforts to return the company to profitability as quickly as possible by reducing costs, adjusting production volumes, and addressing other newly revealed vulnerabilities and weaknesses of the company.

Obviously one of the chief areas of focus was Toyota's manufacturing plants, which account for a major proportion of the company's operating costs. Toyota has historically aimed for its plants to operate profitably at 80 percent capacity (most manufacturing companies require a run rate of 85 to 90 percent capacity to achieve profitability). The 80 percent target was based on historical patterns of demand fluctuation; the company uses temporary labor and overtime to produce at 100 percent capacity during peak periods. The Great Recession showed EPIC and the board of directors that a 20 percent cushion was not enough; demand could swing more wildly than they had planned for. EPIC decided that a new target was necessary: profitability at 70 percent capacity. The figure was based on the company's most efficient plant worldwide, which could operate profitably at just over 70 percent capacity.

Getting to profitability at 70 percent capacity meant cutting fixed operating costs both in the plants and in all support functions. As any factory manager can tell you, cutting operating costs by even a few percentage points is difficult. Cutting operating costs by 12.5 percent would be a multiyear project. Cutting operating costs by 12.5 percent in the most efficient and productive factories in the world in less than two years strains credibility. Yet that's the goal the committee set.

There is one obvious way to cut operating costs dramatically, which is the path that most companies around the world took: laying off workers. A quick survey of news stories from 2009 indicates that 65 percent of the Fortune 100 announced significant layoffs. Toyota could have trimmed its workforce of permanent team members to reach the profitability goal and relied on more temporary workers and overtime in the future. But as we indicated in Chapter 1, Toyota views its people with experience in TPS and TBP as an appreciating asset. With that perspective, it makes no sense to lay off employees to solve a short-term problem. And Toyota hasn't. As of March 2011, no

Toyota manufacturing team member has been involuntarily laid off. Unfortunately, NUMMI, the joint venture with GM, had to be shut down when GM declared bankruptcy and walked away from its obligations to the venture and its workers (see page 35 for a discussion of NUMMI). NUMMI's loss was ultimately a gain for San Antonio, Texas, where the Toyota plant took over production of the Tacoma and added more than 1,000 jobs, and eventually for Mississippi, where the Blue Springs plant, whose opening had been delayed when the recession hit, took over production of the Corolla, creating 4,000 jobs in the process.*

It is interesting to note that the media seemed to respond with indifference or even negatively to this no-layoffs strategy during the recession. For instance, an article in *Automotive News* lamented, "As Losses Mount, No Bold Plan at Toyota."† The article criticized Toyota for its outmoded policy of "slow organic growth" (which is somewhat ironic, given the attention that would be paid to the company's "growing too fast" just a few months into the future), noting that the company hadn't canceled new model introductions, closed down plants in Japan, laid off large numbers of people, or shifted R&D to lower-wage countries. Radical restructuring and massive layoffs were the only plans that made sense to many of the people covering the industry. For Toyota, letting go of workers who had received years of training in continuous improvement and problem solving would be self-defeating. It was these well-trained, experienced employees that the company needed if it was to find ways to cut costs and improve efficiency.

---

* Chester Dawson, "Toyota Revives Dormant Plant," *Wall Street Journal,* December 27, 2010.

† Hans Greimel, "As Losses Mount, No Bold Plan at Toyota," *Automotive News*, March 2, 2009.

It's important to note that Toyota does not guarantee its employees lifetime employment. The promise that the company makes is that all employees are highly valued and respected. That respect means that the company will exhaust all other reasonable possibilities before it lays off a nontemporary employee. One unusual step that Toyota took in reaction to the recession was to offer voluntary separation agreements in the United States—although only after designing a plan to make sure that the employees' choices were truly voluntary. In the end, an estimated 1,200 out of roughly 18,000 eligible employees accepted voluntary separation (less than 7 percent).

TOYOTA, LAYOFFS, AND NUMMI

NUMMI, Inc. was never legally a Toyota plant; it was Toyota's first North American automotive assembly plant, but it was formed as a 50-50 joint venture corporation with General Motors. When General Motors reorganized in bankruptcy, the firm decided to abandon NUMMI. Toyota offered GM everything it could think of to maintain its stake in NUMMI, including building a version of the Tacoma as a GM brand, but to no avail. Toyota was left on the hook for the entire operation and had to decide whether to increase its investment to cover the loss of GM's investment or to close NUMMI. Atsushi Niimi, a board member and head of global manufacturing, explains the background to Toyota's decision:

> NUMMI's operation was almost never profitable but, rather, collected just enough money to release the next model. It is just like a bicycle which needs to be [moving]

(continues next page)

all the time, otherwise it falls. In terms of the volume, we were producing more for Toyota badges than for the GM badges. But when GM made a decision to withdraw from the NUMMI project, and given the high cost structure in the California area, it was not feasible for us to continue this project from a long-term viewpoint.

In the depth of the recession, Toyota already had too much capacity, and so the difficult decision was made to close the joint venture. Toyota went above and beyond legal requirements, paying $250 million in severance to NUMMI employees and providing job placement services. In the meantime, no assistance at all was offered by GM, or the United Auto Workers, for that matter. That wasn't the end of Toyota's association with NUMMI, however. After Toyota invested in Tesla Motors in 2010, Tesla purchased NUMMI and decided to hire back some former NUMMI employees.

Another popular way of confronting a profitability crunch is to cut back on research and development and on new product launches. Toyota did reduce R&D expenditures: it fell from number one globally to number four, according to Booz Allen Hamilton's annual review of global R&D spending, but was the only auto manufacturer in the global top 10 as measured by 2009 spending. In fact, Toyota spent $1.8 billion more in R&D than GM, and almost $3 billion more than Honda or Ford that year.* Global Vision 2020 provided a framework indicating where

* Booz Allen Hamilton's research on global R&D spending can be found at http://www.booz.com/global/home/what_we_think/featured_content/inno vation_1000_2010.

Toyota needed to maintain its investments, particularly technology related to environmentally friendly vehicles. Toyota reduced costs by delaying some new models, focusing on efficiency, and releasing outside subcontractors, but laying off regular engineers was out of bounds. In fact, employees of the Toyota Technical Center in Michigan (its own corporation, which employs more than a thousand key engineering staff members) were ineligible for the voluntary separation program. Toyota wanted to keep all the engineers it had so painstakingly trained.

The task ahead for responding to the recession was to cut costs without layoffs and to ensure that the company was on a sound footing to emerge from the recession stronger than ever. As outgoing President Watanabe put it in a joint speech with new President Akio Toyoda: "We have let [our strengths] become diluted. We have allowed fixed costs and foreign-exchange risks to increase, and our earnings are now overly sensitive to fluctuations in unit sales and exchange rates. Furthermore, the speed and efficiency of our business operations has been reduced."

How did Toyota address these weaknesses? Not by radically changing direction, but by getting more aggressive about what it had always done: continuous improvement, investing in people, and trusting those people to find and implement solutions that would cut costs and improve quality and productivity.

Turning the Recession into Opportunity

With volumes plummeting in late spring of 2008, Tetsuo Agata was named as the new president of Toyota Engineering and Manufacturing North America (TEMA), the organization that runs Toyota's manufacturing, purchasing, and engineering. Agata was chosen from a similar position in Toyota's European operations because he had spent a number of years working in TEMA prior to moving to Europe. The board felt that it needed an experienced hand to manage what at the time was primarily a North American production problem.

Just before Agata's arrival, the decision had been made to cut back production of trucks and SUVs dramatically in response to the oil price spike and falling sales by stopping assembly lines for three months at the Princeton, Indiana and San Antonio, Texas plants and shifting vehicles between plants for maximum efficiency (a decision that we'll return to later). Still, Agata says, "My first message to my staff, from Paris, was that we have to make our best efforts to keep all our staff."

While it's true that Toyota did not lay off any workers, that doesn't mean that Agata and his team didn't think that there was an urgent need to cut personnel costs. As mentioned, Toyota uses temporary workers and overtime for hourly employees as mechanisms for increasing production over the historical 80 percent capacity profitability threshold. During Toyota's steady growth in the United States, its North American plants had been running above 95 percent capacity on average. During those boom years, hourly team members worked lots of overtime hours. In addition to overtime, there was an annual bonus based on the company's profitability and the performance of the plant that regularly paid out more than 10 percent of pay for hourly workers.

As volumes fell and production was dramatically cut back, not only was temporary labor reduced to zero, but team members' overtime and bonuses came to an end. For many workers, that meant more than a 10 percent drop in take-home pay. Agata instituted a shared sacrifice model for TEMA. If the hourly workers were going to be taking home 10 percent less, managers and executives should take larger temporary pay cuts. In addition to canceling bonuses, he instituted a sliding scale, with vice presidents and above, including himself, taking more than a 30 percent salary cut until profitability was restored.

Other cost-cutting measures were implemented as well. The TEMA corporate jet was sold, managers gave up business-class travel, hiring was frozen, and the voluntary exit program mentioned earlier was announced. Team members in the TEMA corporate offices formed *kaizen* groups to look for ways to cut costs, even to the level of saving electricity in the offices. Agata told us, "There were many places we were spending money that didn't affect customers. For example, that is the reason you can see the light, it's not on [in my office]." Saving money became a goal of continuous improvement. Lots of small efforts, rather than a few big cuts made by a senior executive, added up to big savings.

As the Toyota executives had expected, the recession did in fact put Toyota employees in a state of mind to accept levels of change that they might have resisted before the recession. For example, the plant in Kentucky, TMMK, had known only growth and prosperity, and prior to the recession, the biggest complaint that team members had was that they felt pressure to work too much overtime. The initial impact of the oil crisis and the recession was muted at TMMK because the plant didn't build any trucks or SUVs, which had the most sudden and dramatic fall in demand. But as the recession wore on and automobile sales in general declined, the impact became unmistakable on the factory floor. Tim Turner, an hourly team leader who had been at TMMK for 15 years, recalled the exact date that it really hit him how deep the recession had gotten:

> February 12, 2009. That's the date we shut down the plant [a highly unusual occurrence] to have a communication day. The general manager presented lots of

data like the seasonally adjusted rate of sales. Most team members had no idea. The general manager told us, "I already took a pay cut eight months ago and we kept that to ourselves . . . but now we are going to have to ask everybody to cut back a little bit so we can keep everybody working." That's when it really registered that they were really serious about job security.

The stark reality of the fall in demand and what it meant for everyone at the plant immediately led to an intensified focus on cost reduction by team members. In most companies, it is rare for an hourly employee to even see data on cost, and often, as a matter of policy, management does not want these employees to know the real costs. At TMMK, team members used the metrics boards posted in every area of the plant—normally mostly focused on quality and safety *kaizen* projects—to find opportunities to save money. Another structure for *kaizen* is quality circles, which at TMMK are organized voluntarily by hourly employees on paid overtime. The circles use TBP to solve bigger problems then they can handle during a normal day when they are working production. Steve Turley, a 13-year veteran hourly team member who was assigned full time to organize quality-circle activities in assembly, told us:

> In the past we were more focused in quality circles on quality or safety, but with the recession cost jumped right up along with that. We looked at things like reducing scrap and repairs. We could go through our logs to find where we had the most scrap or scratches, and maintenance logs on when they were coming out to fix something, and see the costs associated with that.

These quality-circle efforts, led by hourly team members and team leaders, saved $2 million on just one (of two) assembly line at TMMK in 2009.

For example, one team of hourly team members invented a device to aid in recycling the flow racks (roller conveyors on frames that move parts to the assembly worker), which have to be rebuilt whenever there is a change on the assembly line. The roller conveyors in these racks are highly specific and tended to be discarded when changes were necessary. This team built a machine that could disassemble the rollers and separate them into bins of steel, plastic, and aluminum parts so that each could be recycled rather than thrown away. The invention has been finding its way to other Toyota plants, and the team has submitted the paperwork to get it patented.

All of the cost cutting, though, was done through the lens of future profitability. The idea was to ruthlessly cut any expenses that did not have an impact on customers or on the company's future growth prospects—that's why layoffs and large R&D cuts were off limits. What TEMA and other parts of Toyota found was that even a company that was devoted to constantly finding and eliminating waste can be blinded by rapid growth and profitability. The various teams' success in finding areas where costs could be cut without long-term impact was a powerful reminder of Taiichi Ohno's precept that every process was full of waste and could be improved.

Toyota does attempt to create a scarcity mentality in all employees even in the best of times. In fact, its extreme fiscal conservativism in good times is what gave it the cash to get through the recession and the recall crisis without involuntary layoffs and major reductions in R&D spending (see Saving in Good Times for a Rainy Day, page 42). Still, one of the positive outcomes of the recession was that the firm now has a new generation of team members and leaders who have lived this precept firsthand.

SAVING IN GOOD TIMES FOR A RAINY DAY

One of the seminal events in Toyota's history was the crisis of 1950. The company, still led at the time by TMC founder Kiichiro Toyoda, had been investing heavily, expecting rapid growth that did not materialize. Ultimately the company faced a cash crunch and was unable to meet its payroll, leading to the only prolonged worker strike in the company's history. The company's lenders stepped in and forced the company to reduce payroll by more than 1,500 employees. After asking for volunteers to meet this demand, Kiichiro Toyoda and his executive staff all resigned, taking personal responsibility for leading the company into crisis.

Losing control of the company to the banks has forever cemented the value of "self-reliance" in the Toyota Way culture. That principle has translated into the company's having a very conservative investment strategy to this day, with $25 to $40 billion in cash or equivalents on hand during the boom years. Toyota has been criticized more than once and given low ratings by some investment advisors for this conservative strategy, particularly when competitors were either going on shopping sprees, paying large bonuses, or returning cash to shareholders.

However, this conservative strategy paid off handsomely over the long term as the company faced its worst economic environment since postwar Japan. The only reason Toyota could sustain employment through the recession and then the recall crisis, while continuing its industry-leading investments in R&D, was because of this conservative approach to spending and saving.

That's far more powerful as a learning experience than anything that Toyota could have done during the boom years.

Turning Downtime into Opportunity

As we mentioned earlier, one of the first reactions to the crash in the sales of large vehicles was to shut down assembly lines dedicated to those vehicles and to move the assembly of certain vehicles to different plants to maximize the efficiency of plants and people. Specifically, the Tundra plant in San Antonio, Texas (TMMTX), and the assembly line at the plant in Princeton, Indiana (TMMI), which produced Tundras as well as Sequoia SUVs, were stopped for three months, from August to October 2008. During that time, Tundra production was moved entirely to TMMTX. Meanwhile, the construction of a new plant in Mississippi expected to build the Highlander SUV was halted; instead, TMMI would produce the Highlander once it could reconfigure one of its assembly lines. The shutdown decision was made before the recession hit in full force; when it did, hopes for a quick bounceback in volume were dashed. Sales of large vehicles made in Indiana and Texas continued at only about half their prerecession rates well into 2009.

These assembly-line shutdowns sound a lot like typical manufacturing practices to deal with slow demand, except that the Toyota team members on those assembly lines weren't furloughed or laid off. They continued to come to work each day, putting in eight-hour shifts. Which leads to the question: what were all these workers doing, and how could Toyota be working its way back to profitability by continuing to pay idle workers?

Recall that one of the goals of the Emergency Profit Improvement Committee was for all plants to be able to run profitably at just over 70 percent capacity. The profitability of a factory depends on many factors besides the workers and the cost of the machines. Of course there are maintenance costs, but there are also the costs of defects, inventory, and managing complexity. Complexity in an auto plant is based on several factors, including how many different types of vehicles are produced on each line, how many variations there are in those vehicles (such as different engines, transmissions, and trim levels), and how often new vehicles or variations are introduced. The largest factor of all, though, is how frequently the speed of the line is changed.

When complexity is handled poorly, it causes lots of errors and defects and drives down profitability. But a plant that can handle a great deal of complexity without errors is the most profitable of all—it can dynamically adjust what it is producing to match demand, both upward and downward (even in a strong economy, overproduction leads to price cuts, which harm profitability).

Toyota's plants in Japan are legendary for their ability to manage complexity while maintaining quality. Each plant produces a myriad of vehicles in a variety of versions (including different versions for different countries), with frequent changes in line speed. While Toyota's plants in North America were consistently ranked near the top of American factories, they really weren't close to matching the capabilities of the Japanese plants in terms of managing complexity and achieving high quality rates. For instance, in 2008, TMMI was building at most two different models on one line and operating at 150 defects (these are items that are caught and corrected as the car moves along the assembly line or at final inspection before the vehicle leaves the plant) per 100 vehicles, while the best Toyota plants in Japan were building four to six different models and operating at about 20 defects per 100 vehicles.

Shutting down one of the assembly lines at TMMI (in addition to the line producing Tundras and Sequoias, TMMI has a line producing Sienna minivans that continued operations) presented a huge challenge and opportunity to TMMI's managers. The challenge was keeping half the plant staff, roughly 1,800 people, actively engaged while their normal production jobs were on hold. The opportunity was to match the quality, flexibility, and cost-effectiveness levels of the best Toyota plants in Japan.

Attacking quality issues is never haphazard or ad hoc at Toyota plants. Bringing down the rate of defects started with renewed training in *kaizen* and TBP to sharpen everyone's problem-solving skills before they tackled the daunting task of cutting defects by more than 80 percent (keep in mind that this was a plant that was winning industrywide plant quality awards in the United States at the old level of defects).

Since there were no auditoriums large enough to accommodate 1,800 people in training classes, the plant leaders decided to train team members in their existing work groups and conducted training in small rooms around the shop floor. Instead of computer projectors, they used flip charts. They needed first to train the trainers, since all the training was to be done by managers and group leaders. In truth, this intimate approach worked better, since it made the training more accessible and interactive and allowed the company to apply concepts to the actual production floor. It also significantly raised the training skills of the management team, a benefit that was very important at Toyota, where managers are expected to be teachers.

Anyone who has sat through any amount of corporate training, let alone three months' worth, may rightly ask how three months of training will cut costs and improve quality. After all, training exercises that have no concrete goals attached quickly devolve into training for training's sake—an opportunity for employees to catch a nap and goof off, not necessarily to learn anything that they can put to use.

To combat this tendency, TMMI combined classroom training with hands-on *kaizen* on projects. Concrete goals were set for improved safety, quality, and productivity metrics at the end of the three months, to provide team members with a focus for their activities. In many cases, these hands-on exercises had to simulate the jobs, since the line was not running. But the group leaders and plant managers had data on problems from before the shutdown, and they had the standardized work for each job, so they were able to work on safety, quality, and productivity.

For example, one group of hourly team members dubbed itself the "Ding Kings," as the group members were trying to eliminate dings in the stamped steel body parts that were welded together into panels in the body shop. Small nicks and dents were the number one quality problem in terms of cost for the body shop.

The first step in TBP is to define the problem. As part of this step, the group members classified dings seen in various areas of the vehicle. They found a cluster of dings on the back hatch of the Sequoia and investigated the root cause. One team member suggested that the dings were caused by a jig that holds the part in place. An investigation confirmed the theory. The team fixed the problem by reinforcing the jig and replacing a hard plastic block that presses against the part with a softer, more malleable block. Four months of tracking showed that the fix worked—zero defects.

Teams like the Ding Kings were at work all across the plant, freed up to focus on safety, quality, and productivity by the line shutdown and continued slow demand during the recession. What they achieved is remarkable by any measure. In 2008

TMMI brought down defects from 150 to 31 defects per 100 vehicles. By the middle of 2009, it had broken through the 20 defects per 100 threshold and was performing as well as or better than its Japanese counterparts. When TMMI started building Highlanders in the fall of 2009 on the line that had been shut down, it was able to keep this quality record intact.

Bringing fundamental skills to a new level was another area of focus for TMMI's downtime activities. Before the recession, the paint department had developed a unique training program for team members. Training for a job on a Toyota assembly line means becoming deeply familiar with the standardized work for the job and practicing the necessary steps. Classes of jobs like paint, welding, and assembly have been analyzed, and fundamental skills that apply broadly across those jobs have been identified. The fundamental skills training process begins with performing simulated tasks at artificial workstations (e.g., learning to apply caulk to a welded car body), followed by performing the task on a stationary mock-up of a vehicle, and finally working on a moving mock-up, but not an actual car. The paint department at TMMI had taken this standard approach to training a step further. It created an assembly-line loop out of spare parts, one that was big enough to move real vehicles around so that team members could practice the standardized work on real cars. One of the assembly departments had already built a similar training loop to simulate assembly jobs before the shutdown.

During the downturn, the full-size training loops were made available to all departments to train for the launch of the Highlander. This was one of the reasons why the plant was able to launch production with so few defects.

That was not the only way in which the focused training and *kaizen* activities paid off. TMMI also began setting new records for safety. In 2004, there had been 19.8 safety incidents per 200,000 hours worked; for the entire month of February 2009, there was only one safety incident in the entire plant for more than 200,000 hours of work.

When Toyota shifted production of the Tundra and shut down one of the assembly lines at TMMI in August 2008, it expected demand to mostly bounce back by the fall. The recession ended that hope. By the end of 2008, TMMI's output was down 48 percent from the year before on an annualized basis. Eight months after the initial shutdown, in March 2009, the line was still running at only 60 percent of the previous line speed, leaving 40 percent of the team members available for training and *kaizen*. One hourly employee, a team leader, explained it this way:

> The difference between Toyota and the other companies is that instead of forcing us to go on unemployment, they are investing in us, allowing us to sharpen our minds. I don't think there's one person out there who doesn't realize what an incredible investment Toyota is making.

Walking through the plant in March 2009, it was impossible to tell that 40 percent of the employees were not building cars. In every direction, engineers, managers, and hourly team members were focused and busy. Anyone who was not working on production was planning for line speed changes, preparing for the launch of future models, or working on ways to improve safety, improve plant operations, cut costs, and improve quality.

One way in which the launch of the new Highlander was accomplished at record speed and with record low cost was repurposing the equipment from the old Tundra assembly line. In most cases, the robots and equipment used in the production of a vehicle would be at least eight years old and nearing the end of their life cycle by the time the plant stopped making that vehicle. However, Tundra production had been halted at TMMI after only two years, so the old welding robots and light curtains were salvaged to use again. Carts and racks that would normally have been purchased from outside were built in-house from scrap metal. Even an old overhead catwalk used by maintenance was salvaged and made into carts. Through the initiative and cooperation of team members, a $4 million budget line item was trimmed to just $700,000.

TMMTX in San Antonio was also idled for three months when the bottom dropped out of the truck market in the summer of 2008, but unlike TMMI, it built only Tundras, so the entire plant, along with its 21 on-site suppliers, built absolutely nothing during this period. San Antonio used the time to perform organized training and daily *kaizen*, similar to TMMI. The plant collected all the training modules that it had used at start-up. Gaps remained, however, and the plant developed an additional 30 training modules to fill them. Ultimately, the training included about 90 modules across team members, team leaders, and group leaders. The topics were wide-ranging and quite similar to curricula for some two-year associate degrees—for instance, statistical methods for quality control, ergonomics analysis, work hazards training, line balancing, and equipment maintenance.

Once the training began, it became clear how big a gap there was between the level of capability that Toyota aspired to for team members and the reality of what it had. Even in Toyota's core competency of problem solving, the skill level was less than ideal. TMMTX plant manager Dan Antis explained:

> [Prior to the shutdown,] we had Toyota Business Prac-
> tices training for the manager level and above. Some of
> our engineering groups had already started; they were
> doing pretty well. But on the floor, there was almost no
> training in problem solving. We were unfortunate, but
> fortunate, we had this down period to train.

As the training progressed, the plant was able to take advantage of the unique knowledge of different people. For example, the
assistant manager of security was a former Los Angeles detective.
A casual conversation with a member of a quality team about
how to approach a crime scene led to the security manager teaching a course on investigating quality problems using detective
methods, including how to approach a scene, how to document
evidence with photographs, and even how to dust a car body, as
for fingerprints, in order to see dents and scratches more clearly.

At TMMTX, the quality-circle program was still very im-
mature. When the plant was running full tilt, team members had
very little time during the shift to participate actively in improvement *kaizen*. As a result, few got the chance to lead a significant problem-solving effort. They could develop a *kaizen* idea for
their own jobs, but rarely for a larger, more impactful problem
that affected multiple jobs.

This was particularly important at TMMTX because the plant,
filled with workers who were new to Toyota, was still trying to identify
those team members who had the potential to become team leaders and group leaders. Quality circles provided an opportunity for
the best team members to learn and improve rapidly and for plant
managers to better evaluate the team members' future potential.

Only eight pilot quality circles had been introduced in early
2008, led by assistant managers who had had previous experience

with them at the other Toyota plants. The shutdown presented the opportunity to deploy quality circles throughout the plant. The long-term objective was to have quality circles led by hourly employees, but first their immediate supervisors, called group leaders, had to be experts so that they could mentor their team members. Every group leader was asked to go through facilitator training and then lead a quality circle. As a result, the plant launched 94 quality circles. They worked on safety, quality, and productivity in all areas of the plant. As at TMMI, with the power of all these groups put into problem solving rather than being laid off, the plant was able to achieve its scheduled targets for improvements in cost reduction, quality, and safety a full year ahead of schedule— making major gains in the long-term profitability of the plant.

Learning to Manage Complexity

Another major initiative for improving the long-term profitability of plants was to end the practice of buffering North American plants with Japanese plants. North American plants had never produced all the vehicles sold in North America. Output from American plants was held relatively constant, below actual demand, while Japanese plants dynamically adjusted their production to provide the remaining vehicles to fill demand, buffering the American plants from the complexity of changing vehicle mixes or line speed.

Having the Japanese plants operate as a buffer and shipping vehicles to North America was expensive (in addition to shipping costs, the plants had to duplicate all the tooling in the American plants that they were buffering) and exposed the company to excessive foreign-exchange risk. During the recession, the decision was made to cut costs by ending this duplication of tooling and effort and having the American plants handle the full volume of the unique American cars that they produced (global cars like Corolla and Camry were still shared with Japan). That meant that the North American plants had to be able to manage complexity while maintaining quality as well as their Japanese counterparts did.

Jobs on a Toyota assembly line have been standardized since the days of Ohno. Each worker knows exactly what to do and how much time he has to do it (the line speed is known as the *takt* time, or just *takt*, and is based on the rate of customer demand). However, if the line speed changes to a new *takt* to accommodate a change in demand, the number of workers on the line will need to be adjusted up or down, with each worker taking on fewer or more tasks. Though it may seem counterintuitive, slowing down the assembly line (a longer *takt*) is a harder change than speeding it up. A faster line can usually be accommodated by adding workers and giving each worker a few less tasks to do. Thus, it's only the additional workers who need to be trained when the line speeds up. A slower line means taking workers off the line and allocating their tasks to other workers, so every worker has new tasks to do to fill up a longer cycle of work. In this case, each worker has to learn standardized work for a new job (and some of the standardized work will need to be changed). The more often the speed of the line changes, the harder it is for workers to maintain their standards of quality and productivity.

TMMK, the original Toyota plant in the United States, had been operating for more than 20 years when the recession hit. With the buffer provided by the Japanese plants, TMMK had rarely had to change *takt*, and the vast majority of the changes that had been made had been to increase the line speed. The plant had gotten better and had had more frequent *takt* changes in the years leading up to the recession, but it still made these changes much more slowly than in Japan, and the changes were still rare events.

Now TMMK was going to have to learn to change *takt* as often as demand shifted. Not only that, but it was going to have to adjust to frequent *takt* changes while also moving toward building a larger variety of vehicles (e.g., several models and trim levels of Camry, Camry hybrid, Venza, and Solara convertible) and a dynamic mix of those vehicles. Each day, the mix of Camrys, Venzas, and Solaras and the specific trim options (e.g., power versus manual seats) that was made would change based on market demand.

Planning for the first major slowdown in line speed involved teams from all over the plant studying every job on the line, looking in detail at every task and how long it took, reviewing possible defects associated with each so that countermeasures could be identified, and incorporating all the changes into new standardized work, to improve productivity and reduce defects. Then workers had to be trained repetitively in the new standardized work until they could perform the tasks flawlessly as specified. Phasing in the slower *takt* took six weeks, which at the time was faster and involved fewer defects and safety issues than any of the North American plants had managed in prior *takt* changes.

With overtime cut back dramatically and a slower line speed, many team members were freed up to work on the additional changes the plant was going through that added complexity. *Kaizen* teams were formed to plan for the introduction of additional versions of the Venza. But the place these teams had the most impact was in helping the plant adjust to a dynamic vehicle mix. In the past, TMMK had been able to sequence vehicles and the overall mix of Venzas, Camrys, and Solaras based on what worked best for the assembly line. Now it had to make adjustments based on what the demand was—and that meant lots of *andon* pulls as workers learned to cope with the variety. Teams were formed to analyze every *andon* pull, diagnose the root causes, and find solutions.

Additional teams were formed to continue to work on improving the plant's performance on *takt* changes. Now that it was fully exposed to the most wildly fluctuating demand that the United States had ever seen, the plant would have to make much more frequent *takt* changes. In fact, during 2009 and 2010, the plant made eight *takt* changes, more than in its entire prior history. As of the fall of 2010, TMMK had managed to improve its *takt* change process enough to cut the time for changes from six weeks to four weeks (that does not mean the line is shut down for four weeks)—that means that, in the future, the plant will be able to adjust its speed more frequently while reaching full production sooner, and thus will be more profitable.

Such variability wasn't just limited to TMMK. Recall that TMMTX, the Tundra plant in San Antonio, Texas, was only two years old when the recession hit—and thus had very little experience dealing with change. To make matters more complex, TMMTX had a unique approach to supplier parts. Toyota's just-in-time system depends on long-term, tightly integrated relationships with suppliers that deliver parts frequently throughout the day. This system depends on the suppliers having plants near the Toyota plant, which in Japan means within about a 30-minute drive. TMMTX was built far from the supply base in the Midwest of the United States, so Toyota took the unusual step of locating suppliers on Toyota property, right next to the assembly plant: two-thirds of all parts by bulk are produced on site. That meant that all changes had to be closely coordinated with the suppliers, who were also just learning TPS, because there was literally nowhere for any extra inventory of parts to go. Four of the twenty-one on-site parts suppliers were under the same roof as the Toyota line, with just a few hundred yards separating them.

When a new plant is launched, Toyota's practice is to dub it an infant and assign it a mother plant to guide its growth and development. In this case, the mother was TMMI, which had transferred some of its best managers and group leaders to Texas. Still, under normal circumstances, TMMTX would have been protected from major changes for at least three to five years. The industrywide collapse of truck sales did not allow that luxury. When the plant started back up after the three-month shutdown, it also had to adjust to a slower *takt* time.

TMMTX kept the line slow for months to reduce dealer inventory in preparation for the 2010 Tundra model launch (actually launched in the summer of 2009). With gas prices easing significantly and a popular new model, demand suddenly jumped. The plant was asked to increase the line speed from 109 seconds per vehicle to 73 seconds per vehicle, the largest change in line speed ever for any Toyota plant in North America, and possibly any Toyota plant in the world. This change benefited dramatically from all the training and problem solving that had been undertaken during the shutdown. With such a large change, a decision was made to phase in part of the change over several weeks. Still, the plant was able to fully implement the *takt* change in just four weeks, faster than the six weeks planned and a match for TMMK.

Working with Suppliers

The productivity and profitability of a large manufacturing plant depends on much more than what happens inside the walls, of course. Suppliers are a major part of the equation, particularly in lean production, where there is relatively little inventory to provide a buffer. Toyota depends on suppliers that are reliable and that can meet the quality and productivity standards of its plants. Parts made by outside suppliers account for about 70 percent of a Toyota vehicle, so restricting *kaizen* to the Toyota plants would affect only 30 percent of a car.

When the recession hit, the concern wasn't just about how Toyota was faring, but about how its suppliers were faring as well. If any of the company's larger suppliers were to hit major financial trouble because of dropping volumes and the credit crunch, Toyota's plants would encounter major difficulties. To address the situation and the needs of suppliers, the purchasing department of TEMA had begun an effort to track suppliers' financial status back in 2006, but this required a more intensive effort. The purchasing team set up a war room to begin tracking the financial position of every one of Toyota's suppliers in North America at a finer level of detail. According to Jason Reid, a general manager in Purchasing, "We tried to move very quickly from a reactive assessment model to a more predictive model because we were worried about what was going to happen to suppliers if one or more of the 'Big Three' declared bankruptcy. We were also worried about which suppliers had more exposure to SUVs and trucks versus passenger cars. So based on those predictive models, we started developing contingency plans."

How the company reacted to suppliers that were suffering substantial ill effects is a great illustration of Toyota's aim of improving long-term profitability, not just cutting costs (see Never Bully Suppliers, Your Partners, page 58). Robert Young, a vice president in Purchasing at TEMA, notes that Toyota wasn't interested only in the financial situation of its suppliers, but also in the causes of any problems so that it could assess what, if any, assistance Toyota could provide. "If [their difficulties were] a result of manufacturing inefficiency—something that our team members can go in there and help them with—we did that. In most cases, though, it was a debt refinancing issue, and we couldn't help with that. We're not a bank." But Toyota did have some tools at its disposal to help suppliers that were experiencing a cash crunch. "We modified our tool and payment schedule, so that our payments for tooling were earlier and better aligned with their actual expenditures for their tool shops." In other words, Toyota started paying suppliers *sooner.* The normal response of companies that are trying to restore profitability is to delay payments to suppliers.

But that wasn't the only thing that Purchasing did to shore up suppliers that were facing a cash crunch. The purchasing team developed a plan to do something that Toyota tries to avoid at all costs—deliberately build up a parts inventory. Working collaboratively with some suppliers, the purchasing department actually ramped up orders beyond what it needed for production. The team had to scramble to locate warehouse space—the company doesn't have any of its own—to store these parts. The strategy was twofold: by buying excess inventory in advance, Toyota was creating a safety margin for itself in case the supplier went bankrupt, but it was also helping the supplier avoid bankruptcy by injecting cash into the firm.

Managing supplier relationships was especially high on the priority list at TMMTX, since suppliers were so integrated right on site. Not only were many of the suppliers on site, but most of them were new to the automotive business. When Toyota decided to locate the Tundra plant away from the traditional strongholds of automotive parts supply, it needed to build a new supplier base in Texas. A program was launched to encourage minority-owned businesses. Toyota connected these minority owners, many of whom didn't have experience in the auto industry, with existing suppliers to create joint ventures that were 51 percent owned by the minority partners.

During the recession, Toyota's on-site purchasing group communicated with the suppliers intensively and encouraged them to follow Toyota's lead in keeping their employees on. The TMMTX team invited suppliers to participate in its *kaizen* training and workshops so that they could all "level up" together.

Each supplier had its own approach to dealing with employment security, but all of them diverted some workers to *kaizen*, thus strengthening their operation and their workforce. One of the largest suppliers on site explained: "The *kaizen* projects saved us on tool changes and process steps. It improved ergonomics and increased the productivity and morale of our people."

Some suppliers, without the resources of Toyota, had to find creative approaches to stay in business while also preparing for the future. For example, one company asked for volunteers to go on unemployment while the company continued to pay their full benefits. Enough people took that option that involuntary layoffs were not necessary. When volumes picked back up again, the employees were rehired.

NEVER BULLY SUPPLIERS, YOUR PARTNERS

Taiichi Ohno said, "Bullying suppliers is totally alien to the spirit of the Toyota Production System." In a major downturn, there is a natural tendency to use suppliers as a buffer through tactics like delaying payments, renegotiating contracts, or shifting business to lower-cost sources. Principle 11 in *The Toyota Way*, though, states: "Respect your extended network of partners and suppliers by challenging them and helping them improve."*

That principle is clear in the steps that Toyota took to deal with suppliers during the recession, including offering them

* Jeffrey K. Liker, *The Toyota Way* (New York: McGraw-Hill, 2004).

financial and technical support and *kaizen* training. Another example of the long-term investment that Toyota makes in these partnerships is working with suppliers to buffer them from production changes. For example, when Toyota moved Tundra capacity from Indiana to Texas, Dana Corporation lost the truck chassis business to the incumbent supplier of chassis to TMMTX, a firm in Mexico. However, while it shifted this business away from Dana, Toyota moved other business to Dana, such as parts for the Highlander, which was moving to Indiana, so that there was little net impact on Dana's business.

So it wasn't just Toyota plants that emerged stronger from the recession. Its relationships with suppliers also became stronger, both through the experience of seeing how Toyota treated them in the worst of times—that its commitment to people and to its business partners wasn't just talk—and through their participation in TPS, TBP, and *kaizen* training and exercises. Of course, having stronger suppliers was another win in the efforts to rebuild the company's long-term profitability. With stronger suppliers, operating at a higher level of productivity and quality, the company could be even more flexible in responding quickly to volatile demand and changes in the marketplace.

Emerging from the Recession

The combined effect of these and similar efforts across North America and around the world had begun to turn the tide for Toyota by the summer of 2009. Demand had stabilized with the help of "cash for clunkers"–type programs from governments in the United States, Europe, and Japan. In August 2009, Toyota sold more vehicles under the United States' Cash for Clunkers program than any other manufacturer, holding five of the top ten slots for vehicles sold. In fact, sales were so high that Toyota had a different problem: it could not build cars fast enough. All plants in North America were working overtime, but dealer inventory of the most popular cars—mostly smaller, fuel-efficient cars—was almost sold out. In August, sales were up to about 195,000 vehicles. But the volatility was not over. After Cash for Clunkers ended, sales dropped precipitously in September to 98,000, although this was partially a result of having limited inventory available for sale.

In October, Toyota was able to announce that it had returned to profitability, still without laying off any workers. Toyota's success was a testament to both the strong brand equity that it had built over decades and a policy of miserly spending and saving when times were good. With about $25 billion in cash or cash equivalents, the company could afford to wait out the recession without slashing R&D, closing plants, or laying off large numbers of employees. It certainly looked as if Toyota had pulled off one of the all-time great corporate turnarounds, all the while eschewing any thought of abandoning its core principles or making major changes to its strategy. In fact, it's probably accurate to say that Toyota weathered the Great Recession by simply doing more of what it had been doing before the recession—living the Toyota Way.

In August 2009, Toyota looked as if it were back on its trajectory toward becoming the largest and most admired company in the world. Then a tragic accident in San Diego changed everything.

CHAPTER 3

The Recall Crisis

We recognize that a full understanding of situations and problems requires extensive study and the gathering of all relevant quantitative and qualitative facts with Genchi-Genbutsu.

— *THE TOYOTA WAY 2001*

On August, 28, 2009, in San Diego, California, Mark Saylor and his wife, daughter, and brother-in-law were killed when their Lexus, on loan from a dealer who was servicing the family's own vehicle, careened out of control at more than 100 mph, collided with another vehicle, and crashed into a ravine, setting the car ablaze. The family's high-speed tragedy was recorded live for all to hear via a 911 call. Such a dramatic event understandably captured the nation's attention—especially since Mark Saylor was a veteran California Highway Patrol officer. If a police officer couldn't save his family from an out-of-control car, many hearing the news felt, no one could. If it could happen to them, it was impossible not to think, it could happen to me.

The cursory details that began coming out after the crash contributed to the fear and confusion. The Saylors had been driving a 2009 Lexus ES 350, the current model of a passenger car whose all-weather floor mats had been recalled by Toyota in 2007 because of a possibility that they could trap the accelerator. In the wild ride leading to the fatal accident, the brother-in law made a 911 call reporting that the accelerator pedal was stuck and that the brakes had failed.*

It was easy to leap to conclusions from these sketchy details: either Toyota had failed to fix the floor mat problem in the 2007 recall, or something much more serious was wrong with Toyota vehicles. To many people, the idea that a floor mat could trap the accelerator was implausible. If the floor mat had caught the pedal, why didn't Mark Saylor simply use his foot to free the pedal? Of course, there were additional questions: Why didn't Saylor just turn the car off? Couldn't Saylor or the front seat passenger have shifted the car into neutral?

The questions and suspicions about what had really happened in San Diego set the stage for a remarkable series of events that ultimately proved to be the greatest threat to Toyota since the company's near-bankruptcy in 1950. Over the course of the next six months, Toyota would issue three separate recalls related to vehicle speed control that affected more than 7 million vehicles. Along the way, Toyota would be accused by the media, politicians, and customers of hiding information and putting lives at risk. Some would even allege that defects in Toyota cars had led directly to the deaths of more than 100 people over 10 years. The company's sterling reputation for quality and safety would be seriously

---

* You can hear the recording of the 911 call here: http://www.youtube.com/watch?v=KHGSWs4uJzY.

damaged in the eyes of many. It would lose its leading market position and spend billions of dollars on recalls and incentives to lure back customers. Senior executives would be ordered before Congress and would repeatedly make public apologies.

How did things go so wrong so quickly? How could a company whose quality was legendary suddenly need to issue recall after recall, seemingly unable to find, much less correct, defects in its cars? How could Toyota react so slowly to mounting evidence that customers' lives were in danger? Did Toyota cover up evidence of problems in its vehicles and attempt to avoid responsibility for fixing them? How could Toyota make blunder after blunder in the court of public opinion? Was the idea of quality and putting customers first just nice rhetoric, with nothing behind it? Had Toyota completely lost its way?

Those are all reasonable questions when you take a look at the summary timeline of events from August 2009 through February 2010 (located at the end of the chapter). Answering them, and understanding the mistakes that Toyota made, requires looking at those same events through Toyota's eyes, tracing the history of sudden acceleration claims, and separating fact from fiction.

The Saylor Accident

Given the Saylor accident's seminal role in all that ensued and its coloring of the public's understanding of the allegations of unintended acceleration, it is remarkable how few people are aware of the actual details of the crash. As it does with every fatal accident in its jurisdiction, the San Diego County Sheriff's Department conducted a thorough investigation of the accident. The 29-page report reveals some startling facts that eliminate virtually all doubt about the real cause of the accident: a floor mat from the wrong vehicle, incorrectly installed in the Saylors' car by the Lexus dealer who loaned it to the family.*

One of the first things that the investigating officer noticed when examining the car was that the floor mat in the ES 350 was a rubber all-weather floor mat (AWFM) designed for the Lexus RX400h sport utility vehicle (a vehicle with much more driver floor space) and that the mat was not clipped down. Furthermore, as a result of the fire, "the accelerator pedal had melted and fused to the upper right hand corner of the mat," indicating that the pedal had been jammed in the mat when the accident occurred.

Despite a checklist distributed by Toyota to its dealers that specifically identified the importance of checking the proper installation of the correct floor mats in the ES 350, developed after the 2007 recall of ES 350 all-weather floor mats, Mark Saylor drove away from the dealership with the wrong floor mat. When the investigator placed one of the large RX400h mats in an ES 350 back at the Lexus dealer, he reported: "Each time I depressed the pedal, it became trapped on one of the edges of the AWFM. This was not the case with the ES 350 AWFM. Not only did the pedal become trapped in the SUV mat, but it remained trapped."

The most compelling piece of evidence implicating the floor mat, however, is that a jammed accelerator resulting from having the wrong floor mat in the car isn't just a theory—it had happened to another customer using the same vehicle just a few days before the Saylor accident. Frank Bernard had been issued the loaner vehicle by the Lexus dealer on August 24. The following

---

* All quotes and details here are taken from the official San Diego County Sheriff's Department report, available at http://autos.aol.com/gallery/saylor -crash-report/.

day, while merging into traffic on an area freeway, Bernard punched the accelerator. Once he got up to speed, he took his foot off the pedal, but the car kept accelerating to between 80 and 85 mph. Realizing that the pedal wasn't returning, he stepped on the brakes with his left foot and tried to use his right foot to pull the accelerator back. But the pedal was stuck so firmly that he couldn't free it. Bernard applied the brakes and slowed the car to 50 to 60 mph. By continued braking, he was able to slow the car to about 25 to 30 mph and move onto the shoulder of the highway. Once there, he shifted the car into neutral, brought it to a complete stop, and turned the car off. According to Bernard, freeing the pedal took a considerable amount of effort. He removed the floor mat and went on about his business without further problems with the car.

When he returned the car to the dealer, Bernard warned the after-hours receptionist that there was a problem with the vehicle's floor mat and that it had dangerously trapped the accelerator. He recalls telling the receptionist: "I think the mat caused it, you need to tell someone." His warning went unheeded. Apparently the receptionist thought that Bernard would tell his story to a service technician; Bernard thought that the receptionist would pass the story along. Three days later, Mark Saylor climbed into the car, still with the wrong floor mats, unsecured, and drove off. Just before the crash that killed them, multiple witnesses saw the Saylors doing much the same thing as Bernard had done—they were driving along on the shoulder of the road, going about 30 mph. The police report suggests that at some point before Saylor could fully stop the vehicle, for whatever reason, "the brakes possibly failed due to overburdened, excessive and prolonged application at high speed," and the car began its acceleration again.

It's hard to imagine more compelling evidence of the cause of the Saylor accident. The floor mat explanation also answers a lot of the lingering questions about what happened to the Saylors. The investigators' experiments showed just how easy it was for the accelerator to get trapped if a RX400h floor mat was installed in the vehicle. Bernard's harrowing experience shows how hard it was to free the pedal once it was stuck. The whole situation demonstrates the risk stemming from using the wrong floor mats in a vehicle, and the possibility that, despite specific directives to trained dealer personnel, dangerous floor mats could end up in cars. Conversely, the Saylor accident doesn't suggest any underlying problem with the vehicle, and certainly not with its electronics.

Dealing with Floor Mats

However, the details of the Saylor accident didn't become available until October 25, 2009, when the police report was completed. In the meantime, there was only sketchy information that a Toyota vehicle had accelerated out of the control of a trained police officer, killing four people, and that floor mats may have been involved. The potential involvement of floor mats played a big role in how the story evolved because, as noted, Toyota had issued a recall of all-weather floor mats for Lexus ES 350s and Toyota Camrys (which share the same platform) in 2007. That recall came as a result of five consumer complaints associated with three accidents and one fatal accident that the National Highway Traffic Administration (NHTSA) determined was caused by trapped accelerators.[*]

---

[*] U.S. Department of Transportation, "U.S. Department of Transportation Releases Results from NHTSA-NASA Study of Unintended Acceleration in Toyota Vehicles," February 8, 2011; http://www.dot.gov/affairs/2011/dot1611.html.

The crashes occurred in vehicles using a new all-weather floor mat that had been designed by engineers at Toyota Motor Sales (TMS) in California and that could be added by the dealer.

An investigation of the complaints found that the design and material of the new floor mat created a lip near the bottom of the accelerator pedal. Pushing the pedal to the floor, especially when the all-weather floor mat wasn't secured or was installed on top of the regular floor mat, could cause the accelerator to get stuck. Ironically, the problem was exacerbated by the high quality of the rubber used, which was very thick and rigid. While investigators from Toyota and the NHTSA looked into other possibilities, the new all-weather floor mats were determined to be the culprit and were recalled in 2007. That recall affected about 55,000 customers—only those who had ordered the specific all-weather floor mats sold through Toyota dealerships. The recall didn't cover placing floor mats from a different vehicle into a Camry or a Lexus ES 350 or stacking floor mats on top of each other (which, of course, could trap a pedal in any vehicle). That recall, though, was enough to cast a shadow on Toyota when floor mats were again implicated in the Saylor accident.

While the NHTSA and Toyota had agreed in 2007 that the floor mat recall was sufficient to deal with the issue, the Saylor accident illustrated that using the wrong floor mats (e.g., ones that were too large, designed for a different vehicle) without properly securing them could still cause pedal entrapment. Rather than wait until a full study of the potential issues and solutions had been completed, Toyota announced a recall and what is known as a Consumer Safety Advisory to drivers of eight models, including the Camry, Avalon, Tacoma, and Lexus ES and IS. A safety advisory, as distinct from a recall, is essentially a letter to the public warning of dangerous behavior and advice on how to avoid potential problems. In this case, the dangerous behavior was using the wrong floor mats, stacking floor mats on top of each other, and/or not clipping the floor mats down.

Although it is often the case, a recall does not necessarily take place immediately after it is announced. In this case, Toyota was still determining the best way of dealing with improperly installed or incorrect floor mats, and so drivers were not advised to bring their cars into dealers immediately. Until a more permanent remedy was found to limit the possibility that accelerator pedals could be trapped if drivers ignored warnings about proper installation of floor mats, customers were instructed, via the safety advisory, to remove all floor mats from their vehicles, regardless of style or manufacturer. The safety advisory also provided instructions on how to stop a vehicle with a trapped accelerator pedal (firm pressure on the brake, shift into neutral, turn the ignition off).

Toyota engineers continued to study floor mat entrapment, and—with the floor mat recall announced—now they were getting rafts of reports from dealers about customers doing dangerous things with floor mats. Dealer after dealer was finding vehicles with three, four, and even up to eight floor mats stacked on top of one another. George Tatar, general manager of a suburban Philadelphia dealer, told us, "We were seeing everything. Aftermarket mats for the wrong vehicle was the least of it. We saw bath mats. We saw leftover pieces of carpet from houses. Everything."

That evidence contributed to the decision to handle the September floor mat recall by altering vehicles to increase the space between the bottom of the accelerator and the floor of the vehicle. For most vehicles, this involved cutting off a portion of the bottom of the accelerator pedal. For a few vehicles, it also involved removing some padding from underneath the carpet under the accelerator pedal. While this wouldn't entirely prevent a pedal from being trapped if someone stacked six floor mats on top of one another, it would provide an extra margin of safety against the more common practice of putting an all-weather mat on top of the existing carpet mat for the winter and removing it in the spring.

Toyota began notifying customers of this effort in late October. In its letter to customers, approved by the NHTSA per regulations, Toyota was at pains to clarify that the "defect does not exist in vehicles in which the driver side floor mat is compatible with the vehicle and properly secured." In its press release about the plan to alter gas pedal size, however, Toyota stated that the letter "confirms that no defect exists in vehicles in which the driver's floor mat is compatible with the vehicle and properly secured." The NHTSA quickly rebuked Toyota for that statement because the agency felt that it implied that the NHTSA agreed with Toyota's conclusions. The NHTSA issued a statement saying that the Toyota press statement was "inaccurate" and "misleading" and that removing floor mats "did not correct the underlying defect"; the agency had decided that pedal entrapment resulting from drivers using the wrong—and improperly installed—floor mats was a vehicle defect. Of course, this interaction only served to ramp up the public tensions in the United States. The rebuke from the NHTSA convinced many people that Toyota was not being honest and was not acting in the best interests of customers.

Given what we now know about the very specific situation that led to the Saylor accident, the floor mat recall seems like something of an overreaction: it wasn't floor mats in general that caused the Saylor accident, or even floor mats that weren't clipped down, but using the thick rubber floor mats from a much larger vehicle in a smaller vehicle *and* not clipping them down. Many customers and the general public were understandably skeptical.

If you looked in the average Toyota vehicle with properly installed correct floor mats, you could plainly see that there was virtually no risk of the pedal's getting trapped. George Tatar confirmed the skepticism, "People just didn't take the floor mat recall seriously." This sentiment was shared by other dealers interviewed. The skepticism may have played a role in undermining confidence in Toyota—without the specific details, people simply didn't believe that the Saylor accident could have been caused by floor mats, and therefore the advisory fed speculation that Toyota didn't know what had caused the Saylor accident. The mishandled public communication about the recall and the rebuke from the NHTSA made things worse. By the time the police report on the Saylor accident was widely available, the public and the media had already begun to speculate about other causes, with many pointing the finger at the electronic throttle control and vehicle electronics.

A Brief History of Vehicle Electronics and Sudden Acceleration

The February 2011 release of the detailed NASA investigation of Toyota vehicle electronics has finally put to rest most of the speculation about hidden problems with Toyota's vehicle electronics. As U.S. Transportation Secretary Ray LaHood said, "We enlisted the best and brightest engineers to study Toyota's electronics systems, and the verdict is in. There is no electronic-based cause for unintended high-speed acceleration in Toyotas."* For more than a year, until the report was released, however, there were many who earnestly believed that vehicle electronics in Toyotas were a possible, if not a probable, cause of the reports of runaway vehicles.

---

* Comments by Ray LaHood at press conference, February 8, 2011.

But was there ever any justification for this belief to begin with? Should regulators, drivers, and the media have suspected vehicle computers and electronics?

Looking at the plot devices of thriller movies reveals that human beings have a deep-seated suspicion of machines, particularly computers. Movies like *War Games*, *2001*, *The Terminator* franchise, and *Christine*, to name just a few, embody our concern that machines that we don't truly understand can run amok and put us in danger. Our cars, as they have steadily replaced mechanics with computers, seem to fall increasingly into this category. Fifteen or so years ago, a chain e-mail parodied personal computers, particularly the Windows operating system, by comically depicting what our driving experience would be like if cars behaved more like our computers and just froze without warning. Today, while still amusing, the litany is ironic at best, given that the average passenger vehicle has 10 or more computers built into it that are more powerful than the PCs on which Bill Gates founded the Microsoft empire.

The "Ghosts" in Our Machines

What do all those computers do? Virtually every modern passenger car's engine is controlled by a computer, known in the industry as an engine control module, or ECM. The ECM monitors the engine's performance and can dynamically adjust the mix of fuel and air, detect a loss of vacuum or a buildup of heat, and take any number of other actions that maximize either the fuel efficiency or the output of the engine. Similar control modules govern many other functions in modern cars.

Since their introduction by BMW in the late 1980s, electronic throttle controls (ETCs) have been among these computerized systems. In an all-mechanical system, a cable or a set of rods connects the accelerator pedal to the throttle of the engine, which governs how much air enters the engine's combustion chamber. With electronic throttle control, a sensor monitors the position of the gas pedal and transmits that information "by wire" (which is why they are often referred to as "drive-by-wire" systems) to the ECM, which then sends a message to the electronic throttle control that tells the throttle to let more or less air into the engine's combustion chamber.

As with any system that relies on moving parts, there are downsides to the old-fashioned mechanical throttle control: cables can become stretched or brittle; rod couplings can become worn and loose. Mechanical systems also have limited precision. But most important of all, mechanical systems are "dumb"; the systems can't communicate with one another. An electronic throttle control system coupled with the other computers in the engine and transmission allows for fine-tuning of performance depending on exactly what the situation is. For instance, the use of electronic throttle control, ECMs, and other computers has produced some of the most important safety advances in the last decade, features like stability and traction control. Other computers in the car are responsible for antilock brakes and air bags. Without the use of computers, these features would literally be impossible. These computer-driven safety features are largely responsible for the fact that traffic fatalities in the United States in 2009 were at the lowest level since 1950.

But unlike mechanical systems, electronic systems carry some mystery about them. There's a general belief that if they malfunction, you can't necessarily see what went wrong the way you can with a mechanical system. According to Jeremy Anwyl, CEO of Edmunds.com, one of the leading automotive-information Web sites, that belief is simply wrong. "If a mechanical part sticks or gets jammed, it's entirely possible that the problem would fix itself and leave no trace. You'd never be able to tell. Electronic systems, though, leave a trail of information, making diagnosing problems much easier."* It's only if a mechanical part fails completely—a hose in the brake system cracks, for instance—that the physical evidence is easy to find and diagnose. Electronic systems tend to leave evidence of intermittent problems. While the exact cause of an electronic problem can be hard to pinpoint, the existence of the problem itself is fairly easy to document. Still, people tend to have less trust in electronic systems. What if the electronic throttle control sends the wrong signal to the throttle, causing unintended acceleration?

That was a frightening thought for vehicle manufacturers as well. Moving to electronic throttle control and ECMs, for all their advantages, couldn't happen unless the systems were more reliable than the mechanical systems they replaced. So the manufacturers designed their computer systems accordingly.

Engineers designing vehicle electronic systems employ a methodology called failure modes and effects analysis, which attempts to identify all possible failure points and design in countermeasures. Given the risks, extensive work was done to design ETMs to eliminate the possibility of catastrophic failures, eventually leading to rigorous standards maintained by the Society of Automotive Engineers.

Toyota's Vehicle Electronics, Fail-Safes, and Testing

To give you a sense of the way an ECM and ETC system is designed, Toyota uses multiple redundant sensors and computer

---

* Interview with authors, October 26, 2010.

modules at every stage of the process (see Figure 3.1, a Toyota diagram of its vehicle electronics). These multiple sensors aren't redundant—they aren't designed so that if the first sensor fails, the second can pick up where the first left off. Instead, the systems are designed to snitch on each other. The two pedal sensors send a simultaneous signal to the ECM. If the signals don't agree with each other, the system enters a fail-safe mode. To further guard against errors, the signals from the two pedal sensors are different voltages, offset from each other at a precise interval. Again, if the interval in voltages changes, the system enters a fail-safe mode.

Checks for consistent signals are made constantly. Within the ECM, there are two computer processing units, one that runs the system and a second that confirms that the behavior of the first is following the signals that it is receiving. These two computers are independent of each other: neither controls the other, but either can send the system into one of a number of fail-safe modes to limit the speed or stop the vehicle if it sees the other acting incorrectly. Similarly, the throttle position is monitored by two separate sensors that send signals with different voltages, similar to the pedals.

If any of the sensors or computers fail, or if any of the messages and multiple interpretations of the messages conflict with one another (for instance, if one sensor says that the accelerator is pressed to the floor and the other says that it's only halfway depressed), the system enters a fail-safe mode. Thus, the multiple signals don't protect against failures; they protect against errors. In addition to entering a fail-safe mode, any problem is also recorded in another computer system, and a warning light is turned on. While the specifics of this redundant fail-safe system are unique to Toyota, the basic design is standard in the industry.

FIGURE 3.1 TOYOTA FAIL-SAFE ELECTRONIC THROTTLE CONTROL SYSTEM

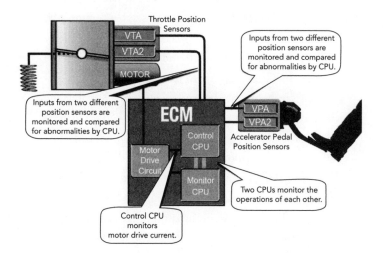

These fail-safe systems to prevent errors in the sensors have worked exactly as expected in testing and on the road. But the vulnerability of electronic systems isn't limited to errors and component failure; these systems are also vulnerable to interference. Any electronic signal can be disrupted or altered by electromagnetic radiation, referred to as electromagnetic interference, or EMI. If you've ever heard the distinctive tapping sound when a cell phone gets too near a landline telephone or a speaker, you've experienced the effects of electromagnetic radiation. Vehicle manufacturers obviously have to protect their ECMs and electronic throttle controls from EMI. Kristen Tabar, general manager of electronic systems at the Toyota Technical Center in Michigan, explains how all manufacturers' vehicle electronics are rigorously designed to protect the systems from EMI:

Shielding the outside of the circuit is one method to protect against EMI, but we also do shielding in the device
itself using a . . . mesh type wire. You can also do that . . .
in the wires bundled into wire harnesses that run through
the vehicle to prevent these waves from traveling along
the wire and then getting into the [modules] through the
wire itself. There are ways to use grounding and capaci-
tors . . . to help [the system] shield itself. Keeping the
right distance between devices and using certain materials to protect from the energy are other design consider-
ations. So, there's more to consider in the design than just
the materials themselves. The circuit board design is probably the most critical: how you ground it, how many layers it has, how you lay out the components on the board.
All of those things are very standardized. There's nothing dramatically unique about Toyota in that respect.

Even with this fail-safe design, Toyota obsessively tests each
component, each subassembly, each complete system, and the entire vehicle inside controlled test chambers and out in the world
in areas that are subject to high EMI. For more on how Toyota
tests electronic systems to ensure that they are safe from EMI, see
Toyota's Electromagnetic Interference Testing, on pages 77 to 79.

Again, we emphasize that Toyota's system for designing and
testing its electronics is incredibly sophisticated, but it is not
unique—all manufacturers, for obvious reasons, require their
electronic systems to meet rigorous design and testing standards.
This point is particularly important to understand because of the
history of complaints of unintended acceleration. Toyota is by no
means the first manufacturer to be accused of having a problem
with sudden unintended acceleration (SUA).

TOYOTA'S ELECTROMAGNETIC INTERFERENCE TESTING

An electromagnetic compatibility (EMC) testing chamber is itself a marvel of engineering. Toyota has built eight chambers in Toyota City, Japan, and each of them is in almost constant use testing components, systems, and entire vehicles. Another chamber is being completed in Ann Arbor, Michigan as we write this. While all systems are also tested in the real world, EMC testing chambers allow Toyota to test the worst electromagnetic interference situations possible.

The largest of these chambers, where entire vehicles are tested, is roughly the size of a small basketball gym. The room has sophisticated equipment that can create every type of EMI, including that produced by high-tension power lines, television and radio broadcasts (up to 10-kW broadcasts), ham radios, aviation radar, and cellular towers. In the center of the chamber is a vehicle-sized platter on which the vehicle being tested sits so that it can be spun around and exposed to EMI from every possible angle. Within the platter is a dynamometer—essentially a treadmill for cars that can measure speed, acceleration, and other characteristics. When a vehicle is brought in for testing, a specialized nonmetallic (to avoid altering the EMI) robot is placed inside. Controlled remotely from outside the chamber, the robot constantly accelerates and brakes at different rates throughout the tests. Cameras positioned on all the wheels and on the dashboard monitor vehicle performance, looking for any hesitations, surges, warning lights, or trouble codes.

In addition to the external EMI, tests for the effects of interference from inside the car, such as cell phones, are also run

(continues next page)

separately and in conjunction with external EMI. All of these tests are designed to exceed the standards specified by the Society of Automotive Engineers, the International Standards Organization (ISO), and the European Union. In general, Toyota aims to test at EMI exposure levels two to four times higher than regulations and standards require.

The chambers are used to test individual components, subsystems, whole systems, and whole vehicles.* Every model that is developed ends up going through more than 1 million hours of testing before going into production. That doesn't include the testing done on individual components by suppliers; for instance, Denso, which makes ETCs, also tests its designs independently of Toyota in its own test chambers.

Testing doesn't stop at the design phase, however. Toyota continues to test older-model vehicles looking for any combination of factors that could either cause a component failure—leading to the system's going into fail-safe mode or setting a trouble code—or exhibiting unintended behavior.

After all this testing on hundreds of vehicles going on for more than 20 years, there has never been a case of interference or component or system failure in a completed design that does not trigger fail-safes. In fact, for a number of vehicles (e.g., the current Camry), by the time they get to the production design, Toyota has been unable to cause the system to fail at all, no matter how severe the EMI induced. While Toyota's testing is extensive, it is not unique. Every major vehicle manufacturer

---

* A video that shows a test chamber in operation and describes the various tests run can be found online at http://pressroom.toyota.com/pr/tms/electronic .aspx?fid=121565&id=E0C19173.

has similar testing chambers running tests on its electronic systems. Even prior to the NASA investigation, there had never been a documented case of EMI-induced failure of an ETC in the field that evaded detection by the vehicle's safety mechanisms or caused unintended behavior. NASA used a similar test chamber to test several Toyota vehicles whose owners had reported incidents of SUA, but was unable to induce acceleration in any of them (though several did enter a fail-safe mode and set a trouble code).

SUA Allegations across the Industry

The most famous instance prior to Toyota was that of Audi in the mid-1980s. The claim then was that Audis were prone to surging at start-up (at that time, Audi did not use a drive-by-wire system). Several children were killed when their parents or grandparents started an Audi and the vehicle surged forward. There were media exposés, including a particularly notorious one by *60 Minutes* that used compressed air to manipulate the transmission of an Audi to cause the gas pedal to operate independently and give the appearance of SUA.* Ultimately, after years of investigation, it was conclusively determined that there was nothing wrong with the Audi vehicles. What was happening was that people were putting their foot on the accelerator and shifting into gear, but then, instead of pressing on the brake pedal to slow down, they were mistakenly pressing even harder on the

---

* Ed Wallace, "The Real Scandal behind the Toyota Recall," *Bloomberg Businessweek*, February 11, 2010; http://www.businessweek.com/lifestyle/content/feb2010/bw20100211_986136.htm.

accelerator. The error was not in the design but in the drivers' behavior—a cause that is known as "pedal misapplication."

The facts weren't enough to prevent huge damage to the Audi brand. It took more than a decade for the company to recover its position in the U.S. market. The blaming of Audi for drivers' mistakes did lead to one positive, the development of the shift interlock. This system prevents a car from being shifted from park into drive unless the driver has her foot on the brake. The system eliminates the danger from one particular type of pedal misapplication. Audi developed the system as a response to the false accusations that its vehicles were dangerous; eventually shift interlocks were required on all new vehicles to prevent children from being able to shift vehicles out of park.

However, complaints of cars acting on their own have continued. They have affected every manufacturer in every era, often leading to lawsuits. For example, Chrysler's Jeep Grand Cherokee has been dogged with hundreds of complaints of SUA, and in 2006 the New York attorney general called on the NHTSA for a "full-gear federal investigation." Even in 2010, after several complete redesigns of the Grand Cherokee, there are claims of SUA unique to that vehicle that are bizarrely associated with driving through car washes.* And while plenty of quality and safety defects have been identified, leading to recalls by every manufacturer, including Toyota (the most recalls across all automakers ever were in 2004, when 30.8 million vehicles were recalled in the United States in hundreds of separate recalls), according to various auto industry experts we interviewed, including Jeremy Anwyl; Edward Niedermeyer, editor-in-chief of *The Truth about Cars*, a

---

* See, for instance, this article about Jeep Grand Cherokees and car washes from the Connecticut Carwash Association: http://www.wewashctcars.com /index.cfm?fuseaction=feature.display&feature_id=3271.

popular auto industry blog; and David Champion, senior manager at *Consumer Reports*, there has never been a proven case of sudden unintended acceleration caused by EMI or a software defect in the electronics of a vehicle. This bears repeating: *there has never been a single documented case of sudden unintended acceleration caused by EMI or a software defect in the electronics of any vehicle from any manufacturer.* That's a 20-year record without a single confirmed incident. In all instances of safety defects affecting electronic systems, the root cause has been a physical defect that could be easily replicated: faulty sensors, wiring problems, or the like.

The fact that electronic systems continue to be blamed, rather than more prosaic causes like driver error or floor mats trapping pedals, is a testament to our mistrust of these systems. It's deeply ironic that the source of arguably the greatest improvements in vehicle safety—the electronic systems that allow vehicles to correct for driver error and for environmental hazards like slick roads—was once again the scapegoat for safety issues. The Insurance Institute for Highway Safety has concluded that electronic stability control (which requires electronic throttle control) would have prevented more than 15,000 fatal crashes in just six years if it had been implemented in all vehicles in 2002. Meanwhile, the highest estimate of fatal accidents allegedly caused by SUA in Toyota vehicles over 10 years was around 100 deaths, more than 80 percent of them reported after the recall crisis hit the news.

Speculation Runs Rampant

Electronic systems have remained scapegoats for some obvious reasons. For one thing, it's always easier to blame vehicles, particularly vehicle electronics, than drivers. The 2008 book *Traffic,* by Tom Vanderbilt, exhaustively details how difficult it is for drivers to gain an accurate perception of their own limitations and errors. Micheline Maynard, a reporter who covered the auto industry for the *New York Times* for a decade, notes that no evidence will ever convince some people: "There will always be people who think it's the electronics." Indeed, in the immediate aftermath of the release of the NASA report absolving Toyota electronics, several of the individuals who had made vociferous claims that Toyota's electronics were at fault simply dug in their heels and insisted that their judgment and insight were superior to those of all of the engineers at NHTSA, NASA, Toyota, and every other automaker using ETC.

Why do people insist on blaming electronics? Well, we all have had experience with faulty electronics or computers that do not do what we want them to do in our daily lives. Those who are attempting to make a case for the vulnerability of vehicle electronics often cite a statistic that there are more lines of software code in a vehicle today than there were in the *Apollo 11* spacecraft that took men to the moon. The statistic is true, but this use of it mostly reveals how little those who quote it understand modern computers and electronics design—there are also more lines of code in an iPhone or a BlackBerry than there were in the *Apollo 11* spacecraft. Jeremy Anwyl also points out that blaming electronics is a fertile field for plaintiffs' lawyers. "It's very hard to prove a negative. You can never say that it could never happen. How do you prove something like that? You can't. . . . From a trial lawyer's perspective, it's not a bad bet. Even though there's no clear proof, it's hard to prove that it didn't happen, and it's not a bad bet to take that to court and see if you can win." That's exactly what happened in the wake of Toyota's floor mat recall—the media, abetted by plaintiffs' lawyers and their consultants working on lawsuits against Toyota, began speculating about a deeper underlying cause for sudden acceleration in Toyotas.

The first media story we've been able to identify that raised the old canard of vehicle electronics, by *Los Angeles Times* reporters Ralph Vartabedian and Ken Bensinger, was published on October 18, 2009. Even after the reporters had access to the official police report on the Saylor accident, they continued to downplay the evidence of the real cause. On December 6, 2009, in a story titled, "Report Inconclusive on Floor Mat's Role in Fatal Toyota Crash," the reporters decided that a single line in the report, in which the investigating officer noted that because of the fire that followed the crash, it was impossible to entirely rule out any other cause, justified calling the evidence inconclusive.

In the meantime, the *Los Angeles Times,* quickly joined by other media outlets, began running stories based on the speculations of various people who were involved in lawsuits against Toyota. While it is a reporter's job to be skeptical of claims made by companies, it is remarkable how little of this skepticism the reporters applied to statements from lawyers and their consultants. For instance, Vartabedian and Bensinger wrote six stories about potential Toyota problems, quoting Sean Kane, of a firm called Safety Research & Strategies, before reporting that the firm is primarily employed to provide research and testimony for lawsuits against automakers. As of this writing, the paper continues to refer to the firm as an "automotive safety consultant," while never mentioning that the organization has no specific expertise in engineering or statistical analysis. On its Web site, the organization lists only one person with even a bachelor's degree in mechanical engineering (and he then went on to become a trial lawyer). The only personnel at the firm with advanced degrees outside of law carry them in "Liberal Studies" and "Library and Information

Science." The firm does not provide any evidence that it has expertise in vehicle electronics or any other area of engineering or that it offers any services useful to anyone other than trial lawyers.

The NHTSA Complaint Database

The major justification for the speculation about underlying Toyota defects came from looking at the NHTSA's database of consumer complaints. As a great deal of reporting since last year has shown, this database can probably best be described as a mess. Investigative work by several reporters has uncovered the fact that the database includes complaints that are impossible (one widely cited example is a complaint about a Lexus accident that killed 99 people in a single vehicle), as well as many, many reports that are dubious. Another prime example is a woman who claimed that her Lexus accelerated out of control even though she had her foot on the brake. The police report following that incident found that she had twice the legal limit for alcohol in her bloodstream. Other complaints, like one recounting how a Toyota Matrix went into a skid as it rounded a corner at more than 40 mph on a wet road while it was snowing, sound a little too much like accidents in which drivers are unwilling to concede error.

The problems of gleaning useful data from the NHTSA database are much greater than the fact that this database includes mountains of unverified data and false claims. Anyone can put in a claim, and it is not necessary to put in any identifying information about yourself or even your car. The person making the complaint classifies the problem into one of a number of broad categories, and it is only if an investigation is launched that an NHTSA staff member audits the complaints to make sure that they are properly classified. The result is that the database conflates many different types of problems into the same broad category. In this case, the category the NHTSA uses is called "Speed Control." In other words, any complaint that involved a vehicle going faster *or slower* than the driver intended is lumped into the same category.

All of these issues aside, given that the NHTSA database did include thousands of complaints about Toyota and acceleration issues (2,290 between 2000 and 2009, according to a count by National Public Radio*), it's worth taking a deeper look to see if there was plausible evidence to suspect a problem in Toyota vehicles. The complaints themselves make compelling and frightening reading, and they certainly sound convincing.

In the summer of 2010, Edmunds.com launched an in-depth study of the NHTSA complaint database. It found that 1 in 10 records were duplicates. To get a more accurate picture from the data, Edmunds.com devoted staff time to going through the complaints one by one. The firm reclassified each complaint into a more specific category and eliminated duplicates and clearly preposterous claims. What Edmunds.com found was that Toyota did have more complaints about sudden acceleration than other manufacturers, but that the true figures were much smaller than a casual look at the database would suggest. From January 2009 until August 2009, Toyota averaged just under 14 complaints of sudden acceleration a month; in comparison, Ford had an average of 7 complaints. To put those figures into perspective, consider that Toyota alone had roughly 16 million vehicles using ETC on the road in the United States during those months. The monthly complaint rate is a little less than 1 in a million. The NASA report estimates the rate of UA complaints at 1 in 1.4 billion miles driven.

---

* The National Public Radio Vehicle Acceleration Complaints Database is available at http://www.npr.org/templates/story/story.php?storyId=124235858.

These complaint levels were not particularly new—sudden acceleration complaints have been made at these levels for decades. The only variation is in which manufacturer leads the complaints. For instance, a later investigation of the data by the NHTSA found that during the period from 2002 to 2009, when it adjusted for volume of vehicles, Volvo actually had the highest level of sudden acceleration complaints per 100,000 vehicles; Toyota was second, and Ford was third. But if you look at shorter time spans, sometimes Ford was the leader in sudden acceleration complaints. On an annual basis, Volkswagen had the most SUA complaints per 100,000 vehicles in 7 out of 10 years between 2000 and 2009.* There are two conclusions to draw from these figures: first, the complaint database does not clearly establish Toyota as an outlier in terms of SUA, and second, SUA claims are regularly made about all manufacturers, but in all cases only as a very small percentage of vehicles on the road.

Forensic Investigations of SUA

Aside from the complaint database, before deciding that there was good reason to suspect an underlying problem with Toyota vehicles, you'd also have to consider the results of actual investigations of SUA. Given that SUA has been reported for many manufacturers for many years, the NHTSA has conducted a number of investigations. One of the first of these investigations is known as the Silver Book (simply because the cover of the report was silver).† This comprehensive study of unintended acceleration was commissioned after the Audi debacle. After a lengthy investigation, a panel of experts concluded that the vast majority of

---

* Based on data from NHTSA and Edmunds.com.

† NHTSA, "An Examination of Sudden Acceleration," 1989, available at http://www.autosafety.org/nhtsa-study-examination-sudden-acceleration-jan-1989.

complaints about sudden acceleration, especially those that happened at low initial speed (such as when pulling into or out of a parking space), were attributable to pedal misapplication. An intensive study by the NHTSA of speed-control complaints in Toyota Camrys from model years 2002 to 2006, done in the summer of 2010, found that 92 percent of the complaints and 96 percent of the crashes were at speeds below 15 mph, characteristic of pedal misapplication accidents, according to the Silver Book.*

Moreover, follow-up research on the issue of pedal misapplication subsequent to the Silver Book found incidents of pedal misapplication to be far more common than previously believed.† Richard Schmidt, a professor of cognitive psychology at UCLA and one of the lead authors of the Silver Book, conducted detailed research on the North Carolina Police Accident Report Database maintained by that state. The database includes the full police report from any accident in the state for which a report was filed. Schmidt and his colleagues began studying the database in the mid-1990s, looking for evidence of accidents caused by unintended acceleration. In that analysis, they found more than 3,700 accidents over the period from 1979 to 1995 where drivers admitted that pedal misapplication was the cause. That averages out to more than 19 accidents per month just in the state of North Carolina. Compare that figure to the average of 14 complaints about sudden acceleration in Toyotas across the entire

---

* NHTSA Informational Briefing for NASA, "Study of Electronic Vehicle Controls and Unintended Acceleration," June 30, 2010. These presentations can be found at the Transportation Research Board of the National Academy of Sciences Web site: http://www.trb.org/PolicyStudies/UnintendedAcceleration Study.aspx.

† Richard Schmidt and Douglas Young, "Cars Gone Wild: The Major Contributor to Unintended Acceleration in Automobiles Is Pedal Error," *Frontiers in Psychology,* November 25, 2010.

United States. Of course, Schmidt notes that the actual number of pedal misapplication accidents is surely much higher, since he counted only accidents where the driver was willing to admit fault.

Another consideration to take into account before drawing a conclusion on the solidity of the evidence for SUA in Toyota vehicles, or any vehicles, back in 2009 is the plausibility of complaints based on the actual functioning of vehicles. All vehicles are designed so that the brakes are more powerful than the engine—the brakes can resist more torque than the engine can create. That's a basic design consideration to make sure that brakes can stop a car. The braking system in modern vehicles is hydraulic—essentially a mechanical system that uses vacuum and liquid pressure to increase braking force. These braking systems are wholly independent of the throttle and engine control modules. Therefore, a situation in which a vehicle did not at least begin to slow down, but rather continued accelerating after the driver pushed the brake to the floor, would require the simultaneous failure of two completely independent systems, one mechanical and one electronic, without leaving any evidence. For example, in December 2009, *Car and Driver* magazine tested the ability of a Camry's brakes to stop the vehicle if the throttle was stuck open, either because of an accelerator pedal being trapped or from some other cause. The *Car and Driver* test found that with the accelerator jammed fully to the floor and the engine running at wide-open throttle from a start of 70 mph, full pressure on the brakes stopped the car in less distance than a Ford Taurus traveling at a similar speed without the accelerator jammed and just 16 feet farther than the stopping distance of the Camry without the accelerator jammed.*

---

* Dave Vanderwerp, "How to Deal with Unintended Acceleration," *Car and Driver*, December 2010; http://www.caranddriver.com/features/09q4/how_to _deal_with_unintended_acceleration-tech_dept

In a July 2009 informational briefing for the Academy of Sciences and NASA teams that the NHTSA engaged to conduct the complete investigation of vehicle electronics that was released in February 2011, the agency reported that in the preceding 25 years it had conducted 109 defect investigations related to unintended acceleration, leading to 34 recalls, while manufacturers had independently issued another 174 recalls related to unintended acceleration. In each case, a specific replicable physical defect could be found. There were no cases of problems caused by EMI or software. In all of these investigations and recalls, the briefing states, "No defect conditions have been identified that resulted in a sudden wide-open throttle and simultaneous loss of brake effectiveness."* NASA's later testing confirmed this finding, noting that in all Toyota test vehicles, "braking systems were capable of overcoming all levels of acceleration, including wide open throttle" and would slow the car.†

One has to question any story that alleges that the brakes couldn't slow an accelerating vehicle. Edward Niedermeyer thinks there is a much likelier explanation for such reports than simultaneous multiple system failure: "As far as I'm concerned, it's proof positive that the driver was pressing the gas, not the brakes." Many other drivers reporting unintended acceleration also claimed that they had shifted into neutral or reverse and/or

---

* NHTSA Informational Briefing, "Study of Electronic Vehicle Controls and Unintended Acceleration," June 30, 2010.

† Brakes will always slow a vehicle no matter what position the throttle is in and will almost always be able to bring the vehicle to a stop in a reasonable distance. The only exception is in the case of a wide-open throttle, NASA noted, as in pedal entrapment, if the driver repeatedly pumps the brakes rather than applying steady pressure. In that case, the brake vacuum assist system can fail, limiting the stopping ability. "Technical Assessment of Toyota Electronic Throttle Control Systems," February 2011 report; http://www.nhtsa.gov/UA.

pulled the parking brake without effect. Those reports would require four separate systems, one of them entirely mechanical (the parking brake), to fail simultaneously.

Thus, the evidence available in the fall of 2009, 18 months before the NASA investigation was completed, was overwhelmingly against vehicle electronics as a cause of sudden acceleration. Yet that did not stop wild, unfounded speculation from carrying the day (or the need to eventually spend $1.5 million of taxpayer monies to prove the speculation incorrect).

A Complete Lack of Evidence

None of these reasons to doubt the claims of runaway vehicles with electronic systems run amok—not the problems with the NHTSA database, not the lack of any forensic evidence of sudden acceleration caused by electronics, not the thorough research by NHTSA into sudden acceleration in the past, and not the unlikelihood of most SUA complaints—was reported in the mainstream media (though blogs and more specialized automotive Web sites did make these same observations). The most visible media stories about "sudden unintended acceleration" focused only on the raw number of complaints from the NHTSA database filed under "speed control," including the deaths from accidents blamed on those incidents (regardless of what police investigations of those accidents found or whether they were cases in which plaintiffs were suing Toyota). With the public skeptical of the floor mat explanation and always willing to suspect electronics, the media stories convinced more and more people that there was something seriously wrong with Toyota vehicles—something that Toyota was hiding, whether the company knew the real cause or not. The nature of the reporting also ramped up the pressure on the NHTSA, which was accused of being soft on Toyota. For instance, one of the *Los Angeles Times* stories was headlined, "Runaway Toyota Cases Ignored." What the news stories failed to dig into was the underlying reasons for ignoring most complaints filed with the NHTSA that we've noted—the content of the complaint is highly suspect, and there is no supporting evidence to back up the claims of the person who is making the report.

The reporting provided fertile ground for the stories to run out of control. There's a well-documented history of highly publicized events, like UFO sightings, leading to a wave of similar complaints, and this phenomenon was clearly evident in the Toyota case.* Once the speculation about electronics, or any other Toyota recall issue, was highly publicized, complaints alleging the issue in question skyrocketed. As a result, the NHTSA database became even less useful. For instance, the NHTSA database includes 11 reports of fatal accidents in Toyotas where the driver alleged unintended acceleration in the period from 2000 to October 2009. After the Toyota recalls and intense media coverage, from October 2009 to June 2010, there were 64 more cases reported. In the June 30, 2009 NHTSA briefing, about 1,300 UA complaints were reported for Toyota vehicles for the nine years through October of 2009, and then a jump to almost 2,500 UA complaints for the next nine months.† With the deluge of daily media reports of sudden acceleration of Toyotas (rarely qualified with "alleged"), it is not surprising that complaints snowballed. For example, in February 2010, Prius speed control complaints were up 13 times compared to January, according to an Associated Press analysis of the NHTSA database. Because of this snowball effect, the NHTSA notes that reports after October 2009 aren't reliable indicators of a trend.

---

*For examples, see Allan J. Kimmel, *Rumors and Rumor Control* (New York: Routledge Press, 2003).

†NHTSA Informational Briefing, ibid.

It is well known in cognitive psychology that people "back-fill" their recollections. That is, they fill in details to make a story logical and complete, often without realizing that they are doing so. This has been shown to have a big impact on eyewitness testimony, as information learned subsequent to the event gets incorporated into a witness's memory, leading the individual to believe it as if it were the actual memory. One of the leading experts on this process, Elizabeth Loftus, explains the development of false certainty by claiming that "the more people think about an event from the past, the more confident they become in their memories. The problem is that they get more confident in their inaccurate memories as well as their accurate ones."*

The severity of the effect is best illustrated graphically (see Figure 3.2). The chart is based on the cleaned version of the NHTSA database generated by Edmunds.com. Before the Saylor accident, while monthly complaints about Toyota were higher than those for other manufacturers, they were not dramatically so—usually below 20. Then, as the media speculation kicked into high gear, the number of complaints experienced a sudden acceleration, reaching a high point of more than 1,300 complaints in February 2010, after several recalls were announced. By September 2010, the number was back down to below 20. (Note that Toyota did not make any changes in its vehicle electronics during that time.)

So while unfounded speculation ran rampant, resulting in no small part from the general public's confusion about how vehicles work, Toyota engineers and executives in Japan believed that any technical or design issues had been resolved via the floor mat

---

* Elizabeth Loftus, *Eyewitness Testimony* (Cambridge, Mass.: Harvard University Press, 1996).

FIGURE 3.2 SUDDEN ACCELERATION COMPLAINTS IN THE NHTSA DATABASE, USING DATA CLEANED BY EDMUNDS.COM

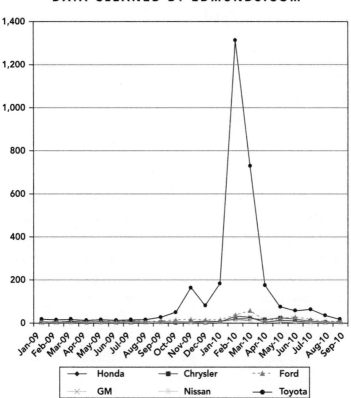

safety advisory and recall. There had been an issue with specific floor mats in the Camry and Lexus ES sedans, and this issue had been dealt with via the recall of the all-weather floor mats in 2007.*

---

* Another source of a large number of complaints was related to how the transmission in Camrys shifted at speeds between roughly 35 and 45 mph, which in aggressive driving situations caused a brief rpm surge; this led to a service campaign to reprogram the transmission for any driver who didn't like the behavior of the transmission.

After the Saylor accident showed the very real possibility of floor mats ending up in the wrong vehicles, the announced recall and safety advisory related to floor mats had been, from this perspective, a decision to go above and beyond any legal culpability to protect customers.

During the course of November and December, the media leapt on any reports of a Toyota with acceleration issues. The *Los Angeles Times* pursued the story with exceptional vigor, publishing several more articles accusing Toyota of hiding data and ignoring customer complaints, still without doing any digging into the forensics of any particular accident or finding any evidence of a defect in Toyota's electronics.

All of these factors—the unfounded speculation about vehicle electronics, the public doubt over the floor mat recalls, the NHTSA reprimand of Toyota, and the insulation of key decision makers in Japan from the realities of consumer sentiment in the United States—created a powder keg, needing only a spark to explode and ravage Toyota's hard-won reputation for quality and safety. That spark came in the form of sticky pedals.

Toyota certainly bears some culpability for what happened next. While there were some technical issues, which we'll explore in detail, the primary problems weren't technical. They were, first and foremost, in how Toyota communicated, both internally and with customers, the public in general, the media, and the NHTSA. The root cause of these errors, Toyota later concluded, was the way in which it had historically handled safety and quality concerns, which was overly centralized in a quality department in Japan and focused on an engineering perspective, while the company had lost direct touch with customer perspectives and concerns (more on this in Chapter 4).

The Saga of the Sticky Pedals

Among the many challenges of switching from mechanical to electronic systems is re-creating the feel of a mechanical system. Since so much of driving is habitual behavior—we manage to control our vehicles without a great deal of conscious thought and attention—it's very important for the driving experience, including the way the pedals feel, to remain constant. In a mechanical throttle mechanism, it requires force to push down the pedal to pull the cable that opens the throttle—and there's force pushing the pedal back to idle as a driver removes her foot. An electronic throttle control system has to re-create these sensations (even though technically they are not necessary) so that the driving experience doesn't materially change.

To do so requires designing pedal assemblies that require an amount of force roughly equal to the amount required to depress a pedal mechanically connected to the throttle and that push back after you remove your foot; this is achieved with a mix of springs, pivots, and dampers. The dampers' role is to provide the right amount of friction so that the pedal moves smoothly, both when it is being depressed and when it is returning to the idle position. Historically, Denso, one of the original Toyota suppliers in Japan, was Toyota's main supplier of pedals, but over the years Toyota has localized the supply of many parts. In the 2005 model year, Toyota began using CTS as a supplier for pedals; the CTS pedals eventually became standard in most North American and some European vehicles.

During the course of 2008, Toyota's European operations had investigated four vehicles where drivers had reported that the accelerator was slow to return or was sticking in a partially open position.* Field engineers recovered the pedals and sent them back to Japan for analysis. Replicating the problem in the lab proved difficult and required months of testing. It wasn't until April 2009 that the testing was able to consistently recreate the problem in the lab. The reason the problem was so hard to replicate was that the stickiness seemingly happened only in high-heat or high-humidity conditions. In such conditions, the synthetic material CTS had used as a damper in the pedal could become sticky. The first European reports all came from right-hand-drive vehicles from the United Kingdom or Ireland. In these vehicles, the driver side heat duct was directed at the accelerator pedal—which the testing engineers from TMC and CTS believed caused high heat and condensation in humid conditions.

With the problem now apparently understood and documented, Toyota engineers got to work on assessing the impact of the stickiness. The primary concern was determining if the sticky pedals affected the ability of drivers to stop their vehicles. This question is the hidden factor around which much of the subsequent controversy revolved: If the sticky pedals kept drivers from stopping or materially increased the amount of time required to bring a car to a halt, then the sticky pedals were clearly a safety defect and required immediate corrective action. If, on the other hand, braking performance was unaffected by the sticky pedals, then, the engineers felt, the pedals were not a safety defect but a customer-satisfaction and component-reliability issue.

As we noted above, testing by independent analysts showed that a Camry with a wide-open throttle could be brought to a stop in less distance than similar vehicles without an open throttle

---

* The details of the sticky pedal investigation are based on reports Toyota has filed with the NHTSA as well as interviews with Toyota personnel.

from other manufacturers. That was the same conclusion that TMC quality engineers in Japan reached. The sticking pedals they were examining were not sticking at wide-open throttle—and the brakes stopped the vehicle in the same amount of time and distance as vehicles without a sticky pedal. Based on those data, they concluded that the sticky pedals were not a safety issues and that therefore there was no need to issue a recall.

This is obviously not a clear-cut decision. There is an argument to be made that any unexpected behavior of a gas or brake pedal is a safety defect and should be treated as such. A driver who finds his vehicle continuing to accelerate or maintaining speed after he has taken his foot off the gas pedal may panic and make poor decisions rather than simply stepping on the brake to bring the vehicle under control. But the Toyota engineers' position—that the sticky pedals were not a safety defect—is also quite understandable. A driver who wanted to bring her car to a stop could do so without taking any action different from what she would do normally.

Buttressing the Toyota engineers' perspective was the fact that no accidents had been reported as a result of the sticky pedals (and the NASA study also did not find any examples of an accident caused by sticky pedals*); the vehicles in question had all been brought to a Toyota dealer by customers who were unhappy with the pedal operation rather than for investigation after an accident. It's also worth noting that this perspective—that the sticky pedals were not a safety defect—has held in Europe, where the sticky pedals were first found. Toyota did not initiate a recall of the European pedals until after discussions with NHTSA led

---

*Matthew Wald, "Electronic Flaws Did Not Cause Toyota Problems, U.S. Says," *New York Times*, February 8, 2011; http://www.nytimes.com/2011/02/09/business/09auto.html.

to the U.S. recall. Toyota has not been fined or reprimanded by any European regulator.

It's easy to second-guess this decision in hindsight, knowing what we do now about the effect that the sticky pedal controversy would have on Toyota's reputation. But the decision that the sticky pedals did not represent a safety defect was made well before allegations of runaway Toyotas came to dominate headlines. So instead of issuing a recall, engineers began designing an alternative version of the pedal to put into production. By July 2009, still a month before the Saylor accident, TMC and CTS engineers had changed the design of the pedal (replacing the synthetic material and altering some pedal components so that, even if the material became sticky, the pedal would operate normally), and a plan was in place to, on a rolling basis, replace the existing design on all new vehicles, beginning with right-hand-drive vehicles in Europe, but eventually expanding worldwide to all vehicles that used CTS pedals.

Toyota Motor Europe issued a technical bulletin to distributors in Europe, warning them to keep an eye out for the problem and to replace any pedals that seemed to be sticking. While some information about the sticky pedals was shared between customer-quality engineering personnel in Europe and the United States, it was still perceived to be a European-only issue.

It wasn't until the period between August and October 2009, when a Toyota Matrix and several Corollas in the United States were found with the same stickiness in the pedal operation, that Toyota engineers in Japan began to suspect that the problem could affect any vehicle with the CTS pedals. The vehicles identified in the United States had the same symptoms as the vehicles in Europe, but just as in Europe, there were no reports of accidents. Engineers in Japan were able to reproduce the stickiness, and, after extensive testing, by December they concluded that the root cause was the same: high-humidity or high-heat conditions. Engineers in Japan carrying out this testing were cut off from the atmosphere in the United States at this time, and they still did not consider the sticking pedals to be a safety issue but simply a customer-satisfaction one. It required attention, but not the urgent response that a safety defect would call for, especially given the very small number of vehicles that were reported with the problem.

So while public concern about Toyota was heating up in the United States, and speculation about Toyota's electronics as the cause was running rampant, Toyota's decision makers on recalls in Japan were looking dispassionately at data about accelerator pedals that were not performing as expected but did not change customers' ability to stop their vehicles by using the brakes. TMS spokespeople in the United States were battling the rumors and speculation as best they could, but they were unaware of the global picture on sticking pedals. That was particularly apparent when, in late December 2009, media attention was drawn to a customer who drove his vehicle to a New Jersey Toyota dealer, complaining of a sticking accelerator. Neither the dealer nor Toyota's external communications personnel were equipped to deal with the issue because they were unaware of the full scope of the sticky pedal issues.

How did this disconnect between quality and safety personnel in Japan and customer-facing personnel in the United States come to be? It was based in the history of Toyota's evolution from a small Japanese company to a leading global manufacturer.

As far back as the founding of NUMMI, Toyota's first attempt to produce vehicles in North America, the company has had the intention of making its regional operations more self-reliant. A major reason for engineering and building cars in North America for the North American market comes back to the Toyota Way principle of *genchi genbutsu*, or "go and see." The idea is that decisions should be made as close to the *gemba*, or work site, as possible. Thus, serving North America can best be done from North America.

It's not enough just to have operations in a particular region, however. The goal isn't simply to have someone locally; it's to have an organization that is deeply trained in the Toyota Way and is capable of making decisions and operating according to the company's principles and plans. Such an operation cannot rely on having Japanese engineers and executives constantly traveling from Japan to "go and see." Not only would that make significant growth impossible from a capacity standpoint, but it would ultimately defeat the purpose of *genchi genbutsu*. The people who are most knowledgeable about a problem should be the people solving the problem. That can't be done by visitors. It has to be done by the people who live with the problem every day.

For a company whose success is built on hewing closely to a very specific way of operating and a very specific culture, that is far easier said than done. For Toyota, before a region can be self-reliant, that region has to have leadership in place that is as deeply steeped in the Toyota Way as the leaders in Japan who literally grew up within the company.

Bucking the trend that has swept most of the world's companies, Toyota has never relied on outsiders or "new blood" to run the company. Every president in the company's history has spent his entire career working for Toyota. The same is true of every Japanese senior executive in the company's history. The only exceptions to this rule are the North Americans, Europeans, and personnel from other nationalities who were hired into the company as it expanded its operations globally.

This desire to achieve self-reliance, coupled with a rock-solid commitment to ensuring that Toyota culture is deeply embedded in every leader, is perhaps the central management tension that the company has been facing for the last 20 years. The North American action plan based on Global Vision 2010 made self-reliance one of its core goals. Yet in 2009, major decisions on engineering, safety, and recalls were still being made almost exclusively in Japan, not in the affected region. Just as important, recall decisions, separated as they were from the region, were based primarily on the input of engineers who did not have direct access to customer feedback. Toyota's culture of fact-based decision making, which has served it so well, essentially excluded from consideration customer complaints or customer sentiment, relying almost entirely on engineering judgments.

The Sticky Pedal Recall

It was not until mid-January 2010 that the engineering executives who deal with safety and recalls in Japan fully informed the external affairs executives who were responsible for communications in the United States about the technical details of the sticky pedal problem and the findings in Europe and how they related to the cases reported in the United States. The American executives, as most famously expressed by communications manager Irv Miller, who wrote that the company needed to "come clean" in an e-mail on January 16 (see The "Smoking Guns" That Weren't on page 102), realized that the media environment demanded a fully detailed public announcement as soon as possible, while the Japan-based executives, who did not consider the sticky pedals to be a safety defect, felt there was no urgent need to issue a recall or make technical details public. While internal debate continued about exactly when the announcement would be made and how much detail on the sticky pedals would be revealed, TMA President Yoshi Inaba and TMS President Jim Lentz met with NHTSA on January 19 to share the latest information and come to agreement on the details of a recall. That recall, announced on January 21, 2010, covered all 2.3 million vehicles in the United States with the CTS pedals.

THE "SMOKING GUNS" THAT WEREN'T

During the height of the crisis, two separate internal communications from Toyota were reported as "smoking guns," purportedly showing evidence that Toyota was aware of safety problems and was actively hiding information from the public.

The more prominent of the two was an e-mail sent by Irv Miller, a group vice president of communications for TMS before he retired from Toyota in February 2010. On January 16, 2010, Miller was involved in an e-mail exchange with Katsuhiko Koganei, a Japanese colleague, over the details of an announcement about the sticky pedals. Koganei expressed hesitation about making a public announcement and sharing technical details of the sticky pedal issue; Miller argued that Toyota had to "come clean" about the sticky pedals. He warned, "We are not protecting our customers by keeping this quiet. The time to hide on this one is over." That certainly seems like evidence that Toyota was concealing information about unintended acceleration.

The other was a presentation given by staffers of Toyota Motor of America's (TMA's) Washington office, which handled the company's interactions with the NHTSA. That presentation, from July 2009, noted that the company had saved $100 million by persuading the NHTSA to accept a limited recall in 2007, involving only all-weather floor mats, rather than asking for a larger recall that would affect more vehicles or a resolution of the problem that involved changes to vehicles rather than replacing the floor mats. After the tragic death of the Saylor family, this presentation seemed to show Toyota boasting about putting savings above customer safety.

In both cases, context matters. The documents look quite different when you know a few of the background details.

The e-mail debate between Koganei and Miller wasn't related to sharing information about sticky pedals with the NHTSA. That process had begun back in November 2009 (when Toyota reported the sticking pedals found in the United States to the NHTSA through technical field reports) and was ongoing. Miller and Koganei were discussing the details of Toyota's public statement about the issues.

While discussions between Toyota and the NHTSA were taking place, communications professionals at TMS, like Irv Miller, who had been the public spokespeople fighting the SUA allegations, were not informed about any of this until mid-January. When they learned of the sticky pedal issue, the TMS communications executives wanted to issue a public release immediately, but the external affairs professionals in Japan wanted to wait until there had been a complete analysis of the problem, a solution had been found, and a plan for fixing the problem was in place. Koganei had moved to California just a few weeks earlier in his new assignment as a liaison between TMS and Toyota Motor Corporation (TMC) in Japan (similar positions exist throughout Toyota's international operations). In the e-mail exchange,

(continues next page)

Koganei was presenting TMC's view from Japan that it was premature to issue a public announcement. Miller felt that Koganei was taking a position without fully understanding the context, or respecting the experience of TMS executives who were at the *gemba*. As Miller explained to us: "I thought our public relations people in Japan were being overly conservative in addressing this particular issue. They wanted to wait until we had a cure for the whole thing rather than saying to the public: 'Hey, look, we are out in front of this thing, we are working on it, we are working with NHTSA, and we are going to do everything possible to resolve this.'"

Toyota's typical approach to communications is to be extremely cautious, saying only the bare minimum that can be absolutely backed up by facts. But this was not a typical environment. Miller clearly understood the political context much better and believed that any lack of detail or delay in the announcement would cause more harm to Toyota than going public before every "t" had been crossed and every "i" dotted. In short, the e-mail exchange was an internal squabble over the details of a press release, not a smoking gun memo about hiding a safety issue from the government.

The story of the $100 million savings presentation is also quite different from what was generally reported. The presentation was created to brief Yoshimi Inaba, when he assumed the role of president of TMA early in 2009, on the activities and importance of the regulatory affairs personnel. As we've discussed elsewhere, every recall is a negotiation, and the NHTSA can push for recalls without a definitive defect or cause being established. The presentation in question was simply an illustration of this fact—by working with the NHTSA, the regulatory affairs department had demonstrated that the design of specific all-weather floor mats, not a generic problem with floor mats or other items that could be related to SUA, such as faulty throttles, was the most likely cause of pedal entrapment. The division members were proud that they had done their job and saved the company a lot of money by preventing a recall of throttles or other equipment that was not faulty and would not have fixed the issue.

The Gap in Perception between Toyota Japan and the United States

The sticky pedal was Toyota's second major recall affecting more than a million vehicles in three months. On top of that, for a public that was confused about unintended acceleration—what it meant and what the possible causes were—this appeared to be yet another grudging admission from Toyota that there were underlying defects in its vehicles, defects that senior executives from TMS had vociferously denied in the November recall announcements and as recently as December 9 in a letter to the editor of the *Los Angeles Times*. Those same TMS executives were not happy to learn in January that TMC in Japan had been so slow to recognize the extent of the problem and the impact it would have on further eroding trust in Toyota. As Irv Miller explained: "When the Avalon incident occurred in December, it was public knowledge. My feeling then and now is that we had to get in front of this, stand up, take our lumps, and start the healing process."

The gap in perceptions between the United States and Japan was large. In Japan, the perception was that the sticky pedal recall was an example of Toyota putting customers first by issuing a recall for a very rare situation that had not caused any accidents and wasn't perceived as a true safety defect. In the United States, however, this latest recall was completely undermining Toyota's reputation for quality and safety and the trust that so many Americans had put in it. All the dealers that we spoke to reported dealing with some customers who, after the recall was announced, were afraid to drive their vehicles at all. Given the reporting that had been done, the customers were in no position to understand the difference between cars zooming out of control at 100 mph and cars with sticky pedals that would stop on command with a normal use of the brakes. For many Americans, trust in Toyota's being fully honest had nearly evaporated.

Further compounding the mismatch and tarnishing Toyota's image in the United States was the fact that when the recall was announced, Toyota didn't have a fix identified. Up to that point, engineers in Japan had been focused on designing a new pedal for future vehicles, not on replacing the pedals that were already in vehicles. As a result, it couldn't tell customers how or when it was going to deal with the issue. Toyota also didn't immediately stop selling vehicles that had been built with the potentially sticky pedals; that announcement didn't happen until January 26.

The media interpretation of what was now a full-blown public relations debacle was that, despite years of denials, Toyota was finally but halfheartedly admitting that there was a defective part that could cause vehicles to accelerate out of control, ultimately killing people. It didn't matter that the part in question couldn't cause runaway vehicles (since the sticking did not affect braking performance), nor that there had not been any recorded accidents as a result of the sticking pedals. The narrative put forth by the media assumed that the unverified complaints that were now flooding in were all real, documented, proven cases. With Toyota's recall, the story that Toyota vehicles were dangerous and were killing people, while Toyota moved sluggishly and without concern for customer safety, seemed to be validated.

The mismatch between public perceptions and Toyota's view is starkly illustrated in news articles published shortly after the recall. For instance, a January 30 article in the *Los Angeles Times* was headlined, "Doubt Cast on Toyota's Decision to Blame Sudden Acceleration on Gas Pedal Defect." In the article, Vartabedian and Bensinger, the reporters responsible for most of the newspaper's Toyota coverage, led off by writing,

> Toyota Motor Corp.'s decision to blame its widening sudden-acceleration problem on a gas pedal defect came under attack Friday, with the pedal manufacturer flatly denying that its products were at fault. Federal vehicle safety records reviewed by the *Times* also cast doubt on Toyota's claims that sticky gas pedals were a significant factor in the growing reports of runaway vehicles.

The most remarkable among several inaccuracies in just the first two sentences of the article is the claim that Toyota was blaming the sticking accelerator pedals for sudden acceleration of the sort alleged by the *Los Angeles Times*. In fact, the Toyota recall announcement goes out of its way to clarify that the pedals *could not* result in a runaway vehicle: "The condition is rare, but can occur when the pedal mechanism becomes worn and, in certain conditions, the accelerator pedal may become harder to depress, slower to return or, in the worst case, stuck in a partially depressed position." This is a far cry from the wide-open throttle acceleration claims that the *Times* repeatedly highlighted in its reporting. At no point in the article do the *Times* reporters provide a statement or quote from a Toyota employee that attributes sudden acceleration complaints to the sticking accelerator pedals. What the reporters do focus on, however, is a statement from CTS in which it denied that its pedals could cause sudden acceleration: "CTS acknowledged that a tiny number of pedals had a rare condition that could cause a slow return to idle position, but it denied that this condition could cause unintended acceleration and said that it knew of no accidents or injuries caused by the issue." This statement is exactly in accord with Toyota's position—this was a rare issue that was not associated with any accidents and was not related to sudden acceleration. Somehow, though, the reporters construed the statement as contradicting Toyota when it was only contradicting the *Times*'s narrative.

Far from blaming CTS, Toyota has had a communications policy of never blaming suppliers for any quality defects. The pedal in question was designed by CTS to Toyota's specifications. And as Robert Young, vice president of the purchasing group at TEMA (which handles suppliers), notes, "We put it in our vehicle. It's our responsibility. End of story." In stark contrast to the finger-pointing between BP, Halliburton, and other companies involved in the Gulf of Mexico oil spill, Toyota has always assumed full responsibility for the sticky pedals. A safety or quality defect that makes it into production is a failure of the system, not of a particular part or supplier.

The mismatch between Toyota's perspective and the popular narrative also served to further blacken the company's relationship with the NHTSA. Understandably, some people within the NHTSA felt that the abrupt announcement of a defect—though wholly unrelated to vehicle electronics—after months of denials from Toyota that there were issues other than floor mats with vehicles meant that Toyota had been dragging its feet on sharing information with the agency. That feeling was amplified as details came out about the months that had passed between reproducing the sticky pedal problem reported in Europe and sharing the full details of the phenomenon with U.S. regulators.*

Finding a Fix for the Sticky Pedals

When the recall was announced, Toyota had not yet identified a viable approach for fixing the sticky pedals. While a new variant of the pedal, one that was not susceptible to stickiness, had gone into limited production in mid-2009, there were not enough of the new pedals being produced to replace the more than 2.3 million in use in the United States, much less all of those in use worldwide. Toyota decided to shut down assembly of all vehicles using the new CTS pedals so that the relatively small number of new pedals could be allocated to repairing customer vehicles. As Bob Carter, group vice president at TMS, explained:

> We stopped production of all 11 assembly lines and transported 27,000 pedals to dealers. We knew that 27,000 was just a drop of water in the Pacific Ocean compared to the 2.3 million we needed. But we wanted to do something for the customer.

---

* The NHTSA's perception that the sticky pedals in Europe were a safety defect and should have been reported much earlier ultimately led the agency to fine Toyota more than $16 million, the maximum fine allowed by law and the largest fine for an automobile manufacturer ever.

Using Toyota's other pedal assembly supplier, Denso, was also not an option because the parts weren't exact analogues; in general, you can't put a Denso pedal in a car designed to use a CTS pedal. A fix for the existing pedals had to be found.

Work was going on furiously in the postproduction engineering teams in Japan as they tested various possible fixes in collaboration with CTS. In North America, the purchasing department at Toyota Engineering and Manufacturing North America (TEMA) was making phone calls to auto parts suppliers and contract manufacturers around the world to find factories that had the capacity to produce the proposed remedies.

By January 28, after round-the-clock testing, a fix for the sticky pedals had been chosen. A small rectangular piece of steel, referred to as a reinforcement bar, was inserted to increase the clearance between the internal mechanisms in the accelerator pedal assembly. This increased clearance would reduce the friction caused by wear and environmental conditions and allow the pedal to operate smoothly for the life of the vehicle. But now millions of these exactly sized steel parts (sized somewhat differently for different vehicles) had to be produced as quickly as possible. Even for a relatively simple piece of steel, that's a tall order. The manufacturer had to have the right machines and the spare capacity to start mass producing the reinforcement bars right away. None of Toyota's major suppliers could do it in the time frame required.

Grand Rapids Spring in Michigan came to the rescue. As luck would have it, the company had a facility with just the right tools that was operating below capacity. Still, starting to produce the parts in volume right away was a mammoth effort. The production line was set up on February 3, and production started 24 hours a day immediately. By the end of the weekend, more than a million reinforcement bars had been made. The next best alternative to Grand Rapids Spring that Toyota could find would have needed two more weeks lead time, an unimaginable eternity given the mass hysteria around the recall.

But the reinforcement bars still needed to get out to the dealers. TEMA set up a special warehouse that Sunday to begin packing boxes for overnight delivery to dealers on Monday morning. Meanwhile, TMS personnel were busy creating training modules for dealers' service personnel to teach them how to install the reinforcement bar correctly. Additionally, letters had to go out to all current owners of the models involved in the recall beginning the repair scheduling process.

While all this frantic activity was happening in the background to deal with the sticky pedal issue, another set of blows landed. Toyota had announced the steel reinforcement bar fix on February 1, telling customers that dealers would begin receiving the parts by the end of the week and that repairs would be scheduled shortly thereafter. On February 3, however, Ray LaHood, the U.S. Secretary of Transportation, having just endured a grilling before a congressional committee about supposed shortcomings at the NHTSA, responded to a question from a reporter about what owners of Toyotas should do now that the fix had been announced by saying, "My advice is, if anyone owns one of these vehicles, stop driving it, take it to a Toyota dealer." Much of the careful work done by Toyota, and approved by the NHTSA, to prepare the logistics for an orderly repair of all customer vehicles as quickly as possible was almost undone by this careless statement.

Carnegie Mellon professor Paul Fischbeck noted the folly of this recommendation by calculating the relative risk of walking versus driving a Toyota, assuming that all of the 19 deaths at the time of the recall (this figure would later grow as more and more past accidents were attributed to SUA, regardless of the actual cause) that had allegedly been caused by sudden acceleration were accurate and were caused by the sticky pedals. "Walking a mile is 19 times or 1,900 percent more dangerous than driving a mile in a recalled Toyota."* Even Sean Kane of Safety Research and Strategies mocked the idea that sticky pedals were a significant source of danger to Toyota drivers. LaHood later had to retract and apologize for the statement, asking owners of vehicles covered by the recall to follow the plans created by Toyota and local dealers.

Prius Brake Feel Further Feeds the Frenzy

But LaHood's comment wasn't the only bad news for Toyota on February 3. That same day, the NHTSA announced that it had received more than 100 complaints about braking performance in 2010 Toyota Prius vehicles. With the frenzy over the sticky pedals at its peak, the announcement was like pouring gasoline on a bonfire. Here, it seemed, was yet another defect in Toyotas that could kill you. Not only did the accelerators stick to the floor, but the brakes could fail, too.

Once again, the frenzy quickly overwhelmed any facts. The basics of the complaint were that the brakes didn't seem to respond immediately when braking at slow speeds on a bumpy and slippery surface (like a wet or icy road with a pothole). It's understandable how worrying this would be to a driver, particularly

---

* Based on a February 25, 2010, article on The Auto Channel; http://www.theautochannel.com/news/2010/02/25/467144.html.

one who was being bombarded with media stories about runaway Toyotas and sticking pedals. But the most important fact about the Prius braking complaints is the word *seem*. The underlying issue was not a true delay in actual braking, but a delay in the feel of the pedal. In these situations, the antilock braking system (ABS) took over control of the braking system from the regenerative braking system, which captures energy from braking to power the vehicle's electric motor. This switchover to the ABS brakes took roughly three-hundredths of a second. But the transition also changed the feel in the brake pedal: the pedal became momentarily "soft," as if the brakes were not working. There was no effect on braking ability or distance, just on the feel of the pedal.

After the launch of the 2010 model in October 2009, Toyota had become aware that customers did not like the way this made the brakes feel and had changed the ABS software in the Prius on the production line in January. Given that there was no effect on braking ability (similar to the initial decision on sticky pedals), the company didn't issue a recall or even a technical service bulletin to correct the issue in Priuses that were already on the road—another misstep by Toyota executives who were too far from the *gemba*.

The fact that the company had changed the production software without doing anything for people with cars on the road was interpreted as yet another example of a company that was hiding crucial information that could affect the safety of customers. For example, in a February 4, 2010 article that was entitled "Software to Blame for Prius Brake Problems," CNN reported: "Toyota officials described the problem as a 'disconnect' in the vehicle's complex antilock brake system (ABS) that causes less than a one-second lag. With the delay, a vehicle going 60 mph will have traveled nearly another 90 feet before the brakes begin to take hold." CNN, like most media outlets, failed to grasp that (1) the issue occurred only at speeds under 35 mph, and that (2) there was no material delay in braking, just in the feel of the brake pedal.

With the Prius braking issues hitting the front pages of newspapers, and amidst all the media frenzy, Toyota announced a new recall on February 9 to alter the software in 437,000 hybrid vehicles that were already on the road around the world. It's worth noting that at about the same time, Ford reported a problem of braking hesitation in its Ford Fusion hybrid as the car shifted from regenerative to conventional braking, but it did not issue a recall, arguing that the hesitation did not pose a safety risk and choosing to handle the issue as a "customer-satisfaction program."*

By this point, Toyota was stuck between a rock and a hard place. Any issue involving the drivability of a car could be used as an example of the company's indifference to its customers, but if it issued recalls for these issues preemptively, it would seem to justify claims that the company had a quality crisis. Toyota decided that it was better to take the hit for perceived quality lapses in the short term to begin rebuilding customers' trust that Toyota would do the right thing. As Steve St. Angelo, who in the wake of the crisis was named chief quality officer for North America, explained: "I'm taking every rock and every stone, and if it looks strange, I'm doing a deep investigation. And if I think it might possibly have any kind of impact on the customer's safety, I will ask for a recall. If we're going to fail, we're going to fail on the side of overprotecting our customer."

---

* "Ford to Fix Brake Problems on Two Hybrid Models," Associated Press, February 4, 2010; http://www.msnbc.msn.com/id/35242362/ns/business-autos.

That new philosophy began to take hold immediately. Shortly after the Prius brake recall, Toyota issued a separate recall for 8,000 Tacoma four-wheel-drive trucks over the possibility of a failure in the vehicle's front driveshaft. While most of the affected vehicles hadn't yet been sold at the time of the recall, it was the third Toyota recall announced in just three weeks.

Toyota and Toyoda Are Called before Congress

Just when it seemed that things could not get any worse, they did. With confidence in Toyota at an all-time low, allegations that the company's legendary quality had collapsed, and questions coming from every side about whether the company was endangering its customers, some political theater was inevitable. Several congressional committees scheduled hearings to grill Toyota executives about the recalls, safety issues, disclosure, and unintended acceleration. This is a fairly well-rehearsed dance on Capitol Hill when a large company receives the kind of negative attention that Toyota was getting. Chief executives are called to Washington to be publicly chastised by members of Congress so that politicians can be seen to be "doing something." Typically these chief executives deny wrongdoing (see Lloyd Blankfein of Goldman Sachs), attempt to shift blame elsewhere (see Tony Hayward of BP), or claim to have been out of the loop and unaware of what was happening (see Kenneth Lay of Enron).

The public and a number of members of Congress expected Toyota to follow this dance. But the invitations to testify went to Toyota's U.S. headquarters and TMA President Yoshi Inaba.

Rather than seizing the opportunity of a public platform for TMC President Akio Toyoda to begin rebuilding trust with customers, the company was initially content for Inaba to appear before the committee. Given the expectations, many in the press interpreted this as indifference on the part of the firm's most senior executive. Congressman Darrell Issa suggested that he would push for a subpoena of Akio Toyoda if he did not appear at the hearings.

This was yet another example of the disconnect between the U.S. political environment and Japan. The TMC public affairs group still perceived the crisis as a U.S. issue that could be effectively handled by U.S. executives. Once the Japanese public affairs group understood that members of the congressional committee expected Akio Toyoda to attend the hearings personally, and a formal invitation was sent, they accepted. It seemed to be this direct brush with the overheated politics of the situation in the United States that finally drove home to Toyota executives in Japan the realization of how deep the crisis really was.

There were several hearings before different committees and subcommittees of the U.S. Congress. The hearing on February 23 before a subcommittee of the House Energy and Commerce Committee began with testimony from Rhonda Smith, who described how in October 2006, her Lexus had accelerated to top speed and would not respond to any of her attempts to slow the vehicle: pressing firmly on the brake, shifting the car into neutral and then reverse, and engaging the emergency brake. Nothing helped, according to Smith, until the car "decided" to slow down on its own, and the brakes were suddenly functional again and able to stop the car.

David Gilbert, professor of automotive technology at Southern Illinois University in Carbondale, followed Smith and described experiments he had run that allowed him to make Toyota vehicles suddenly accelerate without the accelerator being depressed and without triggering a fail-safe mode or setting a fault code. He suggested that electromagnetic radiation in a real-world situation could similarly cause a Toyota to accelerate in a way that the fail-safe system would miss. Further, he claimed that this was a problem that was unique to Toyota, a devastating accusation if it were true.* We'll take a look at Gilbert's testing and what it actually revealed in Chapter 4.

Finally, Sean Kane summarized a report that his firm had written about Toyota incidents based on the NHTSA complaint database, which, as we have noted, is not a reliable source of information. The report itself noted more than 2,000 alleged incidents of SUA in Toyota vehicles, resulting in 815 crashes, 341 injuries, and 19 deaths since 1999.

Through all this testimony, the questions asked by congressional delegates seemed to share the underlying assumption that these were credible witnesses providing factual information. For instance, only one member of the committee asked basic technical questions about Smith's testimony, such as the lack of physical evidence of some of her claims. Edward Niedermeyer, editor-in-chief of *The Truth about Cars*, aptly explained the weakness of the hearings:†

---

* David W. Gilbert, Ph.D., professor of automotive technology, Southern Illinois University, Carbondale, from Prepared Testimony for the Committee on Energy and Commerce, Sub-Committee on Oversight Investigations, Toyota Sudden Unintended Acceleration, February 23, 2010; energycommerce.house .gov/Press_111/20100223/Gilbert.Testimony.pdf.

† Edward Niedermeyer, "The Toyota Testimony Day One," *The Truth about Cars*, February 24, 2010; http://www.thetruthaboutcars.com/2010/02/the-toyota -testimony-day-one-a-comedy-in-three-parts-act-one-the-expert-evidence/.

> Not only are most [congressmen and women] not trained
> to understand the complexities of automotive systems . . .
> the possibility that even a small percentage of the unin-
> tended acceleration cases might have been caused by (or
> at least were not averted because of) human error was, at
> best, only obliquely hinted at for the simple reason that
> congressional hearings always require a satisfyingly sin-
> ister scapegoat.

Just a few questions were necessary to cast doubt on the testimony of these witnesses. Representative Steve Buyer of Indiana
asked Sean Kane whether his company was funded by lawyers,
and he acknowledged that five law firms, all of which were suing
Toyota on behalf of clients, had "sponsored" his firm's report.*
Buyer then questioned Professor David Gilbert, who admitted that Kane had paid him $1,800 in fees, provided $4,000 for
equipment, and promised him that he would get $150 per hour
for any future consulting.

A little research on Rhonda Smith before the hearing might
have called the legitimacy of her testimony into question as well.
The incident happened when she was driving a relatively new ES
350 (one of the vehicles subject to the 2007 recall of all-weather
floor mats) on October 12, 2006. When she took the car to the
dealer after her harrowing experience, technicians examined it
and could find nothing wrong, but did notice that the all-weather
floor mat was not fastened down and was on top of the existing
carpet mat. A NHTSA representative also investigated the vehicle and could find nothing wrong with the car, suggesting in
his 2007 report that the likely cause was floor mat entrapment.
Smith had traded in her vehicle after the incident (for another

---

* Details of the hearings can be found via the U.S. Congressional Record.

Toyota, a Tundra). After the hearing, the NHTSA followed up with the family that had purchased Smith's Lexus. The owners reported no problems with the vehicle. Still, the NHTSA bought the car for further testing and turned it over to NASA engineers as part of the thorough investigation of Toyota electronics. NASA engineers determined that there were no electronic issues with the Smith vehicle, and the NHTSA stands by its original diagnosis of floor mat entrapment.

When Akio Toyoda's turn to testify before the House Oversight and Government Reform Committee came, on February 24, he faced a gauntlet of hostile questioning. His testimony included apologies to anyone who had been hurt in a crash involving a Toyota and a pledge to better listen to customers and further improve the quality of Toyota vehicles:

> As you well know, I am the grandson of the founder, and all the Toyota vehicles bear my name. For me, when the cars are damaged, it is as though I am as well. I, more than anyone, wish for Toyota's cars to be safe, and for our customers to feel safe when they use our vehicles. . . . I intend to further improve on the quality of Toyota vehicles and fulfill our principle of putting the customer first. You have my personal commitment that Toyota will work vigorously and unceasingly to restore the trust of our customers.

Akio Toyoda was in a no-win situation. He knew full well how extensively Toyota vehicles are tested and that no evidence of an electronics failure had ever been found in the real world. But anything that he said in defense of the company's engineering would be taken as excuses; those who assumed that Toyota had major problems that it was trying to hide were hardly likely to believe any statements made by the company's president. He also knew that the company was facing a multitude of lawsuits and that anything he said could be used against the company later.

In his testimony, he did not present the kind of counterevidence to the claims against Toyota that we laid out in this chapter. He did not provide any detail on how Toyota rigorously tests for EMI and designs against it. Nor did he point out some obvious inconsistencies in the testimony of Rhonda Smith or the fact that Kane and Gilbert were both on the payroll of lawyers who were suing Toyota.

While his strategy of apologizing, not blaming others, and taking responsibility has worked in the long term, it didn't do much to change the hostile headlines at the time. Many people in the media and in Congress continued to believe that Toyota had major quality problems, that it was hiding material information, and that it was not taking electronic defects seriously. For instance, after the hearings, Representative Bruce Braley said:

> If you are going to deal with the problem you have to first admit you have a problem. Toyota's focus throughout this recall has been on the mechanical solution involving floor mats and sticky accelerator pedals, but the testimony we heard from the Smith family from Tennessee and from a host of other people, who had problems with sudden unintended acceleration in their Toyota vehicles led many people . . . to question whether Toyota was devoting the necessary time and resources to analyzing and ruling out a potential electronic problem.

An analysis of Toyota-related stories in the *Los Angeles Times*, *New York Times*, and *Detroit News*, conducted by a colleague, found 205 total stories for the month of February alone, of which 196 were negative.* A set of myths about Toyota quality and safety lapses (which we summarize in Table 3.1 along with the underlying facts) had taken hold. Testimony from executives was clearly not enough to turn the tide.

TABLE 3.1 ENGINEERING ERRORS LEADING TO RECALLS: MYTHS AND REALITY

RECALL ISSUE	MYTH	REALITY	CAUSE
1. Pedal entrapment by unsecured or incompatible floor mat	Carpet design causes pedal entrapment, leading to accidents and deaths.	No defect exists with properly installed floor mat. Floor mats that are unsecured, stacked, or incompatible have the potential to entrap the accelerator pedal. Also true for other auto makers.	Improper use of floor mats.
2. Sticking accelerator pedal	Pedal frequently gets stuck, leading to uncontrollable acceleration and causing many accidents.	In rare cases, pedal can get sticky and return slowly to idle or temporarily stick partially depressed. There were no cases of wide-open throttle or uncontrollable acceleration. In all cases, brakes will stop car in normal stopping distance.	As a result of heat, humidity, or condensation, synthetic material in pedal can become sticky. Braking performance is not affected. *(continues next page)*

---

* We thank James Franz for this research. Franz qualified as negative only stories that did not include any positive perspectives on Toyota or qualify negative judgments, and that used disparaging language like "Toyota's reckless irresponsibility."

RECALL ISSUE	MYTH	REALITY	CAUSE
3. Electronic throttle control system failure	Electromagnetic interference or software glitches cause runaway cars that will not stop in a way peculiar to Toyota's design. Has led to accidents and even deaths.	This charge has been made against all car companies, and there has never been evidence of a single case. Millions of hours of tests by Toyota in chambers that generate EMI and in real-world tests in high-EMI areas have never revealed a single instance.	No confirmed problem
4. 2010 Prius ABS problem	On slippery roads, brakes can stop working, severely affecting braking performance.	At speeds below 35 mph on slippery or bumpy surfaces, a switch from regenerative to ABS braking system causes the brake pedal to momentarily feel soft. There is no impact on braking performance.	The software governing the braking system does not provide proper feel in the brake pedal.

How that tide turned, and how Toyota managed to turn the recall crisis into an opportunity to improve the company, is the topic of the next chapter.

SUMMARY TIMELINE, AUGUST 2009
THROUGH FEBRUARY 2010

AUGUST 28, 2009: Saylor accident in San Diego.

SEPTEMBER 29, 2009: Recall and safety advisory on floor mats in 4.2 million Toyota and Lexus vehicles announced. The company advises owners to immediately remove their floor mats and place them in the trunk.

OCTOBER 2, 2009: Toyota president Akio Toyoda publicly apologizes to the Saylor family and to every customer affected by the floor mat recall.

OCTOBER 18, 2009: The *Los Angeles Times* publishes the first of more than 100 negative stories concerning claims of unintended acceleration and safety issues in Toyota vehicles.

OCTOBER 30, 2009: Toyota begins sending letters to owners notifying them of an unspecified upcoming recall related to unintended acceleration and floor mats. In the letters, Toyota says that "defect does not exist in vehicles in which the driver side floor mat is compatible with the vehicle and properly secured."

NOVEMBER 2, 2009: The NHTSA takes the highly unusual step of publicly rebuking Toyota, calling the company's public statements "inaccurate" and "misleading," and noting that the floor mat recall was an "interim" measure and that it "does not correct the underlying defect." Toyota issues a public apology.

NOVEMBER 25, 2009: Toyota announces the specific details of the recall to shorten accelerator pedals or increase the distance between the floor and the pedal in millions of vehicles.

(continues next page)

DECEMBER 28, 2009: A New Jersey man drives his Avalon displaying symptoms of a sticky accelerator pedal to a dealer, where the car remains at an elevated idle even when in park.

JANUARY 19, 2010: At a meeting in Washington, D.C., including TMA President Yoshi Inaba and U.S. sales chief Jim Lentz, Toyota and NHTSA discuss "sticky" pedals. Toyota commits to initiate a recall for the pedals.

JANUARY 21, 2010: "Sticky" pedal recall announced, affecting 2.3 million vehicles.

JANUARY 26, 2010: Sales of all models affected by the January 21 pedal recall are halted, and assembly lines for those models at five North American plants are shut down for one week beginning February 1.

JANUARY 27, 2010: The fall 2009 floor mat and pedal-size adjustment recall is expanded to cover an additional 1.1 million vehicles. The recall now includes the Toyota Venza and more model years of the Toyota Highlander, as well as the Pontiac Vibe.

JANUARY 29, 2010: Toyota announces a recall of millions of vehicles with CTS pedals in Europe.

FEBRUARY 1, 2010: Toyota says that it has come up with a plan to fix the accelerator pedals and that parts are being shipped to dealers.

FEBRUARY 2, 2010: U.S. Transportation Secretary Ray LaHood sharply criticizes Toyota's response to the accelerator pedal concerns, telling the Associated Press that Toyota may be "a little safety deaf" and that "while Toyota is taking responsible action now, it unfortunately took an enormous effort to get to this point."

FEBRUARY 3, 2010: LaHood warns Americans not to drive recalled cars, but later says that this was a misstatement.

The NHTSA says that it has received more than 100 complaints about brake problems from Prius owners.

FEBRUARY 9, 2010: Recall of 437,000 Prius and other hybrid vehicles worldwide to resolve complaints about braking. The announcement raises the number of vehicles recalled by Toyota to more than 8.5 million.

FEBRUARY 12, 2010: Toyota recalls about 8,000 Tacoma pickup trucks from the 2010 model year to fix a problem with the front propeller shaft that could cause the vehicle to lose control.

FEBRUARY 22, 2010: On the eve of congressional hearings, ABC News broadcasts a report that purports to show evidence of the possibility of electronic defects in Toyotas based on Professor Gilbert's device.

FEBRUARY 23 AND 24, 2010: Hearings of various committees of the U.S. House of Representatives, including Akio Toyoda. Toyoda publicly apologizes and pledges renewed commitment to quality and safety from Toyota.

FOUR

Response and the Road to Recovery

We view errors as opportunities for learning. Rather than blaming individuals, the organization takes corrective actions and distributes knowledge about each experience broadly.

— THE TOYOTA WAY 2001

Toyota is never satisfied with restoring the status quo ante or getting back to the steady state that existed before a problem arose. Instead, the goal is always to solve the problem in a way that leaves the company better off for the future than when the problem started. Toyota's strategy during the recession (see Chapter 2), when the company spent a great deal of money in order to build a platform for future profitability rather than just cutting back to match revenues, is a good example of that drive. This striving to make the company better is improvement *kaizen*.

However, many problems don't allow the company to give immediate attention, or even attention in the short term, to improvement *kaizen*. They are crises that require immediate action to put out the fire, stop the bleeding, and contain the problems. That was certainly the case with the recall crisis. For the first few months of 2010, the company was entirely focused on reacting to the crisis before beginning the process of improvement *kaizen*, which would involve identifying and resolving the root causes of the crisis, not just dealing with the symptoms.

Part of the reason that the company remained in reactive mode for so long, of course, is that many parts of the organization, including the most senior leadership in Japan, simply didn't appreciate the depth of the crisis that Toyota was encountering in the United States. In our interview, Akio Toyoda identified the gap in understanding of local conditions and urgency between regions and headquarters as a major contributor to the evolution of the crisis:

> There was a gap between the time that our U.S. colleagues realized that this was an urgent situation and the time that we realized here in Japan that there was an urgent situation going on in the U.S. It took three months for us to recognize that this had turned into a crisis. In Japan, unfortunately, until the middle of January we did not think that this was really a crisis.

Meanwhile, the various parts of Toyota in North America were operating in a frantic reactive mode. Perhaps a more apt description would be shock. For decades, Toyota had worked hard to create a reputation as the highest-quality and highest-value automobile producer in the world—since Global Vision 2010 was announced, the goal of being the most admired auto manufacturer had been explicit. By 2008, the company arguably had achieved that goal. Toyota was ranked fifth on *Fortune*'s list of America's most admired companies, the highest of any auto-maker. Now headlines accusing the company of abandoning its core principles and putting customers in danger were appearing daily. Simply responding to customers, dealers, suppliers, and the media with their urgent questions about Toyota and what was happening was all-consuming. As Jim Wiseman, group VP for corporate communications at Toyota Motor of America (TMA), put it: "When you're getting three or four hundred [media] inquiries a day, you're just doing your best to keep up with them. I don't think any of us were really prepared in the early stages for how big the onslaught could be."

Essentially, Toyota had been growing so rapidly in the United States, moving from a small bit player to the market share leader, that it had been lulled to sleep, and it did not change organizationally as fast as its visibility changed. Bob Carter, group vice president and general manager of Toyota Motor Sales USA (TMS), described what a culture shock it was. "Three years ago, when Toyota became the number one brand in the world, and then last year, [when] Toyota became the number one brand in the U.S., I think that [everyone] started expecting more from us. And perhaps as a company we didn't take ownership of that."

Phase 1: React

The most important reactions by Toyota were not public relations statements but actions addressing the concerns of customers. The combination of wild speculation about vehicle electronics and the reality of the sticky pedals meant that many customers were worried that their vehicles could, at any moment, zoom out of control. Resolving those concerns with actions, not with words, had to be the top priority. The two key contact points with customers were at the dealerships and through calls to Toyota Motor Sales's customer service center.

Dealers Step Up

One key aspect of the sticky pedal recall that is often overlooked is the Herculean efforts of Toyota dealers to bring in customer vehicles and get them repaired as soon as the reinforcement bars became available. Toyota's North American dealers played a huge role in managing the complex logistics and helping customers feel that the company still cared about them. As the front line for most customers, the dealers were acutely aware of just how frightened many customers were. It was not uncommon for customers to refuse to drive their vehicles (LaHood's comments certainly didn't help in this regard) to the dealers for the fix to be installed—illustrating how far out of proportion the whole story had gotten. In these cases, many dealers sent tow trucks out to pick up the vehicles, a service that Toyota eventually offered to all customers who wanted it. One dealer in Virginia was said to have sent a flatbed truck to Florida to pick up a customer's Camry. Several dealers told us that, on a limited basis, they bought back cars from customers who were simply too frightened to continue driving them, even with the pedals repaired—one recalled buying back a car from an elderly couple where the woman was getting physically ill over the stress of worrying that her car would take off on its own. Tellingly, many of those customers bought a different Toyota model. While these customers were concerned, they weren't giving up on Toyota entirely. Almost all dealers extended their service hours, with many of them staying open 24 hours a day during the first week of the recall. Bob Carter praised the reaction of the dealers: "We've got 1,223 dealers. If I could have hugged every one of them, I would have. They did an amazing job overall and thought first about our customers."

One measure of the effectiveness of dealers was the percentage of vehicles repaired. While the media attention certainly played a role, dealers' outreach and logistics efforts deserve much credit. Within six months of the sticky pedal recall, 85 percent of the recalled vehicles had been repaired—an extremely high rate by industry standards.*

Toyota's strategy for developing a dealer network over decades had laid the groundwork for this ability to respond. Unlike the Detroit Three, Toyota deliberately keeps strict limits on the number of dealers it has, preferring large dealers who have the financial resources to invest and survive the ups and downs of the economy. As Carter explained the strategy: "We rejected the notion that if there's a post office in the town, there should be a dealership there. We want our dealers to be financially strong. We are in a cyclical business, and while you may lose a little business at the top, it gets you through times like this."

Avoiding saturation means that the average Toyota dealer sells many more cars, and is more profitable, than dealers selling other brands. For example, in 2009, Toyota (with the largest share of retail sales) had 1,400 dealers, less than half the number

---

* For instance, Ford has recalled over 17.5 million vehicles over eight separate recalls for a cruise control that could catch fire, the biggest recall ever. That recall started in 1999 and continued with 4.5 million additional vehicles recalled in the fall of 2009. NHTSA reported in October 2010 that only 40 percent of the vehicles recalled had ever been repaired. David Schepp, "Feds Warn: Millions of Ford Recalls Still Aren't Fixed," *Daily Finance*, October 22, 2010; http://www.dailyfinance.com/story/ford/feds-warn-about-recalled-fords-not -fixed/19685055/.

of Chrysler and Ford, while GM had more than 6,000. Toyota dealers averaged 1,600 vehicles sold per year, compared to an average of 500 for Ford.* Higher volumes and higher profitability mean that dealers can more easily invest in customer relationships rather than trying to keep costs to a bare minimum. The profitable dealer strategy, which the Detroit Three attempted to copy during the recession by shutting down small dealers across the country, meant that each Toyota dealer could weather the storm of the recall crisis and maintain a positive relationship with customers. TMS also took steps to limit the financial impact on dealers.

Steve Gates, an 18-year Toyota dealer, recalls that at a dealers' meeting in the heat of the crisis, "Jim Lentz [president of TMS] and Bob Carter told us that they would do whatever they could to keep us going and give us the ability to satisfy every customer coming through the door." In terms of direct financial support, TMS put together a fund to help defray dealers' costs. Rather than prescribe specific ways of spending the money, Toyota provided cash and trusted the dealers to spend it in ways that made the most difference to customers. Carter says, "I took $30 million and I cut it up 1,223 different ways [the total number of Toyota dealers], sent a check out to the dealers, and said, 'You know what your customers want.' I'm not going to make the decision whether a customer wants a $50 Starbucks card." Toyota also paid the interest expense on the cars the dealers had in inventory during the sales stoppage. Gates also says that Toyota paid more than a reasonable reimbursement price for the recall repairs, which made a big difference, since repairs are the main profit generators for many dealerships. While it's just one data point, Gates notes that each

---

* Dan Reed and Chris Woodward, "Detroit Wants to Thin the Herd of Dealers," *USA Today*, February 10, 2009.

of his Toyota dealerships made a profit every month in 2010, even during the worst of the crisis, as a result of these steps by Toyota.

Stepping Up at Toyota's Call Center

Dealers weren't the only ones who were facing a flood of customer calls and concerns. At the TMS call center in Torrance, California—where the calls to Toyota's customer service 800 number are received—daily call volume went overnight from 3,000 calls per day to 96,000 calls per day after the sticky pedal recall was announced, and they stayed at that level for a week. The following week, there were still 50,000 calls per day coming in. As Nancy Fein, vice president of customer relations, describes, calling it a difficult situation to manage through is an understatement:

> It was a very tough time with our customers, because our customers had periods where they didn't trust us, or they felt like we were lying to them, or they felt that we were misrepresenting ourselves. Being in customer relations, that means that we had a really difficult role of not just taking care of an individual customer problem with the vehicle, but needing to rebuild our customer's trust. We needed to fix our customers' problems, and we needed to help them have belief, and have confidence in Toyota, the way we have confidence in Toyota.

The TMS call center was perhaps the first place where the Toyota Way began having a major impact on turning the tide. How does a call center manage a 30-fold increase in call volume in 24 hours? The first step that Fein took was to recall everyone in the TMS offices in California who had ever worked in the call center. The call center is one of the places where many employees have their first job at TMS. All of these people were immediately called back to the call center to take calls from customers, no matter where they were at the time or how high they'd risen in the organization. Even some TMS executives took turns on the phones responding to customer calls. Over the years, Fein had also built long-term relationships with three call center staffing agencies that had trained personnel on hand. By the end of the first week, all three of the agencies were providing supplementary staff to the call center. These supplementary staff had already had training as customer service representatives, but they still underwent two to three days of training to prepare them to handle calls according to Toyota's standards.

Fortunately, Toyota had invested in a new call center computer system during the recession, less than 12 months before the crisis, to improve the quality of customer interactions by making more information more easily available to customer service representatives (CSRs). That system proved crucial to enabling the call center to handle 10 to 30 times higher call volume with only three times as many staff members on the phone, all without scripts. Fein explained:

> We never script our call center people. They handle each
> call on a case-by-case basis, and they have to develop a
> relationship with their customer. Through the informa-
> tion system, we provide them with Q&As for all kinds
> of issues. We provide details on whatever the recalls are.
> We provide press release information. We provide all of
> the data that they might need in real time.

Each CSR has two large computer screens full of information about the customers, the history of their vehicles, all recalls for that vehicle, technical information about the recalls, and more. The system allows the CSRs to navigate quickly through a great deal of information while engaged in discussions with customers. The information system was also connected directly to dealers' service centers. That allowed CSRs to make confirmed appointments for customers with a specific dealer immediately over the phone, and if necessary arrange for special services like transportation, rental cars, or loaner vehicles on the spot, a feature that made a huge difference in handling calls from sometimes panicked customers.

The selection and training of CSRs also made a huge difference. Unlike many companies, Toyota had deliberately decided not to outsource the customer call center to low-wage countries. The employees in the call center at TMS who are using the system have been specifically screened for skills in building relationships with customers over the phone. While this is an entry-level job, it is not an easy job to be hired for. Those who have the basic skill set go through a four-week training course, followed by 6 to 18 months of close supervision before "graduating" as a full-fledged CSR.

While their training was not as stringent, the outside agencies that the TMS call center had been working with for some time had also received a great deal of training on the Toyota approach to handling customer calls. So when they were brought in to help with the increased call volume, they needed only some refresher training. Still, the CSRs from the outside agencies were primarily dealing with information requests, such as a customer calling in with his VIN to confirm whether his vehicle was or was not part of the recall, and had Toyota supervisors on site to provide coaching. If a customer had more serious questions or believed that he had experienced sudden acceleration or a sticky pedal, the outside agencies were able to transfer a call to the TMS call center immediately, so that the more experienced Toyota CSRs could work with the customer.

Each of the Toyota CSRs is also empowered to make decisions on the spot to help resolve customer issues. In addition to being directly connected to dealer service centers, a CSR could also immediately approve such expenses as having a car towed to the dealer, reimbursing a customer for renting a car or arranging a loaner vehicle from a dealer, or extending a warranty to cover other issues that a customer might be having. Once a customer talks to a CSR, an attempt is made to connect that customer to the same CSR on any follow-up phone calls. For every five CSRs, there is a supervisor who monitors selected calls, coaches the CSRs, and can authorize more expensive solutions.

Another somewhat unique feature of the TMS call center was the use of quality circles, even during the height of the crisis. Every call center supervisor led a quality circle of 8 to 10 CSRs, meeting once a week to talk about problems, solutions, and best practices. The quality circles were even extended to the call center personnel agencies. These quality circles were led by senior CSRs as a way of giving them experience in leading quality circles and of continuing to ramp up the skills and training of the outside personnel.

The successful rapid reactions by dealers and the TMS call center were possible only because of the Toyota Way culture. Toyota's dealer network had been trained for years in the philosophy of putting customers first, and that's exactly what the dealers did. The TMS call center had, in many senses, implemented the Toyota Production System (TPS) in a nonmanufacturing environment, which allowed it to scale quickly to meet demand while maintaining quality. The investments that the company had made in training the CSRs and giving them the authority to resolve customer issues and concerns paid off time after time. The efforts of dealers and TMS call center personnel served to remind many customers of why they had trusted Toyota in the first place.

Of course, all of these responses to customers cost money—money that Toyota could afford even as the world was still emerging from the trials of the recession because of its policies of thinking long term and keeping large cash reserves. Jim Lentz, president of TMS, described the philosophy:

> Obviously we're tracking spending. But we're doing whatever is necessary to fix any shortcomings that we had in our current processes, make sure that we have the right process, and make sure that we're taking care of customers. . . . For us to be able to rebuild our brand strength, I am not concerned about the dollars we're investing today to keep that strong. . . . It's important for us to keep the strength of our dealer operations so the dealers continue to invest in their operations, as we grow back into a stronger brand and into a stronger marketplace.

Phase II: Contain

At this point, with a growing awareness of the seriousness of the crisis, Toyota as a whole began to move not just to react, but to contain the crisis. The goal of containment is not to deal with the ultimate source of the problem, but to ensure that no further damage is being done while the longer-term efforts at improvement *kaizen* get underway. Perhaps the most important part of containment of a crisis is to ensure that you aren't making decisions that will hamper future improvement *kaizen* efforts.

The reactions of the dealers and the TMS call center in handling the recalls were essentially built in by Toyota's efforts over the years in selecting and training dealers and CSRs, which reflected a more general philosophy across the company. This philosophy might best be summed up in three statements: (1) accept responsibility, (2) don't blame customers, suppliers, dealers, or anyone else, and, above all else, (3) put customers first.

Don't Point Fingers, Respond to Customer Concerns

Mike Michels, vice president of external communications for TMS, put it this way: "It's very easy in the automotive industry to say [a driver is] not using the product as intended. We bent over backwards not to blame the driver. Throughout the early stage of this, there were lots and lots of meetings [asking,] 'How are we going to make this painless, and in fact maybe even a positive experience for our customer?' That got everybody on the same page."

Akio Toyoda described his personal philosophy of communicating during the crisis this way: "I wanted to make people understand that Toyota is not perfect, [we] admit that sometimes we make mistakes, we have defects. But once we know there are defects or problems, we stop and everybody joins forces and we try to fix the problem. And . . . I decided I would never point fingers at somebody else. . . . We were committed to safety and quality and would take responsibility for fixing any problems."

Toyoda's communications during this time were peppered with public apologies to customers. In an op-ed published in the *Washington Post*, Toyoda wrote, "We have not lived up to the high standards you have come to expect from us. I am deeply disappointed by that and apologize. As the president of Toyota, I take personal responsibility. That is why I am personally leading the effort to restore trust in our word and in our products."* Similar statements were made by other Toyota executives in press conferences and in their congressional testimony. There wasn't an explicit policy announced or memo distributed that laid out this "don't blame others" approach. Jim Wiseman explained that it was simply an outgrowth of the existing Toyota culture:

> In every aspect of our operations, from suppliers to our production lines to dealers, we've always tried to live by a "Customer First" mandate. I remember hearing that phrase—"Customer First"—when I first joined the company 21 years ago. So once you live by that belief, it's really impossible to ever put the blame on the customer. So each part of our organization arrived at that place— not blaming the customer—in a natural sort of way.

Recognizing that the way the company had handled quality and safety issues and concerns had abetted the crisis, Toyota also quickly created a new position, regional chief quality officer. An executive from each region (North America, Europe, Asia and Oceania, the Middle East, Africa, and Latin America) was appointed to take on this role. When the role was created, it wasn't fully defined, but the first priority of the chief quality officers was taking ownership of any quality or safety issue and making sure that it was being addressed quickly and getting the needed

---

* Akio Toyoda, "Toyota's Plan to Repair Its Public Image," *Washington Post*, February 9, 2010, p. A17.

attention from all parts of the company. The new CQOs also had the full authority of the office of the president of the company to do what was needed.

Another very visible sign of the containment was the increasing number and pace of recalls beginning in February 2010. Accepting responsibility and putting customers first meant shifting the approach to recalls from "when in doubt, study the issue further," to "when in doubt, issue a recall immediately."

One of the most publicized examples of this new approach and the role of the chief quality officer was the decision to immediately stop sales of the newly introduced 2010 Lexus GX 460 on April 13, the same day that *Consumer Reports* announced that the vehicle had failed one of the magazine's stability control tests and was therefore to be placed on the dreaded "Do Not Buy" list—something that had never happened to a Toyota or Lexus vehicle before, or to any other vehicle for years. According to *Consumer Reports*'s senior director David Champion, the test in question simulates a driver on a freeway entering a sharply curved exit ramp at 60 mph, not taking his foot off the accelerator until the last second, and not applying the brakes. The test is designed to see if the electronic stability control (ESC) can compensate for the lack of braking and make the proper adjustments. In this scenario, the GX 460's ESC kicked in, but reacted too late, after the vehicle had begun a skid. In *Consumer Reports*'s opinion, this could lead to a dangerous situation—it's all too common these days for distracted drivers to enter curves at high speeds. While the stability control prevented the vehicle from rolling over, it might not have prevented the vehicle from hitting a curb or sliding off the side of the road, causing a serious accident.

The test itself was unique to *Consumer Reports*; other vehicle testing organizations don't have a similar test. Toyota didn't test for this specific scenario either (although all other Toyota and Lexus SUV models, including the Toyota 4Runner, which is built on the same frame as the GX, passed the test). In the past, the *Consumer Reports* test results would probably have led to weeks, if not months, of internal debate and testing at Toyota. That was no longer Toyota's approach, and a decision to take action was made first, even before a detailed investigation. As Steve St. Angelo, who had just been appointed chief quality officer for North America, put it, "*Consumer Reports* didn't feel like it was safe for their readers, and I was not going to argue with them. I decided to take action as fast as possible." Toyota stopped sales and then issued a voluntary recall to update the ESC software to account for scenarios similar to those used in the *Consumer Reports* test, delivering the new software to dealers within a week. With the updated software, the vehicle passed the test and was removed from the "Do Not Buy" list.

The GX recall helped build a new sense of action and teamwork across the various parts of the company. St. Angelo explained:

> I think it was a really good example of great teamwork. It was everybody in Japan, and also North America, working together, communicating very effectively, and working very hard to make the programming changes. We called the chief engineer, got him out of bed. And he called his team in to work, and they worked, basically, around the clock to make the programming changes. And within a week, we had those changes ready to go.

The quick action accomplished its goal: reassuring the public by responding to customer concerns quickly and with urgency. Many media outlets, including the *New York Times* and the *Los Angeles Times*, wrote positive stories about the effort, and even

David Strickland, head of NHTSA, publicly praised Toyota for this quick reaction.* St. Angelo explained the new philosophy of recalls in terms of regaining customer trust: "We need to do that to make sure we've taken every rock, every stone, looked underneath, and we can look ourselves in the face and say, 'Look, we've done what our customers expect when it comes to safety.'"

In another highly visible but more global step, Toyoda and the board created a "Special Committee for Global Quality." The committee was made up of the new chief quality officers and a group of executives leading business operations, and was chaired by Akio Toyoda. In its first meeting on March 30, 2010, the committee announced a six-point plan:

1. Improve the quality inspection process.

2. Enhance customer research by establishing customer information research offices in each region to collect information faster.

3. Establish an "automotive center of quality excellence" in key regions to further develop quality professionals.

4. Engage support from outside experts by creating an external quality review panel.

5. Increase communication with regional authorities.

6. Improve regional autonomy, listen carefully to each and every customer, and improve quality based on that.

In addition to this internal committee, an external panel made up of recognized quality experts from outside Toyota was established. The charge to the external committee was to review

* Hiroko Tabuchi and Micheline Maynard, "U.S. Sees a Change of Attitude at Toyota," May 10, 2010; http://www.nytimes.com/2010/05/11/business/global/11toyota.html.

all of Toyota's quality processes and provide feedback on any gaps or areas where quality practice could be improved. A former secretary of transportation in the Clinton administration, Rodney Slater, was tapped to lead this committee.

Of course, Toyota also had to be concerned about sales of its vehicles and the financial health of its dealers. On top of the financial help that it offered dealers to help them with recalls and the week of stopped sales, Toyota launched its largest sales incentive program in history in March and April, according to Edmunds .com. The average incentive on a vehicle moved from $1,700 to $2,400, a 40 percent increase (still about 40 percent below the industry average). The main differences were zero percent financing and two years of free scheduled maintenance, covering items that are normally not covered (such as oil changes). Those incentives helped to bring people back into the dealerships. Edmunds.com's Jeremy Anwyl notes, "People bought into the story that Toyotas were on sale, and that doesn't happen very often. That brought a lot of people in—people who didn't believe there was a serious problem. Obviously if you don't think a car is safe, it doesn't matter how much money you're offered. You're not going to buy it."

Getting ahead of the Story

The cliché prescription for crisis containment is to "get out in front of the story." Certainly Toyota wasn't in front of the story as it was reacting to the crisis in late January and early February. However, several events at the end of February and the beginning of March that at first seemed to further the negative story around Toyota actually helped to turn the tide for the company. First, in late February, ABC News broadcast a story on the eve of the congressional hearings that featured Southern Illinois University Professor David Gilbert, one of the witnesses at the hearings. During the program, Gilbert demonstrated how he could create sudden acceleration in a Toyota Avalon without the vehicle's entering failsafe mode or setting a fault code. Gilbert claimed that the sudden acceleration he had created could happen in real-world conditions and that only Toyota vehicles were susceptible to his method.

Since Gilbert's claims were so sensational, a number of other media outlets as well as Toyota itself went to work to study them. Over the course of a few weeks, a number of details emerged that shed a great deal of doubt on the story. First, almost immediately after the broadcast, several blogs noted that parts of the news report had been altered for dramatic effect. John Cook of the popular blog Gawker wrote a post illustrating how a shot of the vehicle's tachometer zooming toward the red line, which supposedly happened while ABC News correspondent Brian Ross was driving, was actually shot while the vehicle was parked with its doors open. During another portion of the broadcast, Ross exclaims, "The brakes don't work, the brakes give out!" while the video shows him bringing the car to a stop. Even Gilbert never claimed that the vehicle's brakes wouldn't bring the vehicle to a stop.

More important, Gilbert's basic claims—that the vehicle should have set a fault code and that the problem was unique to Toyota—were shown not to hold water. An investigation by Toyota, Exponent [an engineering firm hired by Toyota to study any problems related to sudden unintended acceleration (SUA)], and a Stanford University professor showed that Gilbert had stripped three different wires that connect the accelerator to the engine control module and spliced other electric components into the circuit.* Perhaps the best way to explain Gilbert's engineering is

---

* "Evaluation of the Gilbert Demonstration," Exponent, available at http://a .abcnews.go.com/images/Blotter/ht_exponentgilbert_100305.pdf.

that he added a virtual second accelerator pedal to the system, one that exactly mimicked the vehicle's actual accelerator.

According to Bertel Schmitt, an industry expert who has spent his entire career in the automotive industry, who blogs at *The Truth about Cars,* and who has written extensively about sudden acceleration claims, the vehicle "had no reason to set a fault code. Gilbert fully simulated the behavior of the actual pedal." Schmitt had actually predicted what method Gilbert used just based on the brief video from the ABC broadcast; he believes that anyone who is reasonably familiar with automotive electronics would know that Gilbert's approach would work. All that was required was a bit of tinkering to get the exact voltages for the two pedal sensors right. Indeed, Exponent was able to replicate Gilbert's approach and cause sudden acceleration without a fault in vehicles by Mercedes, BMW, Honda, Subaru, and Chrysler (all of which use an electronic throttle control [ETC] design similar to Toyota's). While Gilbert's claim that his device wouldn't work in other brands of vehicles was technically true, it's almost laughable. To make it work required only matching the specific voltages that each brand used in its ETC. According to Edmunds. com CEO Jeremy Anwyl, all Gilbert's demonstration actually showed was, "[ETC] is an electronic system. If you rewire the thing, you can get it to do almost anything."

The same day that Toyota was releasing its report on Gilbert's rewiring experiment, there was live coverage of a supposed runaway Prius on a San Diego freeway. Live video shot from helicopters showed James Sikes driving his Prius at 80 to 90 mph while a police officer drove alongside him, barking instructions over a loudspeaker, eventually convincing him to use the emergency brake to slow the car and turn off the ignition. Within 24 hours, however, bloggers were able to show that the driver's story was utterly implausible. For instance, despite being advised repeatedly by a 911 operator to shift the car into neutral, he had refused to do so for the 20 minutes that the ordeal lasted. Asked later why he had ignored the advice, he claimed that he had been too scared to take his hands off the steering wheel, although he had been holding a cell phone with one of those hands. He also claimed that he had reached down to the accelerator to pull it free in case it had been trapped, which would have required him to let go of the steering wheel entirely and take his eyes off the road (not to mention having unusually long arms). A local Fox station in California recreated the event on a Prius, only to find that absolutely everything they tried (stepping on the brakes, hitting the emergency brake button, shifting into neutral, and turning the car off) worked quickly to stop the vehicle.

Within days, the actual car was tested by Toyota and the NHTSA, with the results showing that all these systems worked perfectly. The Prius, perhaps unknown to Sikes, was one of the first Toyota vehicles to install a form of "brake override," which cuts engine power if the brake is pressed more than lightly, regardless of the position of the accelerator; a version of this brake override would later become standard on all vehicles.* The investigators also examined the data in the car's electronic data recorder (EDR). It showed that Sikes had pressed the brakes lightly more than 200 times during the time when the car was supposedly running out of control, apparently to make the brake lights come on so that it appeared that he was trying to stop the car. This caused the brakes to

---

* Technically the Prius system is not as sophisticated as the brake override system that became standard in all Toyota vehicles as a result of the recall crisis. It features a self-protection function that cuts engine power if moderate brake pedal pressure is applied and the accelerator pedal is depressed more than approximately 50 percent, in effect providing a form of "brake override."

overheat and burn out. Further investigation, notably undertaken by bloggers rather than by the mainstream media, revealed that the driver had significant financial and legal troubles in his immediate past, suggesting the possibility of an ulterior motive on his part. Toyota did not make any public statements about the driver's motives, sticking with its policy of not pointing fingers, but the facts made the company's case for it.

Just a few days later, another high-profile accident was blamed on SUA by the media and investigators but was equally debunked. In the aftermath of the crash in Harrison, New York, police immediately blamed a "stuck accelerator," even though the incident occurred as the driver was pulling out of her driveway.* Within a week, analysis of the vehicle's electronic data recorder showed that the brakes had not been depressed and the throttle was wide open, indicating, according to the NHTSA, "driver error." The acting chief of the local police department, while at first disputing the NHTSA's finding, noted that he had driven a Prius and had tried pushing the accelerator and the brake simultaneously, and found, "There was no way that car wasn't going to stop."†

What these events created was something that Toyota never could have: public doubt that the claims being made about unstoppable cars were trustworthy. That gave Toyota the opportunity to begin speaking more aggressively, not just about recalls, but responding to misinformation in the public sphere. During the course of March, Toyota issued at least six statements specifically

---

* Lisa Flam, "Police: Accelerator Suspected in NY Prius Crash," March 10, 2010; http://www.aolnews.com/2010/03/10/police-accelerator-suspected-in -toyota-prius-crash-in-ny/.

† James R. Healy, "NHTSA Cites Driver Error in New York Prius Incident," March 19, 2010; http://www.usatoday.com/money/autos/2010-03-19 -toyota19_ST_N.htm.

devoted to countering misinformation that was being reported. For example, in late March, CNN reported that it had uncovered a secret internal document from 2002 that showed that Toyota knew about electronic defects that could cause sudden acceleration in its vehicles. The "secret" document was in fact a public document called a technical service bulletin (TSB) that was available on Toyota's Web site and through several other databases maintained by the NHTSA and independent auto mechanics. Furthermore, it was a bulletin related to a transmission function, not to sudden acceleration.*

The most important sources of information for changing public opinion were the news media and the NHTSA—Toyota's claims of innocence would never be sufficient to change public opinion, no matter how much data the company was able to present. Unfortunately for Toyota, the NHTSA had adopted a very cautious attitude toward disclosing the results of any investigation or its work on sudden acceleration in general, presumably because of the earlier accusations that it had coddled Toyota. Ultimately, because of the pressure on the NHTSA and questions about its capability to carry out a full-scale investigation into vehicle electronics, the agency began working with NASA and the National Academy of Sciences in separate efforts to study the evidence concerning the possibility of SUA in general and in Toyota vehicles in particular. The NHTSA decided to hold the results of

---

* When there is an issue in a vehicle that is not considered a safety hazard, but that affects customer satisfaction, it is standard in the industry to issue a technical service bulletin to all dealers. It outlines the problem and gives instructions on how they should repair it. Customers are not broadly notified of a TSB, but cases are dealt with one by one as the customers come in for service. This TSB covered an update to Camry transmission software that for some drivers caused uneven acceleration between speeds of 35 and 45 mph.

any investigations into specific incidents until the NASA study was completed. That study was originally scheduled to be completed by the end of August 2010, but wasn't completed until February 9, 2011, when the results, exonerating Toyota of electronic defects, were released.

That decision apparently didn't sit well with everyone at the NHTSA. In June, George Person, a newly retired senior staffer, provided the *Wall Street Journal* with the details of the investigations of SUA allegations in Toyota vehicles up to that point. Person provided the data on condition of anonymity, and the *Journal* did not initially report how it had obtained the report. That led to accusations that Toyota had violated confidentiality and leaked the reports. Person came forward a few days later to identify himself as the source. Person told the *Journal* that the decision not to release the report was made at the highest levels of the agency over the objections of some senior NHTSA officials. The report was based on a study of more than 50 vehicles involved in a crash in which SUA was suspected or alleged. In some cases, data were not recoverable. Of the 51 cases for which data were available, 50 turned out to be the result of pedal misapplication (in most cases not pressing the brake at all, but in some cases either pressing it in the middle of the crash cycle and releasing it or pressing it very late in the crash cycle), while 1 was a case of pedal entrapment caused by too many floor mats in the vehicle.

At the same time, more and more analysts and columnists began looking more deeply into the data and the history of SUA and challenging public perceptions. For instance, Jerry Anwyl of Edmunds.com wrote an open letter to Transportation Secretary Ray LaHood, saying: "Every car company has a level of complaint volume from consumers relating to vehicles that suffered unintended acceleration. As poor as their response has been, Toyota is actually the only company I can remember actually doing anything to address these complaints."* *Businessweek, Forbes,* and the *Wall Street Journal* all ran multiple articles debunking many of the myths that had run rampant.†

The news and analysis debunking sudden acceleration claims finally stemmed the tide of negative publicity. Based on our analysis, reporting of incidents became more cautious. For instance, most coverage of a Camry crash in November of 2010 noted that none of the allegations of SUA other than the Saylor accident had been proven. The number of negative articles written about Toyota in six major news sources went from 235 in the month of February to just 7 in August.

Another key decision in containing the damage was not to contest fines related to the series of recalls that were levied by the NHTSA. As we noted in Chapter 3, the NHTSA's frustration with the way information was shared about the sticky pedals, in particular, is understandable. Given the public uproar over the recalls and the suggestions that the NHTSA had been too soft on Toyota, the fact that the NHTSA levied the maximum fines allowable isn't surprising. However the validity of those fines can be reasonably called into question: the regulations that Toyota violated, according to the NHTSA, are vague and ultimately turn on opinions as to whether a particular issue is a "safety" defect or

---

* http://www.edmunds.com/car-news/distracted-driving-summit-letter.html.

† See, for instance, http://blogs.wsj.com/drivers-seat/2010/05/14/why -do-so-many-cars-crash-into-beauty-salons/;
http://blogs.forbes.com/michaelfumento/2010/11/16/in-black-and -white-the-toyota-hysteria-exemplified/;
http://www.businessweek.com/lifestyle/content/feb2010/bw20100225 _403524.htm.

not. Toyota understood, though, that while it might be able to win a dispute over the fines, the cost of doing so would be much greater than the fines themselves. First, fighting the fines would introduce another area of contention between Toyota and the NHTSA, rather than building a better relationship for the future. Second, regardless of the validity of its defense, contesting the fines would be more fodder for negative media stories about how the company was shirking its responsibilities for keeping customers safe. So Toyota negotiated an agreement with the NHTSA to accept the fines while not agreeing with the NHTSA's basis for levying them. That approach enabled the company to focus on what really mattered: improving the company for the future.

Set the Stage for Continuous Improvement

The most important part of Toyota's containment philosophy was its decision to apologize and take responsibility. As data emerged showing that the basis of most of the speculations about vehicle electronics and unstoppable cars was unfounded, that position helped rebuild Toyota's reputation for putting customers first. But the real import of that position is that it turned the energy of Toyota employees worldwide inward, toward continuous improvement.

A critical part of the Toyota Way is the focus on True North, or perfection, as the goal of everything the company does. Given Toyota's run of excellence, many outsiders assume that by now, Toyota should be nearly perfect in everything it does, and any fault becomes evidence that there is some major failure at the company or with the Toyota Way. In fact, even after more than 50 years of continuous improvement, the focus is always on getting better, taking one more step toward True North.

Everyone at Toyota knows that True North, by definition an ideal, is never really achievable. No matter how many times a process is improved or how many problems are solved, there will always be the opportunity for further improvement. The role of leaders throughout the company is to constantly keep people's energy focused on continuous improvement rather than to become satisfied and complacent over past achievements.

During the crisis, the more than 140,000 employees at Toyota and in Toyota dealerships in the United States felt that they were being unfairly attacked. In such situations, it's natural for people to become defensive and start directing their energy outward, attacking and defending. That instinctual reaction is poisonous to both the Toyota Way and continuous improvement efforts. Allowing such an outward direction of energy to take hold would have undermined the company's philosophy of using problems to challenge everyone to improve. For example, the just-in-time approach to parts delivery isn't just about cutting inventory costs; it's about making problems immediately apparent so that they can be addressed.

Akio Toyoda's repeated public apologies, his admissions that the company did not live up to its standards (it never has lived up to the standard of True North, and doing so would be impossible), and his commitments to looking inward and finding ways to improve quality were all devices to encourage the entire company to hold to the Toyota Way principle of continuous improvement. In this regard, the truth or falsity of any of the allegations was irrelevant. Toyota could improve its quality and its operations. Toyota needed to improve its service to customers. Toyota needed to become a more responsive and adaptable company. In fact, in the hypercompetitive environment of the automotive industry, it was—and is—critical to the company's future that it improve in all of these areas every year in the future. And, of course, the drop in trust in Toyota was real and needed to be addressed, whether it was based on truth, confusion, or fiction.

Phase III: Turning the Crisis into an Opportunity

Even at the best of times, no one would have called Toyota a powerhouse of public communications. In fact, arguably the most frequent criticism of Toyota prior to 2009 was that the company was too quiet and boring.

What Toyota does have is a powerful way of responding to problems. The first question is always the same: "What is the problem?" During the heat of the recall crisis, opinions on what was the problem at Toyota were a dime a dozen. Plaintiffs' lawyers suggested that the problem was faulty electronics and a disregard for customer safety; many columnists opined that the company had grown too fast or that it had lost its focus on quality. Table 4.1 shows some of the problems that were suggested by pundits and analysts and the symptoms that would have appeared if the alleged problems had been real.

Improvement *kaizen* and turning the crisis into an opportunity for the company to improve are dependent on correctly identifying the real problems, not just the problems presumed by outside observers. Only then can the underlying root causes of those problems be diagnosed, a necessary step before generating solutions. Akio Toyoda's efforts to ensure that everyone in the company was taking responsibility and turning his energy toward continuous improvement would be useless if that effort was directed at the wrong problems. If the problem really was a fundamental failure of the quality and safety culture at Toyota, that

TABLE 4.1 ALLEGED PROBLEMS, SYMPTOMS, AND PRESUMED ROOT CAUSES

POSSIBLE PROBLEMS	ALLEGED SYMPTOMS	PRESUMED ROOT CAUSES
A disregard for customer safety	• A fall in the safety ratings of vehicles • Increasing numbers of accidents in Toyota vehicles • Failure to seriously test for any and all causes of SUA, including electronics	• Focus on profits and growth over driver safety • A failure to teach the Toyota Way to all employees
A slipping focus on quality	• A significant increase in quality problems worldwide • Rising warranty costs • A significant increase in recalls	• Cutting engineering and design budgets too much • Fast growth, with new employees not trained in quality procedures
Unresponsiveness to customers and the public relations climate	• Poor understanding of how customers use vehicles • Inattentiveness to customer concerns about SUA and potential electronics problems • Poor public relations strategy • Executives not taking crisis seriously	• Communication breakdowns • Overly bureaucratic decision making • Failure to "go and see" with customers • Too centralized to respond quickly to regional context

would dictate one set of steps. On the other hand, if the problem was losing touch with customers and failing to build and defend trust in the company, that would require an entirely different set of steps. Let's take a look at the evidence.

A Breakdown of Quality and Safety?

A careful look at the data shows that the widely held belief that Toyota's quality suddenly took a nosedive during the late 2000s as a result of poor manufacturing and engineering is simply not true. Let's first consider recalls.

In Figure 4.1, we show the number of recalls and the number of vehicles recalled by the top six automakers (in U.S. sales) over the last five years. Note that there is a time lag, so a recall made in 2005 was probably the result of a design decision or a manufacturing error made several years earlier. The only clear patterns for Toyota are that there were an awful lot of vehicles recalled in 2009 and 2010 and that by far the largest number of individual recalls were issued in 2010, when Toyota began taking a much more aggressive stance toward recalls. Take out 2010 and there is certainly no evidence of a general trend toward a greater number of recalls between 2005 and 2009.

The number of vehicles recalled is not an indicator of the number of errors made in design or engineering; it is simply a measure of the size of the manufacturer. That's because, increasingly, design, engineering, and parts are shared by many vehicles—even vehicles made by different manufacturers. Several of Toyota's recalls in 2010 were for parts that were essentially identical in design to parts used by other manufacturers.

A much better measure of design or engineering errors is the number of separate recall events. In 2005 and 2006, Toyota had

FIGURE 4.1 NUMBER OF RECALLS
AND NUMBER OF VEHICLES RECALLED
IN THE UNITED STATES, 2005–2010

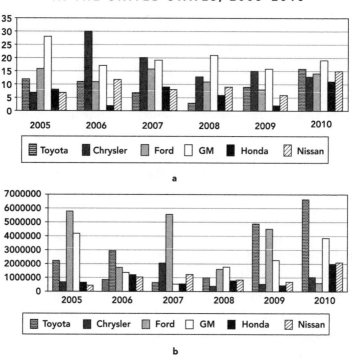

a

b

12 and 11 recalls, respectively, and in 2009 only 9. It was the number of vehicles involved that made the big splash in the headlines. Before 2009, Toyota was relatively low (but was never the lowest, nor did it claim to be) in both number of recalls and vehicles recalled compared to other automakers when we adjust for the size of the company.

For Toyota, both the number of recalls and the number of vehicles recalled rose quite dramatically between 2009 and 2010—from 9 to 17 recalls and from 4.9 million to 6.7 million vehicles.

However, there was a general trend in the industry of increasing recalls, as other automakers evidently felt pressure to recall any problem lest they get on the wrong side of the NHTSA and the media. Among the five largest automakers in the United States (other than Toyota), we see that the number of recalls went from 47 in 2009 to 80 in 2010 and that the number of vehicles recalled climbed from 8.4 million to almost 11 million. These statistics do not support the notion of a general decline in Toyota quality over the decade, leading to steadily increasing recalls; rather, 2009 and 2010 were an anomaly where sociopolitical factors were at least as important as design and engineering issues.

The reason that sticky pedals led to so many vehicles being recalled was that the same pedal design was used on many different types of vehicles, by Toyota and other automakers. Regardless of how many vehicles used the pedal, it is only one defect, one error in design. The other recall that affected more than 5 million vehicles, related to pedal entrapment from stacking floor mats or failure to fasten them down, is difficult to truly blame on Toyota. As Edmunds.com's Anwyl says, "That's not really a vehicle defect. You can argue it's a design issue . . . but there's nothing obviously wrong with the car; and it happens with other [manufacturers'] cars too." For instance, in June 2010 the NHTSA opened an investigation into floor mat entrapment problems in the 2010 Ford Fusion and Mercury Milan, in part based on an Edmunds.com tester experiencing the problem himself.* Ford's official response was that the instructions on the all-weather floor mats state that

---

* Philip Reed, "Unintended Acceleration Reported in Edmunds.com Vehicle," May 25, 2010; http://www.edmunds.com/car-safety/unintended-acceleration -reported-in-edmundscom-vehicle.html. Interestingly, as of February 2011, the investigation has not been resolved, so there does not seem to have been a sense of urgency.

owners should not place them on top of existing floor mats.* As of February 2011, there has not been a recall of Ford vehicles related to floor mats.

Many of the other recalls announced in 2010 involved issues that were not defects but customer satisfaction issues, recalls that would have been handled by a technical service bulletin in the past (e.g., the Prius braking issue), or extra precautionary measures (the recall of leaking brake master cylinders resulting from using the wrong brake fluid).†

We do not mean to imply that errors are okay. Mistakes were made, and Toyota's goal is clear—zero defects. We are saying that the conclusion by some that there were serious declines in the quality and safety of Toyota vehicles as the decade progressed is simply not borne out by the data. The number of defects and errors didn't materially increase in 2009 and 2010. Looking at broader measures of quality and reliability from J.D. Power and *Consumer Reports* in 2009 (just prior to the recall crisis and negative publicity) shows that Toyota's performance on industry rankings met or exceeded its performance in the early 2000s. While it's certainly true that Toyota's competitors had closed some of the quality gap that had existed in the 1990s, Toyota's leadership position in quality hadn't been compromised except in the news media. Consider just a few examples of independent ratings of

---

* Cammy Corrigan, "NHTSA Goes to the Mat with Ford," *The Truth about Cars*, June 2, 2010; http://www.thetruthaboutcars.com/2010/06/nhtsa-goes-to-the -mat-with-ford.

† The recall, announced in October 2010, covered brake systems that could develop leaks if the driver had used the wrong brake fluid. Even in this situation, the brake warning light would come on, and braking performance would suffer materially only if the driver ignored the warning light and did not refill the brake fluid reservoir. More details available here: http://www.toyota.com/recall/avalon-highlander.html.

Toyota vehicles for reliability immediately before the recall crisis and at the end of the decade, when the alleged declines in quality and safety occurred:

- In the 2009 J.D. Power Initial Quality Study, Toyota earned first place in 10 out of 19 categories, more than any other automaker. The Lexus LX had the fewest problems of any vehicle on the road. The assembly plant in Higashi-Fuji, Japan, received the Platinum Plant Quality Award for producing vehicles yielding the fewest defects and malfunctions, averaging just 29 problems per 100, while the industry average in 2009 was 108 problems per 100.*

- In the 2009 J.D. Power three-year vehicle dependability study, Toyota took first place in 8 of 19 categories, again more than any other automaker.

- In the *Consumer Reports* 2009 survey of reliability, Toyota brands took three of the top five slots.

- The Automotive Leasing Group, which tracks various measures of a vehicle's residual value, also tracks customers' view of the quality of a brand (which influences the resale value of a used car). Toyota was the top "mainstream"

---

* The 2010 J.D. Power Initial Quality Study, conducted early in 2010 in the worst part of the recall crisis, was not so kind to Toyota. The Toyota brand slipped to a ranking of 21. The head of J.D. Power explained that the study is based on customer surveys and that the areas in which Toyota had dropped were areas in which it had had recalls, like an unusual number of complaints about braking problems in the Prius, and in fact vehicles that were not recalled showed an increase in quality ratings (e.g., Tundra was the highest rated truck for the fifth year in a row, and Toyota still won the most segment awards of any automaker). He expected a recovery of the ratings by the next survey, as memories of the negative publicity continue to fade.

brand every quarter from 2006 until the fall of 2009. Lexus was the top luxury brand by a significant margin over BMW and Mercedes until the fall of 2009.

None of these rankings indicate a downward trend in the quality and reliability of Toyota vehicles over the decade leading up to the crisis. The small number of defects identified that drove the recall crisis didn't happen suddenly during Toyota's rapid growth. They were made over a long period of time, not just in the last few years, and in different parts of the organization. Toyota Motor Sales had designed the all-weather floor mats that were recalled in 2007 back in 2004. It's unclear that an underlying defect like the technical issue that caused the sticky pedal could have been caught by conventional testing, as finding it would have required extensive life-cycle testing under conditions of high humidity—certainly Toyota wasn't the only manufacturer to miss it and use the CTS pedals. For example, Chrysler recalled CTS pedals in its Dodge Caliber vehicles in July 2010, after reports of sticking. Ford stopped producing (while it made a change in the pedals) a Transit van sold only in China because it used a similarly designed CTS pedal.* Discrete errors in different parts of the organization in different years over the decade do not reflect a general decline in quality and safety.

Judging quality by the number of recalls or the number of vehicles recalled is also problematic because there are other factors involved. Ultimately, the decision to issue a recall is a judgment call, sometimes made by the manufacturer and sometimes by the

---

* "Accelerator Pedal Supplier in Toyota's Recall Has Many Customers," Wheels Blog, *New York Times,* January 28, 2010; http://wheels blogs.nytimes.com/2010/01/28/accelerator-pedal-supplier-in-toyotas-recall-has-many-customers/.

manufacturer and the NHTSA after extensive discussion. That's illustrated most starkly in the fact that one manufacturer may issue a recall over a flawed part, while another manufacturer using the same part does not. We've noted several instances in which Toyota, after January 2010, issued recalls when other manufacturers using similar or identical parts did not. The judgment calls by both parties are also influenced by the political and media environment. All regulatory agencies, not just the NHTSA, toughened up under the Obama administration. The media atmosphere around the Toyota recall crisis influenced other automakers—thus the more than 50 percent increase in recalls between 2009 and 2010 for all manufacturers. It would be foolish to believe that the increase was due to a sudden collapse in quality at every manufacturer simultaneously.

It's also important to keep in mind that even with the huge uptick in recalls, the total number of problems and vehicles recalled is a small percentage of the number of vehicles on the road. Further, the number of times a problem actually surfaces is typically a very small percentage of the vehicles recalled. At the time of the sticky pedal recall in the United States, there had been only 12 vehicles found in the country with the condition—none resulting in an accident—but the recall covered more than 2 million vehicles. Chrysler's sticky pedal recall was due to five complaints. Similarly, the Ford Fusion floor mat entrapment investigation, which theoretically could lead to the recall of 250,000 vehicles, is based on three complaints.*

---

* Stephen Manning, "U.S. Investigates Reports of Dangerous Ford Floor Mats," *Huffington Post,* June 1, 2010; http://www.huffingtonpost.com/2010/06/01/us-investigates-reports-o_n_596625.html.

We dwell on this point simply because understanding how Toyota turned the recall crisis into an opportunity to strengthen the company for the future and move it closer to True North requires an understanding of what the real problems underlying the crisis were and what they were not. First, none of the recalls had anything to do with errors made in Toyota factories—so responding by revamping TPS and the plants would not solve the problem. Second, they were not fundamental engineering or testing problems—meaning that there was not a specific flaw in the core technical process of engineering and validating vehicles that caused all of the defects that led to recalls. Third, the company's commitment to safety and quality did not slip—it did not suddenly become "safety deaf," as Ray LaHood asserted.

But it's not entirely inaccurate to say that the company became deaf. It became deaf to real-world customer use, to customer worries and concerns, to input from nonengineers, to the overall political and media environment it was operating in, and, in some very important cases, to internal communication. In some instances, the organization became deaf to the people at the *gemba*—a serious problem indeed for Toyota, since that is one of the pillars of the company's historic success.

A factual assessment of the symptoms that Toyota was experiencing leads to the conclusion that the problems at Toyota were related to communications, internal and external, and to and from customers and other stakeholders, partially as a consequence of a failure to achieve its goals of regional "self-reliance." The goal is not for each region to act as an island, but rather for each to have the resources and leadership to manage its own day-to-day affairs and a greater degree of influence over larger decisions that cut across regions.

Diagnosing the Root Causes

There's an old phrase in corporate governance that emphasizes the importance of clear roles and responsibilities: "When everyone is responsible, no one is accountable." In other words, diffused responsibility means that you can't hold anyone accountable for a failure because you have to hold everyone accountable. Making everyone responsible provides an opportunity for each person to pass the buck.

To avoid this tendency, "accepting responsibility" at Toyota means something quite personal. When someone at Toyota accepts responsibility, it is not as part of a vague collective responsibility; it is personal and team-level responsibility. Therefore, there wasn't only one corporate-level problem-solving taskforce. Every part of the company launched its own problem-solving process based on Toyota Business Practices (TBP) to examine what the problems were, what role that team or organization had played in causing or failing to address the problem, and what that team or organization could do to contribute to a solution to the problem that would move the company forward. Each part of the company asked itself, "What can we learn from the crisis, and what can we do better?"

These efforts were remarkably similar in their determination of root causes. One root cause identified was that the company was not listening carefully enough to its customers, their concerns and perspectives, and even lacked a sufficient level of understanding of how they used their vehicles. A second commonly identified root cause was that the company's attempts at maintaining close control and efficiency had had the unintended effect of causing too many delays in responding to stakeholders, including customers and regulatory agencies. As Jim Lentz of TMS put it:

> I think the biggest issue is that everyone was so busy chasing so many things at once that we were a little blinded to really listening to the customers. Whether we had a physical check sheet or whether we had a mental check sheet in our mind, when we went out and spoke to customers, we were listening only to have the customers answer questions on that check sheet. And as a result, I think we were missing, in many cases, what the customers were truly telling us.

To fully understand the actions that Toyota didn't take that helped the recall crisis snowball, and the steps that it has now taken to improve and create future opportunity, we first have to explain how Toyota is organized and how decisions on such issues as safety, quality, and engineering were made before the crisis.

Organizational Structure

Toyota's headquarters are in Toyota City. This isn't a cute name for the company's headquarters, but the name of an actual city where Toyota's operations steadily grew as the company became a global player. Toyota's corporate headquarters, its research and development operation, its Japanese manufacturing plants, and even its primary suppliers are all based in or near Toyota City. An exception to Toyota's tightly integrated and colocated corporate structure was the original Toyota Motor Sales. After Toyota's near bankruptcy in 1950, the Japanese government forced Toyota to reorganize into two separate companies, each headed by a nonfamily member. Toyota Motor Sales was eventually reabsorbed into Toyota Motor Corporation, but not until 1982. When Toyota entered the U.S. market, like many expanding multinational firms, its first act was to establish a sales presence: Toyota Motor Sales USA, Inc., was founded in Torrance, California, in 1957. At that time, the company was simply importing vehicles made in Japan and selling them through dealers. Since the dual structure still existed in Japan at the time, Toyota Motor Sales USA was created by Toyota Motor Sales (Japan).

As the company started growing rapidly in North America in the wake of the 1970s oil crises, it needed more than just a sales presence here. In 1977, the Toyota Technical Center, Inc. (TTC), was started in Ann Arbor, Michigan, mainly to perform tests that were unique to the U.S. market and to test supplier parts as Toyota brought on American suppliers. But in keeping with the original model of sales being separated from other operations, TTC was founded as a separate corporation, owned by Toyota Motor Corporation of Japan. Toyota's first real foray into manufacturing in North America was NUMMI, the joint venture with GM, and this was again a separate company. As Toyota built its own plants and expanded in the North American market, a manufacturing subsidiary was created, Toyota Motor Manufacturing, North America (TMMNA). To tie these various corporations together, Toyota created a holding company based in New York City called Toyota Motor of America, Inc. (TMA). TMA also has a branch office in Washington, D.C., to work with regulators and on legislative issues.

From the 1980s, Toyota had a vision to become a global company, with its center in Japan and strong regional branches that were capable of designing, building, and selling cars. Over time, TTC began to take on actual design responsibility for cars that were unique to North America, like the Sienna minivan and the Avalon. In 2006, TTC merged with TMMNA to create Toyota Motor Engineering and Manufacturing North America (TEMA), integrating product development engineering and manufacturing more closely, but leaving TMS and TMA quite separate.

Of course, none of the North American organizations are truly independent entities: they all have to coordinate with and are overseen by the Japanese parent company. For instance, historically the majority of vehicle design and engineering was done in Japan. Each region's engineering department was responsible only for specific customizations of the overall design for that particular region. The simplest example is probably Americans' penchant for cup holders, which took years to sell to the Japanese engineers, as they were not familiar with the idea of going on long trips and having drinks beside you. Similarly, the hard rubber all-weather floor mats that led to the original 2007 floor mat recall were designed in the United States in a part of Toyota Motor Sales USA that has its own engineers for locally installed accessories. Accessory design was done completely separately from the engineering of the vehicle itself.

Despite Toyota's massive growth around the world, core engineering and design, postproduction engineering (dealing with engineering changes to the vehicle after it is on the market), and quality and safety remained centralized in Japan for several reasons. First, the engineers who were most experienced in the Toyota Way, TBP, and TPS were in Japan. Second, modern automotive economics require large scale; in other words, the majority of the design and engineering can't be unique to one vehicle or to one country or region. Camry, Prius, Tacoma, Corolla, and other vehicles are sold around the world. Even vehicles for which the vast majority of sales come in the United States, such as Tundra, Sequoia, Sienna, Avalon, and Venza, often use common pieces of design and engineering from other vehicles. Of course, core technologies like engines, hybrid drive systems, and vehicle control electronics are also developed at headquarters in Japan and shared across vehicles around the world. Third, capital costs for testing equipment and the capability of building large, complex production technology—like robotic welding systems for the car body or today's automated paint systems—are high, and the technology requires a great deal of the specific expertise that is mainly located in Japan.

Thus, it makes sense for these activities to be centralized. In practice, this centralization meant that no region—not even North America, which was by far Toyota's largest—could make final decisions about recalls. Those decisions were made centrally in Japan, based on information received from the various regions.

Takeshi Uchiyamada explained that there was yet another good reason that Toyota had decided to keep the engineers dealing with recalls separate from customer-facing parts of the organization: so that recall decisions could be made by people who did not have to worry about the cost of the recall or potential damage to the brand. The process was set up to make sure that the quality department could put safety and quality ahead of business concerns and was not unduly influenced by the sales or regional units, which were concerned about revenue and profitability. But this intentional separation to create checks and balances created a different problem. In trying to protect quality and safety decision making from sales concerns, the company inadvertently choked off a lot of customer feedback to the quality department. Without that customer feedback, the quality department was left to make recall decisions based solely on the technical details. That obviously played a big role in the way Toyota thought about issues like sticky pedals, which from a strict engineering standpoint it did not regard as a safety issue.

Meanwhile, interactions with the NHTSA in the United States were handled by TMA, since regulatory bodies are country specific, and TMS was the hub for customer data, which it gathered from interactions with customers and dealers. The actual reports to the NHTSA were developed by engineers in Japan who compiled data from the United States. Ultimately, as we've noted, this gave various parts of Toyota quite different perspectives on the brewing crisis in the United States and on what response was necessary. One can imagine the multitude of pathways in this complex web of organizations through which information had to travel when there was a customer concern or a request from the NHTSA.

Before the crisis, this cumbersome organization had never been a big issue because there was rarely pressure for an immediate and definitive response on safety or quality issues. As Bob Carter explained: "Being with the company 29 years, if I had a to-do list of things that needed to change, decentralizing postproduction engineering wouldn't have been on the first five pages. It was never an issue. If I look back, I never had a problem with the decisions we made."

One of the founding principles of the Toyota Production System is to keep every process under pressure by eliminating inventory. When there isn't pressure, according to Taiichi Ohno, problems are hidden and are allowed to continue and perhaps even grow, and that's what happened here. But then the recall crisis applied tremendous pressure within a very short period of time, overstressing the system and leading to a new sense of urgency on the need to change.

Decision-Making Processes

In addition to the complex coordination challenge, in important ways, Toyota's adherence to TBP was a contributing cause of the crisis. This was not because of an inherent flaw in the problem-solving approach but because of the mismatch between the methodical, facts-only core of TBP and the rapid-fire, 24-hour news cycle fueled by rumor and speculation that has defined the American media scene since the advent of cable news and the Internet. To a public that is expecting daily, if not hourly, updates, Toyota appeared to be dragging its feet or, worse, hiding. Even when Toyota was taking action, it was doing so based on a detailed study of engineering and quality issues, ignoring the sensational claims of unstoppable cars with a mind of their own that engineers and executives in Japan were confident were false. But it was those claims that customers wanted and needed to have addressed so that they could feel safe in their vehicles.

There are several aspects of Toyota culture that lead to a slow, deliberate process. The first is *genchi genbutsu*, which we discussed in Chapter 1. A key implication is that decisions are made after a careful investigation of the facts, including seeing for yourself firsthand if possible, for example, retrieving and carefully investigating the actual pedals. Related to this is the concept of *nemawashi*, which means that whoever is leading a project should "prepare the soil" by having deep discussions with all key stakeholders. By the time a decision has been made, the facts are very clearly laid out, and all stakeholders are aware of the facts, the decision, and the rationale and are on board.

This philosophy of slow, deliberate, consensus decision making has served Toyota well. It's what took Toyota to the top with a remarkable record of consistent profitability for 50 years. In fact, many organizations have studied Toyota's approach to decision making and goal setting, hoping to emulate it. Generally it is a great set of practices, but in the midst of a fast-moving crisis that had little basis in engineering analyses or technical specifications, it became a liability. While the company was moving slowly and methodically, it appeared to the outside world as though it didn't know what to do. In the midst of the crisis, stories began popping up in the media that focused on diagnosing how Toyota had fallen so drastically from its perch atop the quality and safety ratings. For instance, *The Economist's* December 10, 2009, cover featured the headline "Toyota Slips Up," accompanied by an image of a banana on wheels.

Communication Problems

Up until February of 2010, as each new recall issue arose, substantive or speculative, Toyota, with decisions being made primarily in Japan, reacted as if these were minor and unrelated incidents. Toyota managers in the United States at TMS, TMA, and particularly the external affairs divisions were feeling the heat rising to an unbearable degree as they responded to thousands of communications a day. Yet, in Japan, there was limited pressure to be proactive to contain the crisis and the downward-spiraling perceptions of Toyota quality in the United States through much of January.

One example is the mounting media speculation about problems with Toyota electronics that began in the fall of 2009. Seeing the media take hold of unfounded allegations of electronics problems, Paul Williamsen, the manager of Lexus College, was asked by the TMS communications group to begin crafting a response that included a detailed explanation of Toyota's electronic throttle control and engine control module systems to debunk the claims that were being made. Williamsen, who had previously repaired cars for a living, oversaw technical training for Lexus, including training mechanics at dealerships. Over the Thanksgiving holiday that year, he developed a presentation on Toyota's ETC, illustrating its many fail-safe mechanisms. However, senior managers in Japan, who were insulated from the brewing storm, didn't make vetting and approving the presentation a priority. It was not until the congressional hearings that a green light was given to release a set of public communications about Toyota's vehicle electronics.

It was a trying time for senior executives and managers in North America, who were dealing with customers, the media, and the NHTSA, who had one set of assumptions about the current situation, and executives in Japan, who had an entirely different set of assumptions. It was similarly frustrating and confusing for the customers, the media, and the NHTSA. Why was Toyota so slow to respond? When pressed for immediate answers to questions, Toyota employees in the United States often had to forward those inquiries to Japan and wait either for information or for approval of their intended message. This disconnect was perhaps captured most starkly in the heated Irv Miller e-mail discussed in Chapter 3 when TMC was hesitant to issue a detailed public release. As Irv Miller further explained: "We [TMS] had been in the box for some time on some key issues and had spent time putting together a draft press release. And basically I was trying to get [Koganei, and indirectly TMC] . . . to understand that our experience plus TMS being on the ground should be the critical factor here."

The mismatch between the perceptions of the current situation held in North America and Japan could be attributed to failure to adhere to the Toyota Way principle of *genchi genbutsu*. Those on the ground who had a detailed understanding of the context and environment were in the United States, while decisions were being made by relatively uninformed engineers and managers in Japan. Toyota had been working for decades to develop regional self-reliance, and it was at the center of Global Vision 2010 in North America. Yet a decade later, the recall crisis showed how far the company still had to go. This was a question not just of the capability of regions to be self-reliant, but of headquarters trusting the regions to act in accordance with the Toyota Way.

Finally awakening to the depth of the problem started Toyota on the path to turning the crisis into opportunity. That meant moving from just reacting to the problem to delving into its source and resolving the root cause in a way that would move the company closer to True North. *The Toyota Way 2001* defines the company's True North as respect for people and continuous improvement. Therefore, the resolution of the underlying problems had to demonstrate respect for customers, the government, communities, partners, and team members, especially those outside of Japan; and the resolution had to be not just mitigation, but a positive step toward bringing the company to a new level of performance.

Weakness in Listening to the Customers

For all of the reasons discussed, Toyota was not living up to its high standards of listening to its customers—a fundamental sin in the Toyota Way. A great deal of work was needed to go back to the basics of customer focus as required by the Toyota Way. It started with improved mechanisms for listening to the customer. Shinichi Sasaki, executive vice president of global quality, explains:

> As you know, Toyota has made a lot of efforts to achieve the classical definition of quality control . . . things like dependability or the durability of the vehicles. But, if there's a [lesson] from the recent recalls, it's that the things we engineers do not think are serious could sometimes create a lot of concerns on the part of the customers. . . . We should not just be talking to the customers from a purely engineering viewpoint, but we have to care more about the customer's feelings.

Takeshi Uchiyamada agreed: "When we finally got the opportunity to do a thorough root-cause analysis and ask 'why' five times, there were two main items from the R&D standpoint. The first item was that from the time that an issue happens in the market to the time when the engineering department responds, it was taking too much time. The second item is about listening to the customer. We have our own Toyota quality and safety standards, which are sometimes more severe than other companies', and we intend to protect that standard of quality. . . . But we did not always understand the customer's view of the product as well as we should have."

Akio Toyoda puts it in a slightly different way: "One of the lessons that we have learned is that safety and peace of mind are two different things. I would say categorically Toyota's vehicles are safe, but we could have done better in terms of explaining [everything about our vehicles] so that the people can feel peace of mind."

The creation of the chief quality officer role in every region was one of the innovations by Akio Toyoda that advanced respect for regional authority, one of the most important steps in reforming the recall process so that input from the regions and from customers fed more directly into it. These executives oversee all quality-related issues before and after production, are a part of the global quality committee, and are key participants in the recall decision process. They ensure that any issues that are discovered in any region are quickly made known to other regions—remember that one of the key failings in the sticky pedal situation was not communicating the findings in Europe to North American leaders. Steve St. Angelo described one of the key conclusions from a meeting of all the managing officers on the quality committee: "As Toyota grew globally, we were still trying to run Toyota within Japan. And I think one thing we learned here is that the different regions understand the customer, understand the regulations, understand the regions much better than you would running it from Japan. We need more autonomy, more self-reliance in the different regions."

All the chief quality officers participate in regular conference calls with one another and with the central engineering group in Japan that is responsible for quality and safety. They also now have access to a global database of issues, so there are no regional information silos on any quality or safety issue. To make sure information continues to be shared widely in North America, Steve St. Angelo convened a North American Quality Task Force that holds a weekly conference call and meets face to face periodically. The task force includes all the managing officers from Toyota Motor Sales, from Toyota Motor America, from TEMA, and from Canada.

Improvements in Listening to Customers

Clearly the existing process of getting information from dealers' service technicians, calls from proactive customers, and the NHTSA complaints database was not sufficient. To start gathering these data firsthand and interacting with customers on their complaints and concerns, Steve St. Angelo's North American Quality Task Force created SMART (Swift Market Analysis Response Teams). These groups of engineers and specially trained technicians were set up around the country to go onsite, with a goal of doing so within 24 hours, to inspect a vehicle and interview any customer who reported unintended acceleration. By August 2010, more than 4,000 vehicles had been examined through the SMART process.* These direct customer contact points didn't find any electronics issues or other unknown engineering issues, but they did reveal how large the chasm was between customers' perceptions of their vehicles' behavior and the Toyota engineers' perspective. The SMART inspections quickly found a pattern of complaints, all related to aspects of vehicle operation that customers simply didn't understand and thought were indications of sudden unintended acceleration, including

- *Cold start idle-up.* An increase in engine idle speed normally occurs just after a cold start on the first drive of the day.

- *Catalytic converter protection.* On some models with manual transmissions, the engine control computer may keep the engine rpm above idle as the driver shifts

---

* Steve St. Angelo, speech at Center for Automotive Research (CAR) Management Briefing Seminars, Traverse City, Michigan, August 4, 2010.

between fifth and sixth gears at highway speeds. This momentary rpm increase is designed to enhance the life of the catalytic converter.

- *Air conditioning or power steering idle-up.* On vehicles with an engine-driven A/C compressor or hydraulic power steering, the engine idle rpm will increase as the feature is engaged. This is especially apparent at a stop or at slow speed, as the engine needs to idle up to prevent the risk of a stall.

- *Intelligent cruise control.* A number of newer-model vehicles have optional adaptive cruise control that can sense the distance of the car ahead and adjust the speed to maintain a constant following distance rather than requiring the driver to constantly disengage and reengage the cruise control. When the cruise control has slowed the vehicle and the car in front moves out of the travel lane, the cruise control automatically boosts the speed to the speed setting that was originally input. For customers who do not understand this feature, it feels as if the car is suddenly accelerating on its own.

The creation and rapid deployment of SMART was possible only because of decisions that were made during the recession, or, more properly, not made. As detailed in Chapter 2, Toyota, unlike its competitors, didn't lay off any of its regular employees during the recession, and as a result of having a full staff, it was able to reassign 140 engineers and 100 field engineers and technicians who were highly knowledgeable about Toyota vehicles and trained in Toyota problem solving to create SMART. Strict adherence to the Toyota Way in the past was rescuing Toyota's future. We saw in Chapter 2 how quickly Toyota was able to restore profitability despite a crash in demand. Of course, it could have achieved much higher profits if it had followed the layoff policies that have become de rigueur in the modern economy. Those profits, however, would have been cold comfort in the depth of the recall crisis, when the company would have had to struggle to react at all after having let go thousands of capable personnel.

The reports coming in from SMART starkly illustrated the need to reconnect customer input to all of Toyota's engineering, design, and customer service processes. These ex post facto customer interactions were helpful, but they weren't a solution to the underlying problem of not having enough direct customer input in everything the company did. The actual engineers who were designing the part, system, or function or were responsible for improving it have to have direct customer contact and see the problems firsthand.

Putting customers first was quite difficult if too many parts of the company didn't really know what customers wanted and how they felt. Toyota's rapid growth and ascent to the number one market share position probably played a role in the emergence of this serious disconnect with customers. When a company is striving to reach the top spot, it is obvious that there are customer needs and issues that are not being met—otherwise the company would already be at the top of the heap. Once a company becomes number one in the marketplace, it's all too easy to slip into a mode of thinking that customer needs are being fully met. The market position becomes all the validation that is needed, and the urgency of ferreting out customer tastes, opinions, and satisfaction fades. Jim Lentz confirmed this view, saying: "As I look at where we were in the past, what we had become . . . with our success . . . as a company, we had a little bit of an attitude. Arrogance is probably the best explanation. What we had always been [was] a very open-minded company, . . . listening to customers."

To rebuild the necessary attention to putting customers first, in June and July 2010, Akio Toyoda's special committee on quality established "Customer First" training centers in Japan, North America, Europe, Southeast Asia, and China to provide team members with additional training on how to integrate customer needs and feedback into their problem-solving and design processes more effectively. This is not a minor investment. Toyota anticipates that in addition to full-time quality professionals, who will go through a three-year training program, more than 300,000 Toyota employees globally will receive 8 to 16 hours of training in the Toyota culture, TPS, TBP, and quality procedures and practices.

The quality division in Japan has created this awareness training and the deeper three-year advanced training program for quality professionals. The professional training goes into great detail about how to inspect a vehicle and what to look for in each specific area of the vehicle. The first center and the original materials were set up in Japan, but a training center was being established in each region at the time of this writing, for example, in Ann Arbor, Michigan, for North America. By Toyota standards, it would normally take a seasoned quality professional two years of training to be a certified trainer, but the development team worked to *kaizen* the process down to one year. That's still an exceptionally long training process relative to other companies' quality programs, which typically involve two to four weeks of training. It illustrates the high standards and unusual commitment to training and developing people in Toyota.

To accelerate the awareness process, Akio Toyoda led an effort to create a small paperback guide entitled "Our Attitude." It is based on 10 attitudes drawn from the Toyota Way that are expected of every Toyota employee. Each page gives an attitude, with a definition, things to keep in mind, a section on warnings of things that can lead you astray (called "Is this happening to you?"), and a cartoon illustrating the concept. These 10 attitudes are posted broadly in Japan, and they show up as the first screen on every employee's computer when she starts work. Deployment outside Japan was in the planning stages at the end of 2010, although the booklet was already available in Japanese and English. The 10 attitudes are

1. Customer first
2. Challenge
3. *Kaizen*
4. *Genchi genbutsu* (go and see to understand)
5. *Shitsujitsu goken* (use money and time wisely and avoid waste)
6. Teamwork
7. Ownership and responsibility
8. Humility and gratitude
9. Integrity
10. We love Toyota (joy and pride from working for Toyota)

Another initiative to increase contact with customers and create more opportunities for listening was making the two years of free scheduled maintenance program permanent. Initially conceived as an incentive to bolster sales after the sticky pedal recall, TMS leaders and dealers realized that the program was a fantastic way to increase the touch points with customers and hear their concerns. Under the program, Toyota dealers will see virtually every customer eight times in the first two years he owns a vehicle.

That will give customers several opportunities to ask questions or express concerns so that, if the issue is a simple misunderstanding of a feature like cruise control, it won't grow into mistrust of the company or the vehicle. At the same time, it will give Toyota a better source of data on customer wants and needs and how customers are using their vehicles. That's particularly important in the United States, with its unique model of independently owned dealers. By law, Toyota cannot own the dealers who are the primary point of contact with customers. Thus, the company has to rely on dealers to capture and relay information from customers. An ongoing challenge for Toyota will be working with the network of dealers to make sure that accurate and complete information is flowing back to the company at a level of detail that will enable any problems or concerns to be thoroughly analyzed, root causes to be determined, and appropriate action to be taken.

Putting Customers First in Engineering and Manufacturing

Under the mandate of the special committee on global quality, various departments also took steps to streamline their processes related to customer information and to increase their responsiveness to customers. Uchiyamada's team had this responsibility for engineering. As Uchiyamada described in his team's root-cause analysis, the process of funneling customer information to engineers was far from efficient:

> A customer would have an issue, and they would report it to the dealer. And then the dealer would send their reports to TMS. TMS sent it to the quality department in Japan. And then the quality department looked at the

field issue, and decided whether or not this was an area that had anything to do with engineering from a design standpoint. If it did, they would request the engineering design group to investigate. So, there were many people that handled the issue before it got to engineering. And there was also the possibility that an issue might be dropped or not passed forward.

Immediate steps were taken to increase the engineering department's access to raw data coming in, but that still left engineers at arm's length. Truly addressing the problem also required a new dedication to the principle of *genchi genbutsu* among engineers.

There have been many changes to the engineering department to bring the voice of the customer into the engineering process. First, the R&D department in Japan reassigned 100 engineers to a Design Quality Innovation Division with a focus on "going and seeing," adding to existing analysis from a human factors engineering standpoint and feeding that information into the design process more directly. The members of this team specifically spend far more time in the field talking to customers and dealers. Trips by Japanese design and quality engineers to visit dealers and customers increased fourfold in 2010. And managing officers who are responsible for the engineering department are also making at least two trips to dealers each year, to try to understand issues.

Second, to ensure that the information gained from this new attention to going and seeing in the field was incorporated into the vehicle design process, the R&D department added four weeks to the vehicle development schedule immediately after the production prototype is complete. Spreading four weeks over the life of the program might have had little impact, but these four consecutive weeks are dedicated to picking apart the vehicle from every possible angle to identify issues that might cause customers concern.

But that was not the only rededication to *genchi genbutsu* that was required. The "go and see" philosophy is not just the idea that the decision maker shows up and looks at the problem before making a decision. It's the idea that the decision maker is close enough to the problem on a daily basis to make a good decision on the best course for addressing it. In Toyota, this is phrased as the *gemba*, or work site. Decision makers should be as close to the *gemba* as possible. This includes not just physical proximity, but close familiarity with the issues so that the individual can anticipate the consequences of decisions and choices. For instance, that's why Toyota CSRs in the TMS call center are not scripted and have the authority to spend significant sums resolving customer issues: they are closest to the *gemba*. Thus, it's not ideal for *genchi genbutsu* to be carried out in the regions by personnel from headquarters in Japan.

The only way around this is to achieve the regional self-reliance that Toyota had named as one of its major goals for North America in Global Vision 2010, but had yet to fully accomplish. Appointing regional chief quality officers was an important part of this process, but it was by no means sufficient for the long term. Regional product quality field offices were set up, so that there is a strong regional engineering presence in each part of North America. Each of the six centers has general responsibility for investigating consumer issues and a particular technical specialty related to unique regional, geographical, or environmental conditions in its area. For example, the New York regional office was developed to investigate vehicle performance in cold-weather climates. Overall, the goal of regional self-reliance is not independence in the sense that regions function without any input from

Japan. The goal is that every part of a region's operations perform at the same level as its counterpart in Japan—and therefore the regions have a strong and respected voice in all decisions that the company makes. That, of course, requires not just that the regions have the capability but that headquarters respects and listens to the input and insight of the regions.

Third, Toyota appointed additional American chief engineers in the United States. In Toyota, the chief engineer has broad responsibility for development of a particular vehicle, from styling to every aspect of engineering the vehicle. Historically, only senior Japanese with more than 25 years of experience at Toyota served as chief engineers. The chief engineer is expected to deeply understand through *genchi genbutsu* how the customer uses the car and what he will value. Chief engineers have taken steps like moving in with a Beverly Hills family during the design phase of a Lexus vehicle and driving a Sienna minivan across North America to experience conditions firsthand. Still, no amount of "going and seeing" by a Japanese engineer will yield the level of insight into the American psyche that an American engineer going through the same process will achieve. In Japan, they use the expression "under the skin." Jim Lentz explained: "We can send all the reports that we can to Japan, but until you're here, living it, you don't have that feeling under the skin of the intensity of something that's going on." Early in 2009, before the crisis, the first two American chief engineers were named. This was quickly increased to four Americans after the crisis hit. These four had formerly been senior program managers, one step below chief engineer, but now they would have the ultimate authority on decisions for vehicles made specifically for the U.S. market.

Fourth, Toyota is making fundamental changes in the way information is communicated to the engineers who are responsible for components and various subsystems of the vehicle. In the past, all the data on customer concerns flowed through the quality division. A new system has been put in place so that data from the call center, field technical reports, the NHTSA database, and various auto-related Web sites will go directly to the engineer responsible for that part of the car.

Toyota also headed back to its roots in how an engineer is trained. At Toyota, every manager is supposed to be a teacher in the traditional sense of the master-apprentice relationship. Originally, a senior engineer was assigned to act as a mentor for a small group of about five direct reports through on-the-job development. Over time, as the company grew, Toyota could not develop engineering managers fast enough, so it increased the number of apprentices reporting to each mentor. A group manager came to be responsible for developing about 20 engineers. Under Uchiyamada, Toyota reversed this decision, adding a role below the group manager (assistant manager) and moving back toward the one leader for five junior engineers ratio for daily mentoring and development. Adding in new layers of management may seem antithetical to a "lean" approach, but that is based on a common misunderstanding of lean. The point of lean is not to eliminate steps or middle management, but to eliminate *unnecessary and wasteful* steps. Toyota has learned that the 5-to-1 ratio is a necessary step for developing engineers with the right capabilities and experience. That's not a wasteful, but a necessary investment.

In another step to advance vehicle safety generally, Toyota decided to invest $50 million in a new Collaborative Safety Research Center near its Ann Arbor, Michigan R&D operations. The new center will take an open-source approach to safety research, working with partners and sharing insights and results with other manufacturers or anyone who can use the research. Even the manufacturing department got into the act, although none of the recalls in 2009 and 2010 were the result of a defect introduced in the manufacturing plants. Art Niimi, who is responsible for global manufacturing and the North American region at the board level, and is a former president of TEMA, shared his perspective that manufacturing has to take ownership of quality issues too:

> We had internal discussions and tried to find out what we can do, what we could offer as a production side. And we decided eventually that in manufacturing we will take the responsibility for quality of the vehicles coming out of the plant. It is the plant that ships the product and delivers the product to the customers. So we say that each plant will take responsibility for the shipment quality.

Each manufacturing plant was charged with reexamining all of its quality procedures, going job by job down to the detail of every step the worker does and the possible quality problems that can occur in that step. Data from the field on defects in any component began coming back to the plant at a higher rate than ever, including, whenever possible, delivering the actual part that failed. Then the problems are analyzed using Toyota's problem-solving method, and countermeasures are defined and implemented. If the countermeasure involves a product change by Engineering, the plant will take responsibility for ushering the change through Engineering. Every work group of about 20 team members has key performance indicators for quality posted next to its work place, and that includes live data coming in on customer concerns. Daily meetings are held to work on quality, and many quality circles have taken on larger projects related to customer quality. The investments in training and *kaizen* during the recession were clearly paying off.

It should be clear that many changes were made, and they were not of the superficial variety to give the public the impression that something was being done. Fundamental changes in engineering, long-term investments in training, shifts in power toward the regions, and enormous investments in communications are investments in the future that most likely would not have an immediate impact on results. Table 4.2 provides an overview of the many investments Toyota made to address the true root causes of the crises.

TABLE 4.2 OVERVIEW OF TOYOTA RESPONSE TO THE RECALL CRISIS

TOYOTA CHANGES	PURPOSE FOR IMPROVING SAFETY—CUSTOMER RESPONSIVENESS
OVERALL STRATEGY AND GUIDANCE	
Akio Toyoda's special committee for global quality	Set global policy
External advisory committee	Outside eyes on quality and safety
REGIONAL INFLUENCE AND CONTROL	
"Chief quality officer" and "regional product safety executive" roles	Respond quickly/appropriately to safety issues and stay informed locally and globally
Additional American chief engineers in the United States	Engineering decisions made at the *gemba* by Americans, who have the best feel "under the skin" for American needs
Board of directors member as liaison for each region	Voice of region directly on board of directors

TOYOTA CHANGES	PURPOSE FOR IMPROVING SAFETY—CUSTOMER RESPONSIVENESS
ENGINEERING AND QUALITY PROCESSES	
Swift Market Analysis Response Teams (SMART)	Initially investigate SUA; expanded to all customer concerns
100 engineers assigned to new design quality innovation division	"Going and seeing" + understanding customer concerns to affect product development
Extra four weeks full prototype quality and safety review	Thoroughly evaluate vehicle from human factors view
1,000 engineers reassigned to quality	Increase engineering focus on quality and safety
Regional quality field offices in North America	Each office investigates customer complaints and has a technical specialty (e.g., cold-weather performance in New York State)
Collaborative Safety Research Center (Michigan)	Funded research in collaboration with safety institutes and universities to improve vehicle safety generally
Hired top U.S. engineering firm Exponent	Independent review of technical SUA and safety issues
Manufacturing took responsibility for quality of delivered vehicles	As last stop, takes ownership of vehicle quality and safety
PEOPLE DEVELOPMENT	
Assistant manager role for mentoring junior engineers	More personalized mentoring like earlier times in Toyota
Customer-first regional training centers	General awareness training on safety and quality philosophy and quality professional training
	(continues next page)

TOYOTA CHANGES	PURPOSE FOR IMPROVING SAFETY—CUSTOMER RESPONSIVENESS
Reduced engineering contractors	Contractors not as trained and indoctrinated into Toyota culture
COMMUNICATIONS	
Executive positions to integrate sales, engineering , and manufacturing	Improve communication and decision making ("One Toyota")
Appointment of regional CQOs, global quality task force formed, and global database created	Communicate effectively across regions to share safety issues
North American quality task force (weekly conference call)	Better communication and decisions
Customer data from multiple sources integrated and directed to responsible engineers	Decisions made at the source; eliminate centralized bottleneck
U.S. TOYOTA MOTOR SALES	
Two-year free scheduled maintenance	More data on customer issues/concerns
Increased use of Internet (e.g., Facebook)	Better communicate directly with customers

Did It Work?

It's impossible to assess any crisis response program without evaluating the impact: Did the company survive the crisis? Did Toyota manage to turn the crisis into opportunity? Of course, that's a long-term question that can't fully be answered just a year after the crisis hit its peak. But there are data available that point to Toyota's recovery from the crisis being remarkable, especially considering the short time frame. We've summarized that evidence in a few key tables and charts. Table 4.3 gives an overall summary of the data. Despite all the troubles in 2010, by the end of the year Toyota was still the number one automaker in global sales, and in the United States, Toyota remained the bestselling brand in retail sales (for the third consecutive year), Camry was the bestselling car for the ninth year in a row, Lexus was the bestselling luxury brand for the eleventh year straight, and Toyota was the leader in certified used car sales.

TABLE 4.3 OVERALL SUMMARY OF DATA TRENDS

MEASURE	RESULTS
Profitability	A short-term profit hit was taken during the worst of the crisis, on an annual basis, but profit continued to recover, replenishing the deep cash reserves depleted by the recession.
Stock price	There was a major fall during the worst of the crisis in February 2010 (21 percent loss), followed by a steep gain by February 2011 (31 percent increase from low point in August 2010).
Market share	Market share became more volatile, and Toyota's share fell one to two percentage points in 2010 (depending on the month), but when retail sales alone are considered, market share bounced back strongly, with 2010 sales exceeding 2009. Conquest sales and consideration rates tracked by Edmunds.com also show a rebound to just below the levels prior to the crisis. Globally, Toyota sales were up 7 percent over 2009 to retain the top spot in units sold.
	(continues next page)

MEASURE	RESULTS
Customer complaints	Edmunds's cleaned version of the NHTSA database showed that complaint levels for SUA dropped 80 percent within months of February 2010 and that Toyota soon rose to second in terms of fewest complaints per 100,000 vehicles.
Quality and safety	Toyota's place at the top of industry awards lists was restored by the fall of 2010. Toyota topped all automakers in end-of-year awards, including those from Polk, *Kiplinger's*, the Insurance Institute for Highway Safety, *Consumer Reports*, Intellichoice, and Motorist Choice.

Net income is summarized in Figure 4.2. We can see the depths of the losses in the midst of the global recession in late 2008 to early 2009, but by the third quarter of 2009, income had turned from negative to positive, and despite a dip in early 2010, at the worst of the recall crisis, Toyota has made money every quarter since.

The hit to Toyota's stock price was also temporary. The stock had risen to its highest point since the recession in January 2010, $91 a share. With the negative publicity after the sticky pedal recall, the price had dropped to $72 a share by February 4, a 21 percent drop, and fell to a low point of $68 a share in August. By February 2011, a day after the NASA report was released, the stock had climbed back to almost $89 a share and as of February 25 had exceeded $93 a share. Of course, the volatility in the stock price is affected by many macroeconomic factors, but it is a good indicator that the market believes the company is headed decisively in the right direction.

One of the most telling statistics relates to the overall brand perception of Toyota—and the fact that Toyota's history insulated it from a great deal of the potential damage from the crisis. Drivers

FIGURE 4.2 TOYOTA NET QUARTERLY INCOME ($ BILLION)

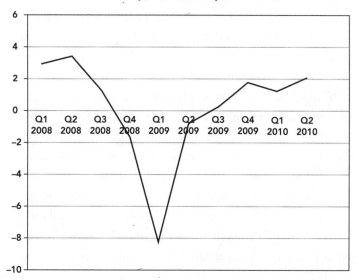

of Toyota vehicles, although they were the ones who were directly affected by the recalls, felt much more positive about the company than people who were not customers. A survey conducted by Rice University and a market research firm in the midst of the worst part of the crisis found tremendous loyalty among current Toyota owners.* On all aspects of the study, Toyota owners proved to have a more favorable opinion of the company than non-Toyota owners. For example, on a 10-point scale, in answer to a question about whether they would buy a Toyota if they were in the market, Toyota owners rated the possibility an 8, while non-Toyota owners rated it an average of 4. This same pattern of Toyota owners being overwhelmingly positive and non-Toyota owners being

---

* Vikas Mittal et al., "Does Media Coverage of Toyota Recalls Reflect Reality?" *The Conversation Blog, Harvard Business Review,* March 9, 2010; http://blogs. hbr.org/research/2010/03/does-media-coverage-of-toyota.html.

overwhelmingly negative applied to statements like: "Toyota appropriately handled issues with the brake-pedal recall; this incident is an outlier; Toyota typically has a strong reputation for quality; and the recall shows Toyota's commitment to customer safety." A separate study undertaken by BizPulse at about the same time confirmed these findings.* The same results also showed up in Edmunds.com's data, which showed that people who had owned a Toyota in the past continued to consider Toyota vehicles at the same level as they had before the recalls. One interesting and counterintuitive finding was that Toyota owners whose cars had been recalled actually reported higher satisfaction and were more likely to buy another Toyota than those whose cars had not been recalled—suggesting that the heroic efforts of Toyota and its dealers had paid off.

Various indicators of sales in Figure 4.3 show a similar pattern of a rapid and impressive recovery, but not fully back to the

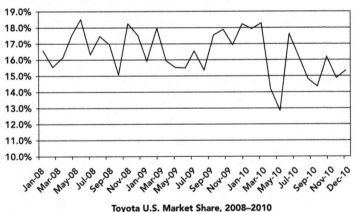

FIGURE 4.3 TOYOTA U.S. SALES EXPERIENCE OVER TIME THROUGH THE RECALL CRISIS

Toyota U.S. Market Share, 2008–2010

* Christine Hall, "BizPulse Results Mimics Rice University Toyota Study," *Houston Business Journal*, March 9, 2010; http://www.bizjournals.com/houston/stories/2010/03/08/daily19.html #ixzz0vTUTWr5u.

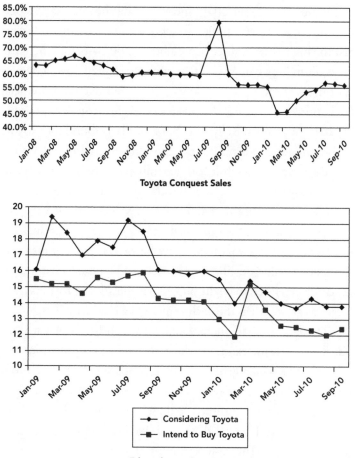

Toyota Conquest Sales

Edmunds.com Consumer Data

levels that Toyota had enjoyed before the recession. U.S. market share dropped to a low of 12.8 percent in February 2010, but rebounded immediately to 17.6 percent in March and then leveled off for the rest of the year at between 15 and 16 percent, below its all-time highs of 18 percent, reached in 2008 and 2009.

Recovery of "conquest sales," the percentage of non-Toyota trade-ins for new Toyota vehicles, was also quite impressive. By the end of September 2010, industry data showed that 55 percent of Toyota buyers traded in models from other manufacturers, the highest level since September of 2009—before the recall crisis. Edmunds.com shows that consideration of Toyota by new car buyers also dipped to a low point in February and bounced back, but stayed below the pre-recall levels through September 2010. In December, Kelly Blue Book similarly found that Toyota had regained its position as the most considered brand among new car buyers, though it had not fully recovered to its precrisis levels.* In January 2011, Kelly Blue Book published a report looking at the impact of the crisis on Toyota vehicles' resale value. Its research found that the crisis had had an impact on residual values, but not nearly what might have been expected. For instance, the average value decline for Honda and Hyundai, two brands generally perceived to be the biggest beneficiaries of Toyota's troubles, was greater than the decline in Toyota residual values.†

The market-share picture looks more positive when we take out fleet sales, for example, those to rental car companies and corporations, which generally are made at a very low or no profit (and drive down future resale values). Toyota has historically limited fleet sales and continued to do so even during the depths of the recession and the recall crisis. If we look only at retail sales (excluding fleet), Toyota was running at 17.9 percent of the U.S. market prior to the recall crisis, and by November of 2010 was at 17.1 percent—just ⁹⁄₁₀ of a point lost (see Figure 4.4). And for

---

* "Toyota Regains Top Spot for Most-Considered Brand; Ford, Honda Close Behind," Kelly Blue Book, December 13, 2010; http://mediaroom.kbb.com /kelley-blue-book-toyota-regains-top-spot-most-considered-brand-ford -honda-close-behind.

† "Toyota: One Year Later," Kelly Blue Book, Special Report, January 2011; http://mediaroom.kbb.com/special-reports.

every month in 2010 after February, and for the year as a whole, Toyota was still number one in retail sales in the United States. Overall for 2009, Toyota's retail share was 18.5 percent compared to 17 percent for 2010, so a hit was taken.

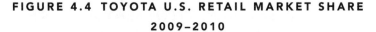

FIGURE 4.4 TOYOTA U.S. RETAIL MARKET SHARE 2009–2010

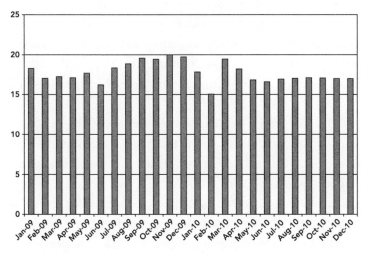

Toyota's rankings in quality and safety awards at the end of 2010 were largely consistent with the past—another indication that there were few true defects in Toyota vehicles. *Consumer Reports* Fall 2010 rankings of the "most reliable vehicles" included 17 Toyota models—the most of any automaker. In December, *Forbes* put five Toyotas on its list of vehicles likely to last beyond 200,000 miles; no other manufacturer had more than one vehicle on the list.* Three Toyota and Lexus vehicles made

---

* Hannah Elliott, "Cars That Will Make It Past 200,000 Miles," *Forbes*, December 8, 2010; http://www.forbes.com/2010/12/08/most-reliable-cars-2010-business -autos-reliable-cars.html.

Kiplinger's list of the "10 best cars of the past decade," more than any other automaker.*

Perhaps even more pertinent to the recall crisis, which focused on the safety of Toyota vehicles, at the end of December 2010 the Insurance Institute for Highway Safety awarded eight Toyota vehicles its top safety award,† in this case tied for second place among all automakers. It is ironic that, at about the same time the Insurance Institute was awarding Toyota for its outstanding safety, seven major auto insurance companies were filing a lawsuit claiming, "certain of Toyota's cars and trucks have a defect that causes sudden uncontrolled acceleration to speeds of up to 100 mph or more."‡

Overall, the various data on the impact of the recall crisis paint a picture of a company that took a significant hit, but recovered quickly to levels near where it had begun. Nonetheless, real damage was done to the brand. For instance, J.D. Power's annual study of customer loyalty showed that Toyota had fallen from the top spot to a few percentage points behind Ford and Honda. Edmunds.com data (see Figure 4.5) on customer consideration of various manufacturers shows that the biggest hit to Toyota was among customers who were predisposed to consider non-Big 3 manufacturers like Honda, Nissan, and Hyun-

---

* "10 Best Cars of the Past Decade," *Kiplinger,* December 2010; http://portal.kiplinger.com/tools/slideshows/slideshow_pop.html?nm=10_Best_Cars_Trucks_Decade_2000_2010.

† "66 Winners of 2011 Top Safety Pick Award," Insurance Institute for Highway Safety, December 22, 2010; http://www.iihs.org/news/rss/pr122210.html.

‡ "Toyota Sued by Insurance Companies over Alleged Acceleration-Related Crashes," *Los Angeles Times,* January 3, 2011; http://latimesblogs.latimes.com/money_co/2011/01/toyota-sued-by-seven-insurance-companies-sudden-acceleration.html.

dai. Another J.D. Power study in December 2010 found that 19 percent of new-vehicle shoppers would not consider a Toyota because of the "bad reputation of the manufacturer," up from 2 percent a year earlier.* In *Consumer Reports*'s main survey of customer satisfaction released in early January 2011, Toyota had regained the top spot, but Ford was right on its heels, virtually tied for first place.† Again, the picture is of a resilient company, but one that has work to do to regain its former competitive status.

FIGURE 4.5 EDMUNDS.COM DATA ON CUSTOMER CONSIDERATION OF AUTOMOTIVE PURCHASES)

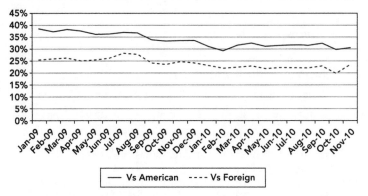

Historically, Toyota has been at its best when severely challenged by the environment, including tough competition. The actions that Toyota took in 2010 put it in a position to compete

---

* Lauren Abdel-Razzaq, "Toyota Reputation Drops among U.S. New-Car Buyers, J.D. Power Says," *Automotive News,* December 14, 2010; http://www.autonews.com/apps/pbcs.dll/article?AID=/20101214/RETAIL 03/101219918/1143.

† David Shepardson, "Ford, Toyota in 'Dead Heat' among Consumer Perceptions," *Detroit News,* January 6, 2011; http://detnews.com/article/20110106/AUTO 01/101060366/Ford--Toyota-in-%E2%80%98dead-heat%E2%80%99-among -consumer-perceptions.

and regain trust and market share, but that will be a continuing long-term battle. Edward Niedermeyer, editor of *The Truth about Cars* site, notes that the competitive landscape has gotten more difficult for Toyota as a result of the crisis:

> Toyota was operating with a halo. And that halo is gone. It's opened up the market for a lot more competition. In a numerical sense, Toyota sales haven't gone down as much as they might have, but in a strategic sense it's in a much, much tougher fight sales wise than it might have been. The strategic loss shouldn't be underestimated.

Anwyl expresses it this way:

> Toyota was the brand of default. [People] would buy their vehicles because they didn't want to have to think about [the decision]. They knew they made good cars. This [crisis] has raised questions, and people are thinking about [their choices] more than they did in the past.

In other words, real harm was done, harm that will have to be repaired over years. That's why the steps that Toyota has taken to improve, not just claw back to its old level of operations, matter so much. That's an important lesson of turning crisis into opportunity. In the next chapter, we'll look at more of the lessons that others can learn from Toyota's experience.

CHAPTER 5

Lessons

Life is a series of experiences, each of which makes us bigger, even though it is hard to realize this. For the world was built to develop character, and we must learn that the setbacks and grieves which we endure help us in our marching onward.

—HENRY FORD

You may have noticed in the quotations from Toyota executives throughout the book how often the word *reflect* appears. You'll hear it whenever you talk to people at Toyota, no matter what their level, because engaging in reflection, or *hansei*, is expected of everyone at Toyota. This isn't esoteric reflection—it's an attitude of constantly looking back at actions and decisions to learn lessons from them and look for opportunities for improvement. *Hansei* is expected at a personal, a team, and a company level. Toyota leaders will tell you that without *hansei* there can be no *kaizen*. Bruce Brownlee, general manager for external affairs at Toyota Technical Center (TTC), explains: "*Hansei* is really much deeper than reflection. It is really about being honest about your own weaknesses. But it doesn't end there. How do you change to overcome your weaknesses?"

We've attempted to engage in *hansei* from an outsider's perspective to draw lessons for others from Toyota's experiences over the last three years. What did Toyota do right, and what did it do wrong? What mistakes did Toyota make that contributed to the crises? What drove positive responses, and what opportunities were missed? What can others learn from Toyota about crisis management and turning crisis into opportunity?

One conclusion rises to the top: turning crisis into opportunity is all about culture. It's not about PR strategies, or charismatic leadership, or vision, or any specific action by any individual. It's not about policies or procedures or risk mitigation processes. It's about the actions that have been programmed into the individuals and teams that make up a company before the crisis starts. In our estimation, Toyota's most important decision in handling the recession crisis was to keep a conservative balance sheet, lots of cash on hand, and an excellent credit rating during the boom years before the recession. Toyota's financial position was what allowed it to keep investing in people and processes even while it was operating at a $4 billion loss. The most important decision for the recall crisis was not to lay anyone off during the recession, but instead to take that time and invest in developing people and deepening the Toyota Way culture. The only big decision that Akio Toyoda had to make in approaching the recall crisis was to go "back to the basics," acting on and further deepening the Toyota Way, a process that had already started in many parts of the company during the global recession. The decisions that made the most difference during the crises were made well before the crises took place. These decisions weren't happenstance, luck, or the insight of a particularly wise individual. They were reflections of how Toyota has always done business. They were a reflection of culture.

From that conclusion, we've drawn four specific lessons for leaders and managers of other companies.

Lesson 1: Your Crisis Response Started Yesterday

Changing the behavior of a large, multinational company on short notice isn't just difficult; it's impossible. There's an old saying that character is what a person does when no one else is looking. Culture is what a company does when senior management isn't looking. Those collective actions that happen outside of a strategic planning workshop or an annual planning process are far more important to a company's direction and fate than anything that a leader, at whatever level, can say or do. Even when a crisis strikes, those actions are unlikely to change much, or for any length of time. They are driven by the culture, and culture simply can't be changed quickly, even in a crisis.

A company with a culture that places blame or denies responsibility won't change just because a senior executive stands before Congress and accepts responsibility. A company that values individual achievement won't work as a team to overcome a challenge just because that executive delivers an impassioned speech on the importance of teamwork at an internal meeting. A company that tolerates disjointed action and large differences in the approach and capabilities of different functions won't start pulling in the same direction just because of a new vision statement or corporate goal. A corporate culture that values short-term profits over long-term success won't change quickly even if the senior leadership team changes the firm's performance metrics. Culture is created over long time frames and can change only over long time frames.

Therefore, the chief questions to ask yourself about how your company will respond in a crisis are not about contingency plans and policies, but about your culture and your people. Have you created a culture that rewards transparency and accepts responsibility for mistakes? Have you created a culture that encourages people to take on challenges and strive for improvement? Have you created a culture that values people and invests in their capabilities? Have you created a culture that prioritizes the long term? Most attempts to change during a crisis fail. Although a crisis helps people accept the need for change, implementing the change takes far too long to make much difference while the crisis is raging.

All of Toyota's positive actions in the two crises were driven by the extant Toyota Way culture that it had been cultivating since the company began. It was the investment in developing team members' problem-solving skills all the way to the shop floor that allowed those team members to contribute materially to the company's future when the recession meant that they were not needed to build cars. Without that investment over many years, those team members wouldn't have been the tremendous asset they were in driving down long-term costs, improving quality, and boosting productivity. If Toyota had tried to cut costs on hourly customer service representatives instead of investing in developing them with the talent, maturity, and judgment to make tough decisions call by call and rebuild trust with customers, it would not have achieved customer satisfaction among those with recalled vehicles that was higher than that for customers whose vehicles were never recalled. If Toyota executives had responded to the incredible costs of the recall crisis by reining in spending on customers and dealers, they would not have been able to maintain the highest levels of customer loyalty in the industry. It was a culture of *hansei* that underlay Akio Toyoda's ability to turn the energy of the recall crisis toward continuous improvement rather than toward finger-pointing and blame. It was Toyota's culture of quality and safety that over decades generated the "brand insulation" that kept customers loyal through the recall crisis.

During the crises, there were no new strategies or radical departures. There were no attempts to change the company's DNA or its priorities. Everything that Toyota did in response to the crises was an outgrowth of what it had already been doing before the crises began. The largest investments that it made in response to the crises were to reinforce or correct areas where the company was not hewing closely enough to its culture. These initiatives weren't efforts to change the culture; they were efforts to return to it and reinforce it.

How Did Toyota's Culture Drive Its Response?

Let's take a look at how the specific elements of the Toyota Way culture drove Toyota's response and the places and ways it invested to reinforce that culture.

Spirit of Challenge

One of the easiest reactions to a crisis is passivity—especially if the crisis seems to be driven by external forces, like the Great Recession. There is a tendency to simply throw one's hands in the air and proclaim, "There's nothing we can do." That's especially tempting in a large, multinational corporation, where it's often difficult for individuals to perceive that their actions matter. This feeling of insignificance is a major barrier to positive action.

The Toyota Way's emphasis on the spirit of challenge is about fighting passivity. *The Toyota Way 2001* puts it this way: "Change is our constant partner. It frustrates and challenges. It brings out the best in all of us. . . . As we meet the challenge of change, we will ensure our vigor and vitality." Emerging from the recession and a $4 billion loss with a company that was stronger—and capable of surviving the recall crisis—required extraordinary action throughout Toyota. It was the culture that allowed the entire company, from the shop floor to the purchasing offices to the customer service center, to focus immediately and actively on cutting costs while protecting capability. There was no single project that made a material difference in cutting overhead costs at factories or returning the company to profitability so quickly. It was the cumulative value of thousands of projects that were launched simultaneously, almost instantaneously, that made the difference. That's the spirit of challenge in action.

For Toyota, the ultimate challenge is perfection. The recall crisis highlighted just how far Toyota had to go to reach that goal. To turn the recall crisis into a growth opportunity required plunging right back into major efforts to improve the company directly on the heels of what many felt had been a tremendous accomplishment during the recession. Maintaining that energy for improvement was again an outgrowth of the cultivation of the spirit of challenge.

Finally, it's the spirit of challenge that Toyota will have to draw on to complete its recovery and continue its steps toward improvement. It will no doubt be tempting for many people in the company to take a deep breath and pat themselves on the back for bouncing back quickly and strongly from the recall crisis. But the work is not done. As Edward Niedermeyer noted, the recall crisis has been a huge boon to Toyota's competitors because it eroded Toyota's "halo." *The Toyota Way 2001* states that "we welcome competition, knowing that we will learn from the challenge and become stronger because of it." Thus Toyota has to be ready to accept a whole new challenge as the recall crisis fades—rebuilding that halo and beating a reinvigorated competition.

RESPECT FOR PEOPLE

The Toyota Way principle of respect for people manifested itself in many ways during both crises. It is respect for people that drives Toyota's commitment to exhaust every other possibility before laying off team members. It's respect for people that drives Toyota's willingness to put extraordinary trust in hourly employees to find and solve problems. These decisions paid off over and over during the last few years. Renee McIntosh, an hourly team member at Toyota Motor Manufacturing Kentucky (TMMK) who was on special assignment leading the quality circles program for her area when the recession hit, saw the payoff from the decision not to lay off team members:

> I never knew anybody who was seriously concerned about losing their job. But you started seeing team members, who were not really pro-Toyota, they started caring more than they did before. . . . There was an attitude change through the whole shop. People really wanted to kick in and wanted to help. . . . People were saying: "We've got to step up."

If Toyota hadn't maintained that commitment to its people during the recession, it would not have had the resources to create SMART teams or an engineering division focused on customer experience.

During the recall crisis, respect for people manifested itself in the decision to avoid finger-pointing and blaming customers, suppliers, dealers, or anyone else for the problems that Toyota was facing. As we noted in Chapter 4, this wasn't a policy edict that was issued by senior executives; that policy didn't have to be issued at all. The approach was a natural outgrowth of the culture of respect for people. Akio Toyoda says that when he was preparing to speak at the congressional hearings, this culture led him to a decision about how he would respond to questions and accusations:

> At the time I was very severely criticized. People suggested that I was trying to escape from the problems in the United States or that I was lying, which was absolutely appalling. It was very difficult for me to face. But one thing that I decided was I would never point fingers at somebody else. I decided I would never blame others.

Not blaming others extended from customers to suppliers to regulators and even critics in the media and expert witnesses for lawyers fighting against the company. We've noted the repeated apologies to customers and the decision to accept responsibility for the sticky pedal design and to deflect negative attention from CTS. One of Toyota's missteps early in the recall crisis was in its communication about the floor mat and pedal shape recall in November 2009, which could be interpreted as disrespectful of the independence of the National Highway Traffic Safety Administration (NHTSA)—independence that the NHTSA took pains to reaffirm when it publicly criticized Toyota's communication on the issue. Since then, Toyota has taken pains to communicate frequently with the NHTSA and become a model of cooperation and responsiveness, including not contesting the fines that the NHTSA levied.

GENCHI GENBUTSU (GO AND SEE TO UNDERSTAND)

The first written communication to the entire company from Akio Toyoda after he assumed the presidency in 2009 was an article for an internal newsletter in which he wrote: "We managed to create a culture . . . where those who learned the truth of the *gemba* were the most respected. In this culture there is no such thing as manager and subordinate. Job titles are unimportant. In the end, who sees wins; and winning means being close to the objects, close to the *gemba*."

The *gemba* is where it is happening—whatever *it* is. It could be where a car is being built, where the engine is being tested, where the car is being investigated by the dealer for problems, or where the customer is driving the car. These are all *gemba* in the Toyota culture. *Genchi genbutsu* is the value of going to the *gemba* and trusting those at the *gemba* to make decisions.

This cultural trait manifested itself during the recession in the number, variety, and autonomy of the *kaizen* projects and quality circles that were launched to cut costs and improve productivity. There is simply no way that senior plant managers could have closely overseen, or even provided meaningful input to, the vast number of projects going on. Those projects were carried forward by the people at the *gemba*. In the same way, the decisions on caring for customers during the recalls were left to the dealers and the customer service representatives—they were the ones at the *gemba*.

We've noted several times that not following through on this value was one of the root causes of the severity of the recall crisis. Decisions on recalls and communication were not being made at the *gemba*; there was too little "going and seeing" on the part of engineers. But it was the deeply embedded cultural value of *genchi genbutsu* that allowed Toyota to muster the resources to fix many of those problems quickly. For instance, that's why the SMART idea took root quickly, why budget was quickly allocated to allow quality engineers to go visit customers and dealerships much more frequently, and, most important, how significant organization changes were made quickly.

Between February and July 2010, the new regional chief quality officer position was created and staffed around the world, the number of American chief engineers with responsibility for vehicle design in the United States doubled, and Americans were appointed as presidents of every American manufacturing plant—all from within. St. Angelo and the other Americans didn't suddenly become capable of filling these roles when the crisis erupted; their adherence to the Toyota Way had been developed over many years. The fact that they hadn't assumed such roles already was a failure to live up to the standard of *genchi genbutsu*, but it was this standard that made it possible for the company to move quickly to correct that failure. There was widespread agreement that these appointments were overdue.

Even after the appointments, there was a renewed commitment to *genchi genbutsu*. St. Angelo remembers running into Akio Toyoda and Yoshimi Inaba in the Cincinnati airport just after he was appointed in February 2010, when the recall crisis was raging and questions about Toyota's electronics systems were still rampant. He took the opportunity to ask Toyoda and Inaba about the allegations of electronics problems directly. After reassuring him that there was no evidence of problems, St. Angelo described how, "Akio Toyoda looked me in the face, and said, 'But, a key element of the Toyota Way, Steve, is *genchi genbutsu*. You can't just take my word for it. You can't just look at a report. You've got to go see and look for yourself. Go to the point of concern and look for yourself.' And then Inaba-san said, 'Steve, take every rock and every stone, lift it up and see what's under there. You've got to look for yourself and make your own judgment. Don't just take our word.' That's the essence of *genchi genbutsu*." Steve followed their advice and developed his own confidence in the electronics systems:

> From March through August of 2010, I traveled to Japan almost every other week. I've been to every engineering area. I've been to the place where they check for electromagnetic interference, that has magnets as big as a room, where they're trying to make the system fail so they can find a weak point to fix it. I visited where they do the crash tests. I've talked to engineers. I've talked to technicians. I talked to people in production. I have visited many dealerships in North America, and they never have found a case of electronic problems causing SUA. And then I spent some time at Exponent. I got there early in the morning and left there about 10:30 at night, and was totally amazed at the amount of problem solving and how they do their problem solving.

The recall crisis revealed that Toyota had missed the mark in its commitment to *genchi genbutsu*, but that renewed commitment also allowed for rapid action when the shortcomings were revealed.

KAIZEN MIND

The role of *kaizen* mind in Toyota's response to the Great Recession and the recall crisis is fairly obvious. At no point did the company panic and start making changes without a thorough analysis of the problems and a search for solutions that would improve the company's operations. The application of *kaizen* mind is what led to the actions that Toyota took.

Toyota repeatedly attributed the recall crisis to communication problems, and it is clear that the process of getting from customer concerns to concrete action to address those concerns was anything but lean. One exception was the call center, but it could not address the real root cause of the problem. What it could do was provide one of the best sources of data on the real customer concerns—it could bring the problems to the surface. Nancy Fein, who was running the call center, discovered that as a result of the crisis, there was far more interest in the data that the center was collecting:

> We were beginning to coordinate across Toyota to pro-
> vide that information and make sure people knew how
> to use that information. Before the crisis, it was more of
> a push to the organization. Now, there is a very strong
> realization everywhere that they need to pull it. People
> are asking for our data now. Our product quality depart-
> ment uses it, public affairs uses it, sales uses it, the legal
> department uses it, and our plants and engineering are
> using it for *kaizen*.

Of course data are only data; they do not solve problems. The problems have to be solved in design, engineering, sales, customer support, and manufacturing. As we saw in Chapter 4, Uchiyamada began bringing Engineering back to the basics. He was concerned that engineers in Japan were too insulated from customers and that, as a result, they spent too little time listening to actual customers: "The previous process was the quality department would look through that database and find the issues and bring them to Engineering. But now, Engineering is looking directly at the data itself, the raw data, and tracking and finding the issues quicker." Uchiyamada also vastly expanded the budget for engineers to get into the field and "go and see" customers, how they use their vehicles, and the problems they encounter.

Reinforcing *kaizen* mind is also the focus of the investment in the new "customer first" training centers that are being deployed around the world. These centers are not just lecture halls where a "customer first" mantra can be repeated over and over again. They are centers where team members practice problem solving from the customer perspective. It is very hands-on work to improve the *kaizen* mind of those who are going through the training.

TEAMWORK

Everyone preaches teamwork, but unfortunately, it is often poorly practiced. We believe that teamwork was practiced quite effectively within departments in Toyota and within sections of the company. Teamwork was evident in the Toyota Motor Sales (TMS) call center during the flood of calls related to the sticky pedal recall. It was evident in the plants as they adjusted to reduced hours and plant shutdowns during the recession, and then adjusted again to self-sufficiency. It was evident in the way various parts of the organization came together to find a solution to the sticky pedals and get parts and training out to dealers.

The communication problems were issues that cut across these divisions, and this was shown to be a weak point. This too violated a core principle of the Toyota Way, perhaps best expressed by former president and chairman Eiji Toyoda: "I want you to think for the entire company rather than yourself alone. Coordinate with other divisions, and lead on, no matter what, to concrete results."

This attitude of thinking about the entire company is all well and good, but in a complex global enterprise, it is impossible for everyone to communicate with everyone else. Each person we spoke to at Toyota thought of himself as a team player. This was drilled into them from the day they entered the company. Yet working in whatever teams they were part of was not enough. There needs to be a constant focus on understanding the weak points in teamwork and communication and looking to improve those blockages that prevent the right people from communicating about the right things. This is an endless journey for every company.

In response to these cross-company communication weaknesses, Toyota put enormous resources into streamlining communication, adding engineers to focus on quality, dramatically increasing travel to go and see, bypassing the bureaucracy to get customer data to the right people, creating weekly quality conference calls of executives across functions, and more. Yet, we guarantee that this will not fix the problem forever. As the company recovers and begins to grow again, it will take constant vigilance to avoid creeping bureaucracy that blocks communication and teamwork across the company.

A Never-Ending Cycle

We can't emphasize enough that Toyota's efforts in response to the crisis were neither radical changes nor short-term "projects." The efforts were to a large degree the same agenda that Akio Toyoda had set when he first became president, more than six months before there was any thought of the recall crisis: to strengthen core Toyota values.

Akio Toyoda grew up in the family that had founded Toyota values. It is evident to anyone who spends time with him that he still cherishes the core principles today in a very personal way.

When Liker visited Japan to do the interviews for this book, Akio Toyoda made a point of telling the story (memorialized in the Toyota museum) of his great-grandfather, Kiichiro Toyoda, taking personal responsibility for fixing a customer problem. One day Kiichiro happened to drive by a broken-down Toyota truck. He stopped, climbed under the truck, and helped the driver repair it. Back at Toyota headquarters, he went to the engineering department to explain the problem and give the engineers the task of finding and fixing the root cause. Later, he went to the factory to make sure that the fix had been properly implemented and that no future Toyota vehicle would suffer the same problem. The point of the story is not that senior executives should be climbing under vehicles or replacing sticky pedals; it's that everyone in Toyota, no matter what level she is in the company, should take errors and defects personally—and do everything she can to make sure that the root cause is found and the problem fixed. A problem that affects a Toyota customer is never "someone else's problem."

As soon as Akio Toyoda was appointed president, he began preaching "back to the basics" and an intensified focus on *genchi genbutsu*. He promised to be "the most active president in Toyota history at the *gemba*." He recognized that the company had lost some of that deeply felt spirit of taking ownership of customer problems as it grew to become a global powerhouse. He saw the gap between the plans for regional self-reliance that had been worked on for decades and the reality of leaders in Japan having difficulty letting go, what he referred to as "micromanagement." He saw the fragmentation of the organizations in North America, which meant that the critical connection in his grandfather's time—between caring for the customer, recognizing the problem, taking immediate action, and following through to be sure the customer concerns were solved—was weakened.

Putting real force behind this never-ending cycle of getting back to the basics and strengthening the culture was something of a silver lining of the recall crisis, according to Toyoda:

> If you ask me if I want to go through the same experience again I would say absolutely no! . . . But because of the issues I was able to wholeheartedly communicate my core values to the 300,000 employees globally and also to the suppliers and dealers. So, I think that by now this has become an asset for me. I can take advantage of that as I continue to manage this company into the future.

Lesson 2: A Culture of Responsibility Will Always Beat a Culture of Finger-Pointing

It's common sense that organizations that encourage taking responsibility and solving problems perform better than those that allow finger-pointing and passing the buck. But how much can any person or company take responsibility for? Should a company take responsibility for being hit hard by the Great Recession or for the damage done by misleading media reports?

Various Toyota leaders took responsibility for both crises. Even areas like manufacturing, which had nothing to do with the recall crisis, engaged in *hansei* to determine what could have been done better.

This may seem more like ritual self-flagellation than like a productive stance, but there is an important nuance to understand about Toyota's culture of responsibility and problem solving. There is no value to the Five Whys if you stop when you find a problem that is outside of your control. There will always be factors outside of your control. When you reach a cause that is outside of your control, the next why is to ask why you didn't take into account forces outside of your control—either by finding an alternative approach or by building in flexibility to adjust to those forces.

In the case of the Great Recession, taking responsibility doesn't mean looking for ways in which Toyota could have prevented the Great Recession. Rather, as Art Niimi did in our interview, it asks, why didn't Toyota sense the evidence that it was in a bubble and a downturn of some kind was coming? And if anticipating the crisis was impossible, why didn't the company have much greater flexibility built in? Why did it allow fixed costs to get so high?

Niimi's observation that "our truck inventory was building up from the end of May through the beginning of June" was more than lamenting. As someone who had been personally trained in the Toyota Production System (TPS) by Taiichi Ohno, he knew that the company had violated a fundamental principle: avoid overproduction, the most fundamental waste. Ironically, one of the events that solidified the Toyota Production System as the system to emulate in Japan was an oil crisis, the 1973 oil embargo, which led to skyrocketing fuel prices and in the United States even fuel rationing. At that time, Toyota recovered faster than any other large Japanese company because it had not over-produced, had very little inventory of parts or finished cars that would not sell, and had the flexibility to quickly ramp up production of the small, fuel-efficient cars that Americans now craved. While almost all other companies were helpless to adapt to the crisis, Toyota navigated through it relatively smoothly. Now, 35 years later, in a similar crisis beginning with rising fuel prices,

Toyota had overproduced and was not flexible enough to adapt. That was the problem Niimi saw that the company needed to work on to strengthen it for the future.

In terms of the recall crisis, taking responsibility isn't just about poor communication or perspectives on whether sticky pedals are a safety issue or not. It means examining why rumors and innuendo were able to take hold of the public consciousness. It means examining why so many people were willing to make the leap from limited technical issues and gray areas like floor mats and sticky pedals to believing that Toyota was producing dangerous cars that could zoom out of control at any moment. It means examining why so many people would believe that Toyota was knowingly producing dangerous vehicles and hiding from the consequences. Toyota executives believe that if Toyota had done a better job of listening to customers and building trust, even the sticky pedal problem would have been unable to make a dent in the company's public image. The fault lies in not building a stronger base of goodwill.

Akio Toyoda has been illustrating this concept with an analogy about homemade versus mass-produced food. No matter how safe mass-produced food is, it doesn't give you the same peace of mind as a meal made by your mother. Even if you get sick after a meal, and someone starts a rumor that your mother's cooking was at fault, you are unlikely to believe the rumor. According to Toyoda, the strong relationship and trust between mother and child insulates against virtually any attack: "Even in such a case, the relationship between the child and the mother would not be changed. I think their relationship has been totally insulated from the noise outside. . . . So the way we talk to customers who are not already committed to Toyota really has to be improved to give peace of mind to those people as well."

If respect for people is at the foundation of continuous improvement, then we could also say that mutual trust is the foundation for respect for people. Perhaps the greatest casualty of the recall crisis was a breakdown in the customer trust that Toyota has taken decades to build up—not so much among the core of loyal customers, but among those who were on the fence and those who knew little about Toyota but were potential Toyota loyalists. James Wiseman, who in the midst of the crisis was named as the group vice president for communications at TMA to oversee all communications in North America, is convinced that Toyota was too risk-averse in the early stages of the crisis and should have done more to clearly explain technical issues, speak directly to customers, and explain Toyota's efforts to resolve problems and improve, taking some personal responsibility for this: "Generally I wish we had been more proactive, especially on TV, to speak for our company and all our employees and partners in America. We should have been more visible, including me."

When Toyota teaches Toyota Business Practices (TBP), it is a natural tendency for the student to answer one of the whys by blaming some factor or department that is outside his or her control. Perhaps in solving a quality problem in assembly, the answer to the third why is, "Engineering designed the car so it is difficult to assemble." In such a case, the coach might say: "You may be correct that the engineer could have done a better job of designing for ease of assembly, but we cannot change that right now. How can we answer the next why in a way that will allow us to take positive action?" Then the student might answer the next why as: "We in assembly did not exert our influence to participate in the design process early enough to help the engineers design for assembly," or, "Our training in assembly is not good enough to allow us to assemble difficult designs without defects."

The answer to the fifth why might be: "We have been too busy building vehicles to dedicate the time and effort to working up front with Engineering or to train our team members to assemble challenging designs without defects."

The point is that when you define the problem as something that is within your domain of control, when you take responsibility, there is always something that you can do to improve the situation, but pointing fingers freezes innovative thinking. A true culture of responsibility allows you to perceive opportunities for improvement everywhere, even in areas that at first seem to be beyond your control.

Lesson 3: Even the Best Culture Develops Weaknesses

There's no question that, after years of studying the company, we believe that Toyota's investment in a shared culture of continuous improvement is remarkable and practically unique. For evidence of the success of that investment, one need look no further than the company's nearly continuous rise over the last 60 years. Despite that commitment and investment, however, the company still encountered difficulties that were directly attributable to weaknesses in its culture. Toyota failed to live up to its own standards in a number of areas.

The lesson here is that even the best culture can and will develop weaknesses. If Toyota, despite all it does to inculcate the Toyota Way throughout the company, is susceptible to a weakening of culture, then everyone is. There is simply no realistic way to avoid it. Toyota's experiences show that the greatest threat to a culture of continuous improvement is success.

During the recall crisis, many commentators suggested that Toyota's rapid growth was at fault, leading to breakdowns in safety and quality. Even Akio Toyoda has suggested that the company grew too fast. As we've illustrated through the data, there's little evidence of the purported decline in quality or concern for safety at Toyota. So what did Toyoda mean when he stated that the company may have grown too fast? "The problem was that the pace of growth was faster than the pace of human resource development. . . . It is not the growth pace itself, but it is the relation between the pace of growth and the pace of people development," he told us.

Toyota was certainly growing rapidly during the 2000s, more rapidly than the company's ability to keep up its patient approach to developing people within the Toyota Way, and teaching TPS and TBP by giving people mentoring and opportunities to practice problem solving. Toyoda noted how impatience played a role in the cultural breakdown and contrasted it to his experience being trained at an organization set up by Taiichi Ohno:

> The process of arriving at the root cause when I was on the staff of OMCD [Operations Management Consulting Division] took me about two months. But the person just above me, he was able to get the root cause in two weeks. But if you go to a higher level of expertise, the head of OMCD, he could get the answer within two minutes. The problem, however, is that . . . when people are working under the pressure of time, the mentors are irritated, and mentors would give the answer to the juniors. But you have to differentiate, depending on the maturation of the trainee; sometimes you have to give him two months so that he can arrive at the true cause on his own.

Under normal circumstances, the growing weaknesses in the culture would quickly become apparent as problems were encountered and not optimally solved. But along with rapid growth, Toyota was experiencing unprecedented success. The five years leading up to the recession were the most profitable in the company's history. It had successful vehicles in almost every category of the market, from compacts to hybrids to large SUVs. This success allowed the weakening of the culture to be hidden from view.

Long periods of success are actually the most difficult times to put values front and center. Fulfilling demand, expanding capacity, introducing new products, and planning for growth take up all the available energy. There seem to be no negative consequences from taking shortcuts and choosing "good enough" over excellence. Those shortcuts create weaknesses that steadily build, and when success starts to drain away, the consequences can be severe and difficult to deal with.

One of those consequences that Toyoda saw within the company was a drift away from a true understanding of the company's vision, as encapsulated in Global Vision 2010's target of 15 percent market share:

> I realized that sometimes the people were mixing the goals and the means. To put it in a different way, for Toyota, the goal is to contribute to society through the automotive business. As a means to get to that goal, we need to sell more vehicles so that we have resources to reinvest. But if you put more sales and profit in front of the goal, we are going to make a big mistake.

That's a mistake that can be directly traced to weakness in inculcating the Toyota culture, helping team members to not just know the words of the Toyota Way, but understand how those words should drive their actions and their decisions.

A crisis can help you sort through your priorities. And that's what the crises at Toyota did. The recession awakened the company to its overexposure to market volatility and drove renewed investment in *kaizen* and problem solving to increase flexibility and productivity (thereby driving down costs and risk). The recall crisis illustrated cultural breakdowns, communication inefficiencies, and creeping bureaucracy that was inhibiting customer focus.

Toyota did not suddenly go from a model company with one of the strongest, most customer-oriented cultures in the world to a basket case. The fundamentals of the strong culture that made Toyota so successful were largely intact, yet critical weaknesses evolved when the company grew too fast to fully develop its people in the Toyota Way. Even with everything that Toyota does right, it was still possible for the company to lose sight of its core goals and to lose touch with its customers.

That brings us to another crucial point about culture. To survive the weaknesses that inevitably develop, a corporate culture has to have clear and objective standards, codified in such a way that self-correction is possible. Having a culture that recognizes a loss of direction is absolutely critical to long-term survival. Perhaps the best analogy here is the U.S. Constitution. The Constitution is in many ways a codification of the ideals of American political culture. More often than many Americans would like to admit, the American polity has wandered from the ideals expressed in the Constitution, but the Constitution has provided the basis for these errors to be corrected. Ending slavery and segregation didn't require a completely new Constitution; it required following the Constitution more closely, ensuring that its guarantees applied to everyone. The Constitution and the Bill of Rights express the True North for the country. The Toyota Way functions in the same way for Toyota, with its True North of excellence and service to society. Thus, when the weaknesses in the company were exposed, there was a clear guide and will to right the ship.

Akio Toyoda often cites Jim Collins's book *How the Mighty Fall* to remind listeners that Toyota is not immune from mistakes and problems; without constant vigilance, the company is in danger of a downfall. Collins's model of downfall has five stages, several of which could be applied at some level to Toyota in the lead-up to the crises: hubris born of success; undisciplined pursuit of more; denial of risk and peril; grasping for salvation; and capitulation to irrelevance and death. The fourth stage of the model describes the steps that many once-successful companies take when a crisis strikes deep: making a big acquisition in an attempt to transform the business at a single stroke; embarking on a program of such radical change that the business's underlying strengths are forgotten or abandoned; destroying momentum by constant restructuring; pinning hopes on unproven strategies, such as dramatic leaps into new technologies or businesses; or hiring a visionary leader from the outside who has little understanding of what made the company great in the first place. That fourth stage is where Toyota's actions diverge from Collins's model. Those are the actions of a company that does not have, or does not have faith in, a strong culture. Toyota did not do any of these things.

What Toyota has done is follow the recipe that Collins advocates: old-fashioned management virtues such as determination, discipline, calmness under pressure, and strategic decision making based on careful sifting of the evidence. He suggests that the leader who is best able to halt a downward spiral will be an insider who knows how to build on proven strengths while simultaneously identifying and eradicating weaknesses. That's a fair description of Akio Toyoda.

None of this is to suggest that a good culture is a static culture. One step that Toyota has taken recently to invigorate the culture with outside influence is the investment in and collaboration with Tesla that was announced in May 2010. Toyota is already learning lessons by seeing its culture reflected in Tesla's lens. One of those lessons is about bureaucracy within its design efforts. Tesla was able to create a concept for an all-electric RAV4 in less than eight months and have it ready for display at the Los Angeles Auto Show in December 2010. Several executives we spoke to suggested that it would have taken Toyota about two years to do the same. The Toyota design team is now studying how Tesla works on designs to learn lessons about how it can better incorporate a sense of urgency and rapid development into its culture.

Toyota board member Yukitoshi Funo, formerly the CEO of Toyota Motor Sales in the United States, warns that Toyota needs to continue to embrace greater diversity to continually challenge its most basic assumptions:

> A lesson from the recent issues is that we need a system to share the potential problems of an intangible nature— like customers' concerns and customers' anxiety, the political landscape, and economic situations—those kinds of things we were not able to share across the company. But in order to create an efficient system to share such intangible problems, I think you have to take into consideration the culture, mindset, or ethnicity of the team members. To address both problems—the problem of information and also the problem of sharing intangible

problems—I think that both of them need a diversification of Toyota. And of course we need to globalize. It is a must.

Lesson 4: Globalizing Culture Means a Constant Balancing Act

The strength of the Toyota culture is that it is shared. Developing a shared corporate culture across varied national cultures is perhaps the biggest challenge facing modern multinational corporations. It was Toyota's biggest worry when it was expanding into the United States, so much so that it formed the NUMMI joint venture with its chief competitor, GM, to insulate the company from the risk that the Toyota culture simply could not be translated into an American context. That worry was belied by the immediate success of NUMMI and the continuing growth of a strong Toyota culture throughout North America.

Its success in the United States emboldened Toyota to believe that the Toyota Way could be taught effectively anywhere. The United States, with the strong value it places on individualism and its tendency toward short-term thinking, was probably Toyota's toughest challenge in that regard.* It has taken different approaches in other geographies, though. For instance, in India, Toyota has founded its own high school next to an assembly plant, following the model of Toyota's technical high school in Toyota City, Japan. The goal of the high school is to produce graduates who have not only the technical skills, but also the Toyota Way culture and approach to problem solving, so that they will

---

* For a comparison across different nations on the variables individualism versus collectivism and short-term versus long-term thinking, see Geert Hofstede, Gert Jan Hofstede, and Michael Minkov, *Cultures and Organizations: Software for the Mind*, 3d ed. (New York: McGraw-Hill, 2010).

be able to hit the ground running should they decide to join Toyota after graduation.

Still, despite the progress that Toyota has made, the balance between centralized and decentralized, global and local, is even harder than most people think (and most people think it's very hard). Toyota's commitment to a specific culture has positives and negatives in that regard. The clarity of its values and its culture is absolutely essential to enabling the inculcation of that culture across national boundaries. On the other hand, the expectation that everyone in the company will rigorously learn and internalize the culture, no matter where she is or what her prior background may be, requires massive investment. Toyota cannot simply hire new people and delegate; it needs to first spend time and money to grow the Toyota culture in every employee. The tension at Toyota is captured in the commitment to the culture and the fact that the culture includes the value of *genchi genbutsu*. There is an inherent demand here that *especially* the people who are at the margins, at the periphery of the organization, be deeply steeped in the culture, and that they are to be trusted to make decisions because they are at the *gemba*.

One of the factors that has been identified as a root cause of the recall crisis was overly centralized decision making. The reasons that those decisions were centralized make a lot of sense, and there are obvious dangers in the regionalization strategy that Toyota has chosen to pursue coming out of the crisis. Typically you don't fix information flow problems by decentralizing. You bring the people who are involved in a decision closer together. In other words, you centralize the function. What Toyota has done instead is put pressure on its commitment to inculcating its culture deeply everywhere. If it doesn't succeed in that challenge, then regional decision making on design, engineering, and safety will become fragmented, and the company will encounter even more problems in the future. As in most companies, Toyota's concern about not having leaders around the world who could consistently react in the Toyota Way drove centralized control. Toyota is learning that it has to trust the leaders it has trained or the whole system begins to break down.

It is well known in organizational design that communication is easiest within self-contained units, and most difficult laterally across different parts of the organization. Clearly there is critical information centralized in Japan that will stay centralized in Japan. Finding the balance between that centralization and figuring out the boundaries of self-reliance within regions so that they can make as many self-contained decisions as possible will be an ongoing learning process as Toyota moves forward.

One thing Akio Toyoda realized when reflecting on Global Vision 2020 was that it was developed in Japan without sufficient overseas input. Five non-Japanese managing officers have been tasked with proposing revisions to Global Vision 2020 to ensure that it truly is a global vision that adequately reflects the input of the regions. A new version of Global Vision 2020 was scheduled to be issued in the spring of 2011.

What If?

In the previous chapter, we attempted to document the damage to Toyota from the recall crisis and how it has bounced back. But the story does beg two questions: what if the recall crisis had happened to a company that was in a weaker position, be it in terms of finances, reputation, or capability; and, what benefit has the public received from the sensationalism and rumormongering that surrounded the recall crisis?

The answer to the first question is fairly obvious. It's likely that the crisis would have cost a significant number of people their jobs. Certainly some people's careers would have been destroyed. It's also likely that the overall investment climate for foreign companies would have been undermined, perhaps further damaging a weakened U.S. economy. A recent book by Micheline Maynard documents the value of foreign investment for the U.S. economy. These companies haven't just brought money; they've brought innovative ideas and created many of the good jobs that pundits lament are disappearing.* Given this threat, was anything gained?

Several experts that we talked to pointed to one benefit from the recall crisis: greater focus on safety issues and human factors in vehicle design. We've noted that the industry has lowered the bar for recalls, initiating them more often and for issues that probably wouldn't have been dealt with via a recall in the past. At the same time, it's not by any means clear how many of the increased recalls actually benefited drivers in a material way. Kevin McDonald of the George Washington University School of Law suggested in a paper published in 2009 that for many recalls, the costs to drivers and society as a whole far outweigh the benefits. Those costs, according to McDonald, include "the risks of crash and injury, not to mention fuel consumption and pollutant emissions, posed by otherwise unnecessary trips to car dealerships to repair 'safety defects.'"†

Perhaps a clearer benefit of the drama of the Saylor incident is the needed attention to the fact that vehicle technology has

---

* Micheline Maynard, *The Selling of the American Economy: How Foreign Companies Are Remaking the American Dream* (New York: Crown Business, 2009).

† Kevin M. McDonald, "Do Auto Recalls Benefit the Public?" *Regulation*, vol. 32, no. 2 (June 21, 2009), pp. 12-18. Available at SSRN: http://ssrn.com /abstract=1432448, p. 1.

evolved much faster than drivers' ability to understand and use the technology. For instance, many people who were driving vehicles with push-button start/stop functionality did not know how to turn off the engine in an emergency, and many vehicles now have transmission shift gate designs that make it unclear how to put the car in neutral. Such issues might lead to the NHTSA's setting a standard for push-button ignition systems and for the layout of transmission shifters so that drivers won't need to learn how these systems behave in each different vehicle. There's no doubt that a greater focus on human factors by vehicle manufacturers will benefit everyone, but there's still a long way to go. *Consumer Reports*'s David Champion notes that research shows that antilock brakes haven't provided much safety benefit— not because the technology doesn't work, but because most drivers don't use them correctly, easing off the pedal when they feel a skid starting rather than pressing more firmly and letting the antilock system take over. Edward Niedermeyer also believes that the manufacturers often aren't thinking about the right issues: "I see more manufacturers talking about how to integrate Twitter and Facebook into their cars . . . than manufacturers trying to figure out how to make sure that drivers know how to drive the vehicles."

But there are limits to what manufacturers can do. No matter what safety mechanisms are put into cars, for the time being at least, human beings will be driving them, and those humans make mistakes. Richard Schmidt, coauthor of the Silver Book, and his colleagues have found that pedal configuration has virtually no effect on pedal misapplication.* The most significant cause of pedal misapplication is simply that our bodies don't always do

---

* Doris Trachtman, Richard Schmidt, and Douglas Young, "The Role of Pedal Configuration in Unintended-Acceleration and Pedal-Error Accidents," *Proceedings of the Human Factors and Ergonomics Society,* 49th Annual Meeting, 2005.

what our brains tell them to. Schmidt points out that even the most highly trained and skilled basketball players can make only 9 out of 10 free throws. That may sound impressive on a basketball court, but consider the idea that 1 out of every 10 times someone pushes the gas pedal in his vehicle, he gets it at least somewhat wrong. More prosaically, just think of all the times you've accidentally put your car in motion thinking that you were in reverse while the car was actually in drive, or vice versa. We all do it. We all make mistakes. Vehicle electronics have saved thousands of lives by correcting for some human error, but short of removing people from vehicles, some errors will persist—and they will cause far more accidents than all vehicle defects combined.

Given the modest benefits of the recall crisis, and the costs to Toyota and to society, it's impossible not to ask what the media could have done to actually make drivers safer rather than crying wolf. Micheline Maynard, who recently left the *New York Times* after covering the auto industry for a decade, including the recall crisis, notes that the *Times* is one of the few media outlets that continues to have both robust news reporting and reporters focused on reviewing cars. She says that meant that, unlike in most media, every story she worked on was reviewed by someone who truly understood how cars work today—a difference that is evident in her coverage of the crisis. Jeremy Anwyl told us that the lack of a "discussion rooted in facts" is why Edmunds launched a contest, with $1 million to be paid out to anyone who could prove that there are problems with vehicle electronic systems, in an attempt to clear up, once and for all, whether there are actual vulnerabilities in electronic throttle controls (ETCs) and vehicle electronics. "We felt that in the Toyota situation, the core issues were getting lost in the media coverage," Anwyl said. "There are a lot of incentives for the media to push the boundaries of a story.

There are very powerful financial incentives for being 'first' and for being extreme. . . . What you tend to see is these stories start to grow . . . to take on a life of their own."

That's a sad commentary on the state of the news media today—but there's ample evidence of Anwyl's point. ABC's manipulation of footage in its Toyota story was reminiscent of CBS's alteration of an Audi and NBC's packing of a GM pickup truck's tank with explosives. Indeed, the *Los Angeles Times* reporters were finalists for the industry's premier award, the Pulitzer Prize—this despite the fact that based on our review of their coverage, it seems that the reporters failed to ask basic questions about vehicle mechanics, component design, and the incidence of sudden unintended acceleration (SUA) around the world and never wrote a single story that actually investigated an alleged incident in detail. Shoddy reporting has a real cost, and not just to the direct victims, notes Anwyl: "In the United States, popular opinion can create policy very easily. . . . If those opinions are ill formed, that creates risk. Where media scrutiny becomes intense, does it create the appropriate sort of actions?"

But it wasn't only the news media that drove public attention to phantoms and rumors. The U.S. government, particularly Congress, deserves its share of the blame. Journalist Ed Wallace suggests that if Congress were serious about uncovering facts, it would have interviewed real experts:*

> Even in the hearings in Congress, it appeared that most witnesses were tied to safety advocates, litigation attorneys, and traumatized victims; that's like trying a case

---

* Ed Wallace, "The Toyota Witch Hunt"; http://www.businessweek.com/life style/content/feb2010/bw20100225_403524_page_3.htm.

in court with no defense attorneys. The outcome is almost preordained. If only to resolve the rabid focus on Toyota's problems, it's past time to turn this over to the engineers. Innuendo, emotion, and speculation are not how one resolves an issue such as this.

David Champion points out that even if all of the incidents that the media uncovered and managed to somehow blame on SUA and vehicle electronics were real, they would have accounted for a little more than 100 deaths over 10 years. Every preventable death is a tragedy, but over that same period, roughly 400,000 people died in accidents on American highways. "There are over 6,000 teens killed every year, but we don't have any congressional hearings . . . to find out what we can do for teens. Alcohol-related deaths due to driving are around 10,000 [a year], but we don't have congressional hearings looking at shift interlocks to keep the worst offenders off the road." A recent study found that one of the most common causes of accidents, accounting for 17 percent of road deaths, is sleepiness of drivers.* Champion believes that the funds spent on the NASA investigation of SUA and vehicle electronics could have done much more good for the public if they had focused on the issues that we know cause thousands of deaths a year.

Indeed, Secretary of Transportation Ray LaHood admitted at the February 2011 press conference where the NHTSA presented the results of the NASA/NHTSA investigations of Toyota's electronics that the only reason for the study was to convince members of Congress. The NHTSA was fully confident that there

---

* Larry Copeland, "Study: Sleepiness a Factor in 17% of Road Deaths," *USA Today*, November 8, 2010.

were no electronics issues to be found: "Look, the reason we did the study that we did is because if you went to the hearings that I testified at in the House of Representatives and the Senate, just about every member of Congress believed that we had not found the problem. . . . And just about every member of Congress that questioned me said, 'It's got to be the electronics.' So to try to prove the case that it wasn't the electronics we hired the experts. . . .We have some of the best safety people in the world working at DOT, that know what they are doing, that did a thorough investigation." One can ask whether reassuring Congress is the best way that NHTSA could have used $1.5 million. It seems obvious that a much greater bang for the safety buck could have come from improving the NHTSA complaints database, which will, without alteration, presumably continue to provide fertile ground for baseless accusations and media frenzies.

What if the news media and the U.S. Congress paid more attention to finding facts and solving actual problems, themselves practicing *genchi genbutsu* and some version of TBP, rather than chasing headline-grabbing stories fueled by speculation and trial lawyers? It's hard to believe that we wouldn't be better off.

We do not mean to imply that making the world safer is a trivial task and as simple as writing more accurate newspaper stories or having the U.S. Congress focus on the most important issues. After announcing a set of fines related to Toyota's handling of recalls, NHTSA administrator David Strickland commented that Toyota had made efforts "to make improvements to its safety culture."* While we obviously don't agree that significant changes

---

* Josh Mitchell, "U.S. Hits Toyota with Fine on Lapses," *Wall Street Journal,* December 20, 2010.

to Toyota's safety culture were needed, the more important question to ask is, what efforts are needed to improve the U.S. safety culture?

Take, for example, the forces that shape communications about product (not just automotive) recalls. When communicating a recall, a manufacturer has to balance many concerns, few of which have anything to do with actual safety. First, the recall has to be communicated in terms that are serious enough to induce customers to act. If too few bring products in for repair or replacement, the manufacturer is subject to fines. Meanwhile, the manufacturer has to communicate in such a way as to protect itself from the worst charges that will inevitably be levied by lawyers suing the company. The result is communications that are often very difficult to understand, mired in legalese, and tragically uninformative to the people who matter most: the owners of the products.

Many of the automobile safety scares that have received heavy media coverage in the last 25 years—Audi surges, Suzuki rollovers, Firestone tires, exploding Crown Victorias—either were patently false or seem to have been overblown when you examine all the facts.* What does that say about the United States' safety culture?

Our safety culture continues to focus on headlines and bogeymen while ignoring major sources of risk. Our safety culture pushes companies to cover themselves against lawsuits, resulting in warnings to avoid ironing clothes while wearing them, but doesn't address human errors as a major cause of accidents.

---

* Ed Wallace, "The Real Scandal behind the Toyota Recall," *Bloomberg Businessweek*, February 11, 2010; http://www.businessweek.com/lifestyle/content/feb2010/bw20100211_986136.htm.

Our safety culture spends $1.5 million to find that "pedal misapplication" was the major cause of sudden acceleration incidents, but forces Ray LaHood to say, when presenting these results, "Nobody up here has ever insinuated the term . . . 'driver error.'" Our safety culture leads to enough people avoiding childhood vaccines to allow measles and whooping cough epidemics to re-emerge. Our safety culture in the health-care system leads to far too many deaths attributable to human error, yet programs to reduce this have been largely ineffective.* Our safety culture leads to hundreds of millions of dollars annually paid out in lawyers' fees (the first cases in the class-action lawsuits against Toyota won't start being heard until 2013!), but no significant changes in vehicle accident rates. There is clearly a need for change in the U.S. safety culture that is not just about regulators, politicians, and the media—but they are good places to start.

---

* A case in point is the drive to reduce medical errors that cause thousands of unnecessary deaths each year in the health-care system. Steven Spear became a student of the Toyota Production System as a doctoral student and later applied what he learned to the problem of improving safety in the health-care system. He was part of a team at the Institute of Medicine that studied health care and published the famous report "To Err Is Human," finding "one in every few hundred [patients] was hurt, and one in every few thousand was killed by medical misadventures." The solution was to identify and proliferate medical "best practices" across health care. A great idea, but unfortunately it has not worked. A 2010 study published in the *New England Journal of Medicine* reports that "In the 10 years since publication of the Institute of Medicine's report *To Err Is Human,* extensive efforts have been undertaken to improve patient safety. The success of these efforts remains unclear." See Steven Spear, "Why Best Practices Haven't Fixed Health Care"; http://blogs.hbr.org/cs/2011/01/why_best _practices_havent_fixe.html; and Christopher Landrigan et al., "Temporal Trends in Rates of Patient Harm Resulting from Medical Care"; http://www .nejm.org/doi/full/10.1056/NEJMsa1004404.

A Final Lesson

Toyota's resilience in the face of two major crises in three years has been remarkable. Despite plunging demand, first from the Great Recession and then from the recall crisis, the company has restored profitability and clawed back most of its retail market share, both globally and in the United States. But the real outcome has yet to be written. Toyota's reputation has been pulled down so that it no longer holds a dominant position, but is just another of the companies scraping for a piece of the pie. The final judgment on Toyota's response to the crises will be written over the next 10 years as Toyota works to regain its sterling reputation and again become a role model for companies throughout the world. That's the vantage point from which we can judge whether Toyota used the crisis to truly become a better and a stronger company than it was in the past—that is, after all, the metric that Toyota has always used to measure its response to a crisis.

Admittedly, these were the biggest crises that Toyota has faced since World War II. But the philosophy is the same today as it was for Taiichi Ohno: you must drain the water to see the problems and then fix them in pursuit of perfection. Jim Lentz, president of TMS, used that very analogy:

> As we went through this [crisis], and the water level dropped, we started noticing some of the rocks that had been there all the time, but they were kind of hidden by success and by a big marketplace. So, I guess, in the long run, going through all this is a good thing, because we're able to assess what the problems are, make sure we have the right processes in place, make sure we're developing

people and we have strong manufacturing, strong suppliers in place, get back to understanding root problems, but don't be so focused on the technical side that we miss the human side.

Challenge is the source of energy to go beyond goodness to greatness. While these crises were severe, they were just another of the challenges that Toyota constantly creates for itself to drive continuous improvement. Just as the performance of a factory is expected to improve each year, to advance another step toward True North, the board of directors will assess the company's performance based on whether it operates better this year than it did the year before. The goal is never a steady state or returning to the status quo.

That's the final and perhaps the most important lesson of turning a crisis into an opportunity. Expectations and goals matter. A company that is simply trying to survive a crisis, to get back to the status quo ante, is never going to do better than that. A company that is dedicated to continuous improvement, to constantly moving the goalposts to a higher level of performance, will expect much more from its crisis response. In fact, the crisis becomes less an obstacle to be overcome and more another tool in the arsenal of continuous improvement. With that perspective, it's far more likely that a firm will do more than just endure a crisis. It will conquer crisis after crisis and emerge stronger from each. That's the standard by which to judge all of Toyota's history. Time will tell how this generation of Toyota leaders has lived up to the standards of its predecessors.

Index

About the Authors

Jeffrey K. Liker is the author of the bestselling *The Toyota Way* and 10 other related books. He is a professor of industrial and operational engineering at the University of Michigan and consults and speaks through his own consulting firm and The Toyota Way Academy.

Timothy N. Ogden is cofounder of Sona Partners and a writer and editor who has developed nearly 20 business books for major publishers. His work has appeared in *Harvard Business Review*, *Stanford Social Innovation Review*, *Strategy+Leadership*, and Miller-McCune, among others.